NAVIGATING YOUR FUTURE

An Interactive Journey to Personal and Academic Success

Bruce J. Colbert

University of Pittsburgh at Johnstown

PEARSON
Prentice
Hall

Upper Saddle River, New Jersey
Columbus, Ohio

Library of Congress Cataloging-in-Publication Data

Colbert, Bruce J.
  Navigating your future : an interactive journey to personal and academic
success / Bruce J. Colbert.
      p. cm.
  Includes bibliographical references and index.
  ISBN-13: 978-0-13-196084-8 (pbk.)
  ISBN-10: 0-13-196084-9 (pbk.)
  1. Success 2. Conduct of life. 3. Academic achievement.   I. Title.
  BJ1611.2.C647 2009
  646.7088'378198—dc22

                                        2007042349

Vice President and Executive Publisher: Jeffery W. Johnston
Executive Editor: Sande Johnson
Editorial Assistant: Lynda Cramer
Development Editor: Jennifer Gessner
Project Manager: Kerry Rubadue
Production Coordination: Thistle Hill Publishing Services, LLC
Managing Editor: Pamela D. Bennett
Design Coordinator: Diane C. Lorenzo
Cover Designer: Candace Rowley
Photo Coordinator: Shea Davis
Cover Image: i-stock
Operations Specialist: Susan Hannahs
Director of Marketing: Quinn Perkson
Marketing Manager: Amy Judd
Marketing Coordinator: Brian Mounts

This book was set in Weidemann Book by S4Carlisle Publishing Services. It was printed and bound by Courier/Kendallville. The cover was printed by Phoenix Color Corp.

Photo Credits: Najlah Feanny-Hicks/Corbis SABA Press Photos, Inc., p. 6 (left); Sue Ogrocki/Corbis/Reuters America LLC, p. 6 (right); David Cannon © Dorling Kindersley, p. 19 (left); Rubberball/Alamy Images Royalty Free, p. 19 (center); Corbis Royalty Free, pp. 19 (right), 107; Susan Oristaglio/PH College, p. 26 (top left); Prentice Hall School Division, p. 26 (top right); David Young-Wolff/PhotoEdit Inc., pp. 26 (bottom), 75 (left); STOCK4B-RF/Getty Images, Inc.–Stockbyte, pp. 27 (left), 136 (left); David Mager/Pearson Learning Photo Studio, pp. 27 (right), 194; Michael Newman/PhotoEdit Inc., pp. 33, 91 (bottom left); Eunice Harris/Jupiter Images–Index Stock Imagery, p. 35; Laima E. Druskis/PH College, pp. 75 (right), 210 (top right); Richard Haynes/Prentice Hall School Division, p. 91 (top right); Rhoda Sidney/PhotoEdit Inc., p. 91 (right); Jay Penni/Prentice Hall School Division, p. 136 (right); PH College, p. 139; Barbara Stitzer/PhotoEdit Inc., p. 143; Corbis Digital Stock, p. 157 (left); Getty Images, Inc./Photodisc, p. 157 (right); Cathy Melloan/PhotoEdit Inc., p. 162; Patrick White/Merrill, pp. 181, 185; Biophoto Associates/Science Source/Photo Researchers, Inc., p. 207; Myrleen Ferguson Cate/PhotoEdit Inc., p. 210 (top left); Patrick Watson/PH College, 210 (bottom); Dennis MacDonald/PhotoEdit Inc., p. 223

Pearson Prentice Hall™ is a trademark of Pearson Education, Inc.
Pearson® is a registered trademark of Pearson plc
Prentice Hall® is a registered trademark of Pearson Education, Inc.

Pearson Education Ltd.   Pearson Education Australia Pty. Limited
Pearson Education Singapore Pte. Ltd.   Pearson Education North Asia Ltd.
Pearson Education Canada, Ltd.   Pearson Educación de Mexico, S.A. de C.V.
Pearson Education–Japan   Pearson Education Malaysia Pte. Ltd.

10 9 8 7 6 5
ISBN-13: 978-0-13-196084-8
ISBN-10:   0-13-196084-9

DEDICATION

To the loving memories of Robert and Josephine Colbert,
who taught me how to journey through life.

To all the teachers who serve as travel guides to lifelong
learning and to all the students who embrace the journey.

PREFACE

Why This Book?

This project grew from several years of fun, interactive workshops on academic and personal success with both students and teachers. From these interactions, two main concerns stood out. First, many students felt overwhelmed and unprepared for their transition to higher education. Second, when they took academic success courses, they again became overwhelmed with all the exercises, programs, and information. They found it hard to sift through it all to find the most positive and immediate strategies for their new and, yes, sometimes chaotic lives. This project was written to show students how to be successful in a very tangible, interactive, and practical way—in other words, to get back to basics.

What Are the Goals and Guiding Principles of This Text?

The main goal is to encourage students to assess their current skills and to develop specific action plans for improvement. A secondary, but very important goal is for the readers to enjoy a fun, interactive journey toward self-improvement.

Guiding Principles

The development of this book was based on the following principles:

Short, Simple, and Effective Techniques: This text does *not* offer, for example, "10 steps to stress management," crowded with copious amounts of information and losing students in numerous steps and long lists. It keeps concepts simple yet focused. Students will see quick results, which will motivate them to move forward.

Relevant Learning and Language: A simple, conversational style helps students to learn and personalize their strategies for skills development. Examples relate *why* these skills are needed and *how* to develop them fully.

Personalized Assessment and Techniques: The text and CD materials allow students to assess their strengths and need areas, and then to develop personalized action plans. The CD interactively reinforces the material and gives the student the ability to track their progress.

In summary, this book strives to personalize the material, making it easier for students to internalize and actually use the ideas presented during—and beyond—their postsecondary education.

TO THE STUDENTS

Why This Ordering of Chapter Topics?

Most academic success textbooks place stress management in the middle or end; however, this text emphasizes it from the start. A 2004 National College Survey at the University of Minnesota at Duluth indicated that stress is the main barrier to academic success. If new students cannot manage stress and their minds race a million miles per hour, how can they go on to develop critical and creative thinking skills, set proper goals, manage their time, and study effectively? Imagine trying to make an effective study schedule or implementing time management techniques while feeling stressed out and overwhelmed. The skills presented here follow a progressive, logical learning sequence.

The first six chapters focus on *you* and your internal (or *intra*personal) success skills. Stress management lays the foundation so you can harness your stress in a positive manner to enjoy a positive attitude and set personal goals (Chapter 2). With motivating goals in mind, you can now develop effective time management techniques (Chapter 3) to free up valuable study time in the midst of your busy schedule. With this solid foundation, you can then sharpen your study strategies (Chapter 4). Chapter 5 adds material on learning styles, improving memory, and test taking. Chapter 6 then fine-tunes your higher-level skills in critical and creative thinking. You are now prepared to move into the *inter*personal skill areas to maximize your external success skills.

Whereas the first six chapters focus on how to do well "within yourself," the last four deal with succeeding "within your program and beyond." These skills focus on communication, group interaction, team building, and leadership development (Chapters 7 and 8). A full chapter is devoted to job-seeking skills and methods to thrive in your chosen career after graduation (Chapter 9). Finally, Chapter 10 explores enhancing your personal health and wellness along your journey toward success—in your academic studies and in your career.

Should You Use the CD?

Using the CD will enhance your understanding of the concepts in the text. The text and CD focus on making positive behavioral changes rather than learning tons of theory. It is important for you to realize *why* each particular subject will benefit you and *how* you can implement positive change. Therefore, the CD symbol shown here will be placed at the end of each chapter. After you have read the chapter and performed the interactive exercises and assessments, you will then be directed to the corresponding CD chapter, which provides examples and exercises to help you further practice the strategies discussed in the text.

Have a great journey!

ACKNOWLEDGMENTS

There are so many people to acknowledge for a book of this scope. First and foremost, I want to thank Sande Johnson for her faith, wisdom, and guidance in the development of this vision. Without her, this would still be an unrealized passionate idea rattling around in my brain. Jennifer Gessner deserves special thanks for helping me clarify my words and guiding me along the writing process. My thanks to all the production staff at Prentice Hall who worked hard to produce the book and CD professionally. Finally, my special thanks to my secretary, Jan Snyder, and two students, Jamie Kusher and Nikki Weaver, who read through several versions of the chapters and whose comments and experiences helped enhance this project.

CONTRIBUTING AUTHORS

I was very fortunate to have two great authors and friends help me in the writing of this material. They contributed to Chapters 4, 5, 8, and 9 with both their expertise and passion for helping students. Thanks go to:

Susan Dawkins, assistant director of Academic Support Center, University of Pittsburgh at Johnstown.

Doug Reed, MBA, assistant professor, Business Department, University of Pittsburgh at Johnstown.

Also, a special thanks to Susan for helping in the final editing phase and to both Doug and Susan for their valuable contributions to the CD.

Kathryn Kasturas deserves thanks for her assistance in editing the original proposal and her initial research and contributions to the early chapter drafts.

CD Developer

Jim Booth deserves a tremendous amount of credit for his creativity and technical skill in making my vision of the CD come to life. I still don't know how he did it. I also want to thank Tim Doyle, the videographer, for his skill, creativity, and humor in setting up and recording all the raw video needed for the CD.

REVIEWERS

A special thank you to all the reviewers involved with this project. Your guidance, wisdom, and experiences honed many rough drafts into a more focused and relevant learning text. I also appreciated the encouragement along the way.

Glenda A. Belote, Florida International University

Michelle Buchman, Everest College

James Cebulski, University of South Florida

Philip Corbett, South University

Gigi Derballa, Asheville-Buncombe Technical Community College

Goldean Gibbs, Ohio Institute of Health Careers

Shirley Jelmo, Pima Medical Institute

Marilyn Joseph, Florida Metropolitan University

Margaret G. Kennedy, Lansing Community College

Sharon Occhipinti, Florida Metropolitan University–Tampa

Kate Sawyer, Lincoln Educational

Allison Schmaeling, Capps College

Kimber Shaw, Boise State University

Mary Silva, Modesto Junior College/YDDC

Jill Strand, University of Minnesota–Duluth

William E. Thompson, Texas A & M–Commerce

Theresa Tuttle, ECPI College of Technology

Dr. Dale Weinbach, Miami International University of Art and Design

Katie Winkler, Blue Ridge Community College

ABOUT THE AUTHOR

Bruce Colbert is the director of the Allied Health Department at the University of Pittsburgh at Johnstown. He has authored five books, written several articles, and has given over two hundred invited lectures and workshops throughout the United States. Many of his workshops provide teacher training on making learning engaging and relevant to today's students. In addition, he conducts workshops on developing effective, critical, and creative thinking, stress and time management, communication, and team building. He is an avid basketball player, even after three knee surgeries, which may indicate he has some learning difficulties.

SUPPLEMENTAL RESOURCES

An interactive CD accompanies this working text. Conveying simple, focused concepts in a personal tone, the CD personalizes the development of each student's success skills. WHY are these skills important? HOW should you fully develop them? The CD allows students to assess themselves and create personalized action plans that will work in their lives. Students will experience quick results, reinforcing their progress.

INSTRUCTOR SUPPORT

Resources to simplify your life and engage your students.

Book Specific

Print	Print Instructor's Manual	ISBN 0-13-196086-5
Technology	Online Instructor's Manual	ISBN 0-13-227568-6
	Online PowerPoint Slides	ISBN 0-13-196087-3

"Easy access to online, book-specific Teaching support is now just a click away!"

Register today at www.prenhall.com to access instructor resources digitally.

Instructor Resource Center Register. Redeem. Login. Three easy steps that open the door to a variety of print and media resources in downloadable, digital format, available to instructors exclusively through the Prentice Hall IRC.

www.prenhall.com

Instructor Resource Center

Returning Instructors

Please Login

Login Name:

Password:

Login

☑ Forgot Password?

Welcome new Instructors!
College instructors: please register to gain access to all the media resources available from the IRC.

Register

Already have an Access Code?
If you already have an access code, you'll need to redeem it before you can log in.

Redeem

"Choose from a wide range of Video resources for the classroom!"

Prentice Hall Reference Library: Life Skills Pack, ISBN 0-13-127079-6, contains all of the following videos:

- Learning Styles and Self-Awareness, ISBN 0-13-028502-1
- Critical and Creative Thinking, ISBN 0-13-028504-8
- Relating to Others, ISBN 0-13-028511-0
- Personal Wellness, ISBN 0-13-028514-5

Prentice Hall Reference Library: Study Skills Pack, ISBN 0-13-127080-X, contains all of the following videos:

- Reading Effectively, ISBN 0-13-028505-6
- Listening and Memory, ISBN 0-13-028506-4
- Note Taking and Research, ISBN 0-13-028508-0
- Writing Effectively, ISBN 0-13-028509-9
- Effective Test Taking, ISBN 0-13-028500-5
- Goal Setting and Time Management, ISBN 0-13-028503-X

Prentice Hall Reference Library: Career Skills Pack, ISBN 0-13-118529-2, contains all of the following videos:

- Skills for the 21st Century – Technology, ISBN 0-13-028512-9
- Skills for the 21st Century – Math and Science, ISBN 0-13-028513-7
- Managing Money and Career, ISBN 0-13-028516-1

Prentice Hall Full Reference Library Pack, ISBN 0-13-501095-0, contains the complete study skills, life skills, and career skills videos on DVD.

One Key Video Pack, ISBN 0-13-514249-0, contains Student Advice, Study Skills, Learning Styles, and Self-Awareness, Skills for the 21st Century—Math, Science, and Technology, and Managing Money and Careers videos on DVD.

Faculty Video Resources

- Teacher Training Video 1: Critical Thinking, ISBN 0-13-099432-4
- Teacher Training Video 2: Stress Management and Communication, ISBN 0-13-099578-9
- Teacher Training Video 3: Classroom Tips, ISBN 0-13-917205-X
- Study Skills Video, ISBN 0-13-096095-0
- Building on Your Best Video, ISBN 0-20-526277-5

Current Issues Videos

- ABC News Video Series: Student Success 2/E, ISBN 0-13-031901-5
- ABC News Video Series: Student Success 3/E, ISBN 0-13-152865-3

"Through partnership opportunities, we offer a variety of assessment options!"

LASSI The LASSI is a 10-scale, 80-item assessment of students' awareness about and use of learning and study strategies. Addressing skill, will, and self-regulation, the focus is on both covert and overt thoughts, behaviors, attitudes, and beliefs that relate to successful learning and that can be altered through educational interventions. Available in two formats: Paper ISBN 0-13-172315-4 or Online ISBN 0-13-172316-2 (Access Card).

Noel Levitz/RMS This retention tool measures Academic Motivation, General Coping Ability, Receptivity to Support Services, PLUS Social Motivation. It helps identify at-risk students, the areas with which they struggle, and their receptiveness to support. Available in Paper or Online formats as well as short and long versions. Paper Long Form A: ISBN 0-13-072258-8; Paper Short Form B: ISBN 0-13-079193-8; Online Forms A, B, and C: ISBN 0-13-098158-3.

Robbins Self-Assessment Library This compilation teaches students to create a portfolio of skills. S.A.L. is a self-contained, interactive library of 49 behavioral questionnaires that help students discover new ideas about themselves, their attitudes, and their personal strengths and weaknesses. Available in paper, ISBN 0-13-173861-5; CD-ROM, ISBN 0-13-221793-7; and online, ISBN 0-13-243165-3 (Access Card) formats.

Readiness for Education at a Distance Indicator (READI) READI is a web-based tool that assesses the overall likelihood for online learning success. READI generates an immediate score and a diagnostic interpretation of results, including recommendations for successful participation in online courses and potential remediation sources. Please visit www.readi.info for additional information. ISBN 0-13-188967-2.

"Teaching tolerance and discussing diversity with your students can be challenging!"

Responding to Hate at School Published by the Southern Poverty Law Center, the Teaching Tolerance handbook is a step-by-step, easy-to-use guide designed to help administrators, counselors, and teachers react promptly and efficiently whenever hate, bias, and prejudice strike.

"For a terrific one-stop shop resource, use our Student Success Supersite!"

Supersite www.prenhall.com/success Students and professors alike may use the Supersite for assessments, activities, links, and more.

"For a truly tailored solution that fosters campus connections and increases retention, talk with us about Custom publishing."

Pearson Custom Publishing We are the largest custom provider for print and media shaped to your course's needs. Please visit us at www.pearsoncustom.com to learn more.

STUDENT SUPPORT

Tools to help make the grade now and excel in school later.

"Time management is the #1 challenge students face." We can help.

Prentice Hall Planner A basic planner that includes a monthly and daily calendar plus other materials to facilitate organization. 8.5" × 11".

Premier Annual Planner This specially designed, annual 4-color collegiate planner includes an academic planning/resources section, monthly planning section (2 pages/month, weekly planning section (48 weeks; July start date), which facilitate short-term as well as long-term planning. Spiral bound, 6" × 9". Customization is available.

"Journaling activities promote self-discovery and self-awareness."

Student Reflection Journal Through this vehicle, students are encouraged to track their progress and share their insights, thoughts, and concerns. 8 1/2" × 11". 90 pages.

"Our Student Success Supersite is a one-stop shop for students to learn about career paths, self-awareness activities, cross-curricular practice opportunities, and more!"

Supersite www.prenhall.com/success

"Learning to adapt to the diverse college community is essential to students' success."

10 Ways to Fight Hate Produced by the Southern Poverty Law Center, the leading hate-crime and crime-watch organization in the United States, this guide walks students through 10 steps that they can take on their own campus or in their own neighborhood to fight hate everyday. ISBN 0-13-028146-8.

"The Student Orientation Series includes short booklets on specialized topics that facilitate greater student understanding."

S.O.S. Guides Connolly, *Learning Communities* (ISBN 0-13-232243-9) and Watts, *Service Learning* (ISBN 0-13-232201-3) help students understand what these opportunities are, how to take advantage of them, and how to learn from their peers while doing so. New to the series, Hoffman: *Stop Procrastinating Now!, 10 Simple and SUCCESSFUL Steps for Student Success* (ISBN 0-13-513056-5) will provide the basic strategies for acknowledging, addressing, and ultimately overcoming procrastination to ensure one's success in college and beyond.

BRIEF CONTENTS

CONTENTS

PART II
A ROAD MAP
FOR PROFESSIONAL
SUCCESS 131

7. Communication in Action: Presenting Yourself to Others 132

8. Group Interaction and Team Building: Working Together Works 154

Job Seeking and Leadership Development: Your Future Begins Now 176

Enhancing Your Personal Health: Take Care of Yourself Along the Journey 202

Note: Every effort has been made to provide accurate and current Internet information in this book. However, the Internet and information on it are constantly changing, so it is inevitable that some of the Internet addresses listed in this textbook will change.

PART I

Traveling Toward Personal Success

Stress Management

The Skill That Affects All Others

OBJECTIVES

What you will discover by the end of this chapter:

- The meaning of *stress*
- The types of stress
- The effects of stress
- How to differentiate "good stress" from "bad stress"
- How to develop your very own *two*-step stress management system

WHY LEARN THIS SKILL?

Stress management is the one foundational skill that will increase your chance of having a healthy, happy, and successful journey through life. If your stress is out of control, so is your physical and mental health, academic and job performance, decision making, and personal relationships. Ironically, schools and employers are offering more and more stress management seminars, yet stress levels seem to keep on rising. Mastery of this skill is critical.

Many stress management systems are complicated and difficult to use. Have you ever read an article that gives you the 10 to 20 steps to a stress-free life? Just the idea of learning 10 to 20 steps is stressful! This text and CD present a simpler, more realistic two-step system.

Another problem is that many of the stress management systems are cookbook recipes expected to work for everyone, even though everyone's life is different. Just because a particular method works for the professional speaker who developed the program, it does not ensure that it will work for a student who is juggling multiple roles, such as being an employee, student, and single parent. This text and CD will help you assess and develop your own personalized stress management system. By reading this chapter, completing the exercises, and using the fun, interactive, and personalized CD, you will develop a simple and effective stress management system that will work *for you* in your academic, personal, and professional life.

Going to school and learning should be a positive and uplifting experience, but a lack of good stress management skills can make you feel like Figure 1-1. If you can relate to Figure 1-1, think about the following questions: Is the "after-school" picture how you really want to

FIGURE 1-1

Do you sometimes feel like this?

Before School   After School

feel for a large portion of your life? Do you think you will make good decisions, perform well academically, or even feel well if you remain in the after-school mode for extended periods of time? Unfortunately, some people are constantly stressed out and always feel like the after-school image. Keep this picture in your mind as you travel through this chapter.

Before you can look like the "before-school" picture, you first need to understand what stress is all about. This chapter provides an understanding of stress that will serve as the foundation for your personalized stress management system. Instead of letting stress work *against* you, you will learn to make it work *for* you.

Before you begin to develop your stress management system, it is important to get a baseline assessment of your current stress levels. In Exercise 1-1, let's find out where you are now to see how much you can improve in the coming months and years once you begin to integrate this simple system into your life.

EXERCISE 1-1
Your Stress Number

Rate the following statements with numbers 1 through 4 as follows:

1 = Rarely   2 = Sometimes   3 = Frequently   4 = Always

_____ 1. I have low energy and feel tired.

_____ 2. I worry a lot about problems or how things are going to turn out.

_____ 3. I can spot all the things others are doing wrong.

_____ 4. I feel the need to be perfect at what I do.

_____ 5. I skip my workout/exercise sessions.

_____ 6. I feel sad.

_____ 7. My mind goes a million miles per hour.

_____ 8. I take on everyone else's problems.

_____ 9. I try to control other people.

_____ 10. I can't do anything right.

_____ 11. I avoid risks for fear of failure.

_____ 12. I let my work pile up.

_____ 13. I feel like I'm being pulled in all directions.

_____ 14. I have a pessimistic attitude.

_____ 15. I get headaches.

_____ 16. I have too much to do and too little time to do it.

_____ 17. I overreact to situations.

_____ 18. I feel guilty if I relax and do nothing.

_____ 19. I talk very quickly.

_____ 20. I get angry easily.

Now add up your answers and see where you stand: _____

60–80:	This chapter could be a life-changing experience.
50–59:	Your stress is out of control, and you desperately need this material.
40–49:	Your stress is causing problems for you, and you would gain moderate benefit from this chapter.
30–39:	Stress is affecting you and this chapter will help with the stress in your life.
20–29:	You are doing pretty well, but you can still improve.

WHAT IS STRESS?

What is this thing we call stress? One of the misconceptions about stress is that we need to wipe it out of our lives, and our goal should be to become "stress free." Nothing could be further from the truth. Stress is needed for our very existence.

For example, your body temperature must be maintained within a narrow range. Most environments are colder than body temperature (98.6°F) and thus produce stress even though you may feel comfortable. Your body senses and interprets this stress in order to adapt, and it adjusts to cold temperature both to produce and retain heat to regulate the temperature within normal range. The body maintains many conditions, such as oxygen levels, blood values, and so on, all within narrow ranges by making changes based on internal and external stress or stimuli. Your body does this often without you even knowing it. In this way your body regulates your physiologic stress for you to survive.

Another example of good stress is when your muscles receive "stress" from exercise. This is needed so they adapt and rebuild themselves to become better and stronger. Using this concept, your mind can also use mental stress to better itself.

A Working Definition

So what _is_ the best definition of stress? If you read books on stress, you will find many different definitions. According to the American Institute of Stress, Hans Selye, the father of stress theory, defined stress as "the non-specific response of the body to a demand made upon it." Although this statement certainly rings true, we will define stress in more user-friendly terms. We have already established that some stress is needed to maintain optimal body functioning. However, at times we let this stress get out of control, and instead of helping us, it causes serious harm. What we are concerned with is how does the body _react_ to stress? Here's our working definition of the **stress reaction:**

> **STRESS REACTION**—How our _mind and body_ react to an environment that is largely shaped by _our perceptions_ of an event, person, or situation.

Mind–Body Connection.

Let's take a closer look at this definition. Notice how it begins with "how our mind and body react." This shows the close relationship between the body (physiologic responses) and the mind (psychological responses). Many in the medical community now claim that stress causes a significant number of health problems in the United States. You may have read elsewhere that heart and lung disease are among the top illnesses. However, think about *why* many individuals develop heart or lung disease. Much of lung disease is caused by smoking, which is an unhealthy response to stress. Likewise, heart disease is often caused by poor diet, smoking, and lack of exercise. These are all indicators of someone who doesn't properly handle stress in his or her life. Just think about the following common statements as they relate to stress and the mind–body connection:

- I couldn't catch my breath.
- My heart was racing.
- My brain was fried.
- My stomach was twisted in knots.

Our Perception Defines Our Stress.

Now let's continue on with the rest of the definition: "react to an environment that is largely shaped by *our perceptions* of an event, person, or situation." Notice how the words *our perceptions* stand out. We can drive this point home using the noble example of giving blood. Study the pictures of the two volunteer blood donors in Figure 1-2.

FIGURE 1-2

Differing perceptions to the same procedure.

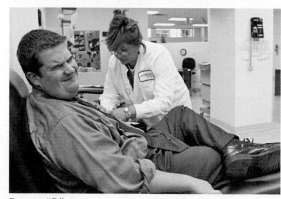

Donor "B"

Donor "A"

Donor "A" is calm and relaxed throughout the whole procedure and even smiles and jokes with the technician. Donor "B" is highly stressed, has an increase in vital signs, is sweaty, and in general is just a "nervous wreck" throughout the whole procedure. However, both patients had the *same* procedure, with the *same* technician, with the *same*-size needle. What was the difference?

Obviously, the perception of the first donor was more positive, whereas the second donor was full of dread. Their *perceptions* made the difference in their very different stress reactions. Keep in mind that most stress occurs as a result of how we *interpret* and *react* to a situation, person, or event. It is sometimes hard to admit that we cause most of our stress, but the good news is that if we do cause it, then we actually can control it.

Hans Selye developed many of the terms associated with stress. He referred to anything that causes stress as a "stressor" or "trigger" (American Institute of Stress, 2007). It's important to become aware of the stressors in your life to learn to manage them. Give Exercise 1-2 a try.

List and describe the top three stressors or triggers in your life.

1. _____

_____

_____

2. _____

_____

3. _____

EXERCISE 1-2
What Triggers You?

TYPES OF STRESS

We've established that stress is a physical and emotional reaction based on our perceptions. Let's further define stress to include two broad categories called **external stress** and **internal stress** (Posen, 1995).

External Stressors

External stressors include your physical environment, social interactions, major life events, and daily hassles. In other words, external stressors represent everything outside of you. Please see Table 1-1 for examples of some external stressors in our lives.

Internal Stressors

Internal stressors include such characteristics as lifestyle choices, personality traits, and negative thinking styles, such as being pessimistic or too self-critical. Thinking styles are the

TABLE 1-1	
Examples of External Stressors	
External Stressors	**Examples**
Physical environment	Noise, heat, bright lights, confined spaces
Social interaction	Bad relationships, aggressive interactions
Major life event	Starting school, moving, getting married, getting divorced, job loss or change, family sickness or death
Daily hassle	Commuting to work or school, car repairs, and paying bills

internal "mind talk" we engage in. You will learn in Chapter 2 just how powerful this internal dialogue can be and how it can work either positively for growth or negatively for serious adverse outcomes. For example, someone who is a perfectionist might have unrealistic expectations. Imagine the self-critical "mind talk" if that person makes a mistake. Please see Table 1-2 for some examples of internal stressors.

TABLE 1-2	
Examples of Internal Stressors	
Internal Stressors	**Examples**
Lifestyle choices	Lack of restful sleep, smoking, drug abuse
Personality traits	Workaholic, perfectionist
Negative thinking styles	Pessimistic, self-critical, rigid thinking

Survival Stress

Survival stress occurs when your body quickly adapts to maximize your reaction to a physically or emotionally life-threatening or challenging event. This is our "fight-or-flight" response, which rapidly turns on in times of perceived danger. This response is much greater than the normal day-to-day physiologic responses and adjustments to minor stresses such as environmental temperature changes.

HARMFUL EFFECTS OF STRESS

It is a fact of life that we all have temporary stressors. Currently you may be studying for that big exam, deciding on your career path, or going on a job interview. The question is, Will you handle your temporary stressors and turn them into a positive experience? Let's first explore what happens if you cannot—the harmful effects of stress. We will then finish this chapter by learning how to face stress in a positive way.

Chronic Stress

No matter what the change or challenge may be, it is important that you do not let stress adversely affect your performance and health. It is especially dangerous when you remain in a chronic (long-term) state of stress. **Chronic stress** equals poor performance, poor decisions, and poor health. It can affect you physically, mentally, emotionally, and behaviorally.

Physical symptoms of chronic stress can include sweating, muscle aches, digestive problems, loss of appetite, headache, and dizziness, to name just a few. Mentally, chronic stress manifests itself as anxiousness, forgetfulness, confusion, panic attacks, and loss of humor (American Medical Women's Association, 2007). Do any of these sound familiar? Emotional changes include anxiety, nervousness, fear, irritability, impatience, and even depression. Behavioral changes may include increased alcohol intake, appetite changes, smoking and drug abuse, restlessness, nail-biting, and increased aggressiveness.

Stress and Disease

Let's look more closely at the connection between stress and disease. Forty years ago, health professionals might have denied that stress can make you sick. Since then, extensive research has indeed shown that stress can contribute to illness. Now we have enlightened attitudes in the health professions toward stress. Chronic stress has been related to conditions such as cardiovascular disease, decreased immune function, personality disorders, depression, ulcers, and migraine headaches. Some say it is the leading cause of health problems in our hectic, high-paced society. Look at some of these facts concerning stress (American Institute of Stress, 2007; Burt, Cutler, Roccella, Sorlie, & Hughes, 2004; Gudka, 2002; Laurence, 2004; Women's Heart Foundation, 2005).

- Chronic stress has been shown to weaken the immune system.
- It is estimated that cardiovascular disease causes over a third of all deaths in the United States. Stress can play a major role in these diseases.
- The majority of heart attacks occur on Monday mornings.
- The stress-related disorder of hypertension is estimated to affect as many as 65 million Americans.
- Research shows that stress plays a role in osteoporosis in women because of increased hormonal levels.
- Sales of antidepressant medications, often used to help cope with stress, have increased greatly.

Stress and the Workplace

Stress also has major effects in the workplace. According to NIOSH (National Institute for Occupational Safety and Health, 1999), job-related stress generates more health complaints than

An Alarming Fact

It is estimated that $300 billion, or $7,500 per employee, is spent annually in the United States on stress-related compensation such as workers' compensation claims, reduced productivity, absenteeism, and medical and insurance costs (American Institute of Stress, 2007).

other life stressors. Studies cited on the American Institute of Stress website (2007) indicate that 25% of employees say that work is the main stressor in their lives, and 75% of workers believe job stress is worse than it was just one generation ago.

GOOD STRESS VERSUS BAD STRESS

Hans Selye was once quoted as saying "stress is the spice of life." His quote was meant to show that boredom itself can be stressful. Selye used the term *eustress* to describe positive stress. "Eu" means easy or normal. Conversely, Seyle used the term *distress* for negative stress (American Institute of Stress, 2007). We are going to keep it much simpler and use the not-so-technical terms of **good stress** and **bad stress**.

Stay in *Your* Zone

The main goal of this chapter is to help you develop a personalized system to keep you in your "good stress zone," so you can perform at your best and seize personal and professional opportunities.

Let's revisit the notion that not all stress is bad for you. Survival stress is an important and necessary stress. If confronted by a life-threatening event, part of your nervous system called the sympathetic nervous system—the fight-or-flight system—will kick in. The impact on the sympathetic system causes certain responses that will maximize your chance for survival. In other words, your body gets ready to either fight or flee the dangerous situation. Your physical and psychological responses may include (Posen, 1995):

- Increased adrenaline levels for more energy
- Faster heart rate to supply more oxygen to muscles
- Increased blood pressure to get more blood flow to the brain
- Pupil dilation to bring in more light to see better
- Faster and deeper breathing to bring in more oxygen
- Heightened state of awareness to focus on the job at hand

> ### Strange But True Fact
>
> There are many stories of people performing herculean feats when their fight-or-flight response, or adrenaline rush, kicked in. Stories include people of average strength and weight lifting cars to save someone trapped underneath or carrying items such as refrigerators while running from a fire.

All of these responses can help enhance your performance. In other words, you can have "good stress." Now we don't always want to be in a fight-or-flight response and should reserve that for truly life-threatening situations. However, a little bit of stress is good for you while performing important tasks. The key is balance and moderation.

Good Stress

The fight-or-flight response shows a good stress response in life-threatening situations. But what about everyday events such as a big exam, a job interview, or giving a speech in front of the class? Studies show that you actually perform better if you have moderate stress and are not totally "cool as a cucumber." If you are not under enough stress, your performance may suffer because you are bored or unmotivated. A little stress will get you "up" for the task. However, if you let stress get out of hand and you panic, you have entered into bad stress. In bad stress, your anxiety rises to the point where you perform poorly or even not at all.

So let's begin the first step of the two-step stress management system. Here you learn to become aware of *your* good and bad stress zones. Exercise 1-3 will help you recognize your good stress zone.

Write at least three adjectives or phrases that describe you when you are in "your good stress zone." In other words, select words that describe you when you are functioning well, running on all cylinders, hitting your peak, and so on. To get you thinking, some adjectives may include *happy, focused*, and a *sense of humor*. Remember, choose words that best describe you when you are doing well in *your* life.

_____

_____

_____

Keep these in mind because we will soon use them in developing your personalized stress management system.

Bad Stress

The first step in treating any illness is good assessment. This is also the first step in a good personal stress management system. First, recognizing your own stressors and the symptoms they cause can help you determine when your stress is out of balance or in other words, when you have entered your bad stress zone. These signals can be valuable to your good health and positive attitude. They represent a wake-up call that says you need to cope with what's going on in your life before it overtakes you.

As already stated, a certain amount of stress is normal. We need it to develop and grow. However, going beyond your good stress zone and "losing it" by entering your bad stress zone can be harmful. You need to determine when you are losing balance. The best way is to look for physical and emotional signs or indicators that the stress is too much. From our previous discussion on the harmful effects of stress, it should be clear as to what high levels of bad stress can cause. It's no wonder that individuals who can't handle stress have more accidents, poorer attendance, and difficulty studying and learning. If bad stress persists and becomes long term or chronic, it can become destructive. The American Institute of Stress lists several effects of stress in the *bad zone*, including:

- High blood pressure, heart attack, or stroke
- Stomach pain

REAL-LIFE APPLICATION
Preventive Medicine and Early Intervention

Preventive medicine has gained much attention in recent years as opposed to the traditional disease model in which the medical community waited until individuals got sick and then treated them. Tension headaches indicate you have been in your bad stress zone for some time. If you can identify earlier signals that precede a headache, for instance, and intervene right there and then, you can prevent many headaches from ever happening. One thing to look for is nervous habits such as biting fingernails, pulling your hair, shaking your leg, or clicking your pen. These are usually early signs that you have just entered your bad stress zone. Again, if you intervene right away, you can prevent yourself from developing more serious problems. This self-awareness is often difficult because many of these habits are so automatic that we just ignore them. So if you catch yourself shaking your leg and intervene, you can prevent the subsequent muscle tightness, upset stomach, and headache that may follow.

- Lack of sleep or insomnia
- Decreased immune system functioning
- Depression and personality changes
- Problems with learning
- Frequent headaches

YOUR TWO-STEP STRESS MANAGEMENT SYSTEM

Now that you have the background information, you can develop your personalized stress management system. Take your time with each step, and remember that this system will evolve over time and with continued use.

Step 1: Become Aware of Your Good and Bad Stress Zones

You defined your good stress zone in Exercise 1-3. You want to do the things necessary to maintain your good stress levels and reduce your bad stress levels. Now, in Exercise 1-4, let's go on to develop awareness of your bad stress zone.

EXERCISE 1-4
Finding Your Bad Stress Zone

List several mental *and* physical changes that occur when you are in your bad stress zone. In other words, come up with a list of things that happen to your body and mind when you are "losing it," not clicking on all cylinders, and not functioning well. To jog your memory, some possible examples could include stomachaches, forgetfulness, nervous habits, eye twitching, making mistakes, irritability, headaches, or muscular tension. Remember to list your own responses. Some may be the same as the examples given, but they must relate to *your* life.

_____

_____

_____

_____

_____

You have now developed a contrasting picture of your good and bad stress zones from Exercises 1-3 and 1-4, but we need to take it just a little further. In Exercise 1-5, you will now develop your personal stress chart or continuum.

Using Figure 1-3, place your descriptions from Exercise 1-3 in the Good Stress Zone. Now look at your list from your bad stress zone (Exercise 1-4) and place it in *chronological* order starting with what occurs first when you just begin to enter your bad stress zone. You can also see Figure 1-4, which shows a completed stress chart or continuum as an example.

EXERCISE 1-5
Making Your Personal
Stress Chart

FIGURE 1-3

First, place your descriptions from Exercise 1-3 in the good stress zone. Then put the items from Exercise 1-4 in chronological order in the bad stress zone. You can add lines or spaces if needed.

Good Stress Zone   **Bad Stress Zone**

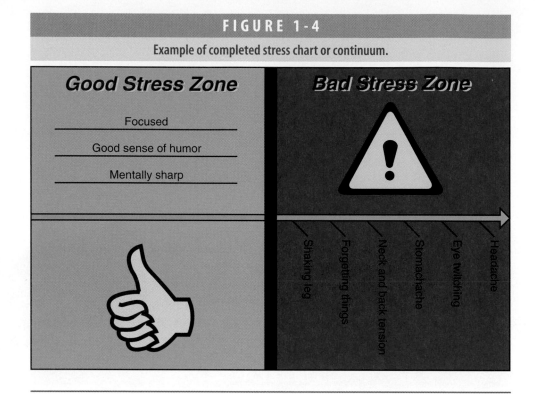

FIGURE 1-4

Example of completed stress chart or continuum.

Good Stress Zone

Focused

Good sense of humor

Mentally sharp

Bad Stress Zone

Shaking leg

Forgetting things

Neck and back tension

Stomachache

Eye twitching

Headache

You have now completed step 1, "Become Aware of Your Good and Bad Stress Zones." Your personalized system now shows you how to recognize when you are in your good stress zone. Most importantly, it will show you how to recognize when you are *just beginning* to enter your bad stress zone so you can quickly intervene to prevent all those bad things that can occur later.

For example, look at Figure 1-4. If this person intervenes as soon as his leg starts shaking (step 2), he can quickly go back into the good stress zone. If he doesn't intervene, he will move further down the continuum to more serious consequences such as headaches.

People who get frequent tension headaches (four to five per week) have used this system to reduce their headaches down to one or even *none* per week. They recognize the early warning signals—such as shaking their leg or rolling their neck because of tension—and stop and do something about it before it builds into a headache.

Please note that your stress continuum will continue to develop over time. Here are some helpful hints:

- As stated previously, often a nervous habit such as tapping a pen, shaking a leg, or biting your nails is an early warning sign you are entering your bad stress zone.
- Make sure your list contains both mental and physical signs.
- Visit your continuum every few months to see if you discovered something new to add. (Your CD can help you here.)

SUCCESS STORY

Often you are not aware of a nervous habit. During one workshop, an attendee who had a headache 5 days per week vigorously denied any nervous habits that led up to the headaches. When pressed, she began to click her pen at  a very high rate and still deny any nervous habits until it was brought to her attention. She said, "I didn't even know I was doing that." Then a friend said, "Yes, and you always chew on your hair" and another coworker said, "You drive me crazy when you tap your pencil and grind your jaw." In 15 minutes she had a fully developed stress continuum with many early indicators that could signal an alarm to intervene before her headache began. Within 6 months she indicated she was down to one to two tension headaches per week! What a positive change in her quality of life!

- Pick something (like a headache) that occurs at the latter part of your continuum, and chart your progress in reducing the number of occurrences.
- Pay attention when people close to you provide personal insights about yourself, like your nervous habits or overreacting. They may see things you do not.

Congratulations! You now have become aware of and have developed your personalized stress continuum. Now we move on to step 2, which basically says once you recognize that you are in your bad stress zone, you can intervene in a healthy manner to get back to your good stress zone.

Step 2: Perform a *Healthy* Intervention

Notice that the word *healthy* is emphasized. If every time you enter your bad stress zone, you drink alcohol, take other drugs, or reach for something to eat, you can develop addictions. That is an unhealthy way to cope with stress. So what are the healthy interventions? There are many, and they depend on your particular situation. This chapter ends with some positive interventions to consider. Please note that not all of these will work for any given situation; they are presented here as a start to give you options to think about.

Exercise.

Physical exercise relieves stress. The type of exercise is up to you and can be as simple as taking a brisk walk. If you are more physically fit, you may want to include jogging, bicycling, or lifting weights. Finding a good workout partner or participating in team sports increases the likelihood of consistent follow-through because of the spin-off socialization aspects.

Aerobic exercise also releases *endorphins*, which are the body's natural pain killers and mood-elevating chemicals. Exercise can be used on a regular basis to help *prevent* you from entering your bad stress zone. It can also be used when you find yourself crossing into the bad stress zone and just need to take a brisk walk to clear your mind.

Now you can't always drop everything while at work or taking a test, and just begin exercising when things get stressful. This is why it is important to have a variety of interventions to choose from for any particular situation. People who have office jobs and spend a lot of time sitting at the computer can do certain office exercises, such as periodically stretching to help relieve their tension. Some workplaces even have office aerobics and exercise sessions built into the workday.

Nutrition/Sleep.

Good health practices such as sleeping the proper amount and good nutrition increase the probability that you will remain in your good stress zone, even when triggers do come your way. It is like hydrating yourself before physical exercise instead of waiting until you are dying of thirst. Adequate sleep is a must for us to function at our peak and handle stress. Research has shown that lack of sleep makes you more susceptible to illness, more irritable, and less able to focus. Health experts recommend that most adults get between 7 and 9 hours of sleep a night.

When the body is run down because of sleep deprivation or poor nutrition, every little trigger will cause you to enter and most likely stay in your bad stress zone. Remember what happens when people stay in their bad stress zone for extended periods of time, creating chronic stress—high blood pressure, diabetes, and heart attacks are just a few possible outcomes.

Good nutrition is a must for our growth and development. It also helps to fight bad stress and disease. One part of practicing good nutrition is to drink plenty of water. Water makes up the majority of our body, and it aids in digestion, absorption of nutrients, and removal of waste products. Although water is found in most foods, drink at least 6 to 8 glasses each day for good health.

Caffeine, found in coffee, tea, and many sodas, is a potent central nervous system stimulant. Large amounts can make you anxious, nervous, and can prevent you from getting a good night's sleep. Maintaining a well-balanced diet in moderation is important to your long-term health. More is discussed on these areas in Chapter 10.

Leisure/Hobby/Music.

Taking leisure time helps you to deal with stress in a positive manner. Both the body and mind need to get away and recharge their batteries. Getting lost in a hobby or listening to your favorite music can slow down your mind. Slowing down your mind can help you take a calmer look at perceived stress.

Did you ever have a major problem come into your life and the more you focused on it, the more stressed and emotional you became with no solution in sight? It is hard to come up with ideas and use good decision-making skills in this frame of mind. Even taking only 15 minutes of leisure time can help greatly.

When a problem is causing unrelenting stress, take a break and get away from the problem by doing something else. In many cases, the solution will then just come to you as if by magic. It's not magic, just your subconscious mind working for you, a phenomenon discussed in depth in Chapter 2. Basically, by stepping away from the problem and emotionally detaching into a hobby or music, the calmer mind may come up with the solution.

Humor Therapy.

It has been estimated that children laugh 100 times a day. Maybe there is a lot to be learned from children. How often do you think adults laugh in one day, compared to children? How much do *you* laugh?

> *Laughter is the vaccine for the ills of the world.*
> —Joey Adams

Humor also has psychological effects, such as helping to resolve problems and to reduce stress and anxiety. You have probably been in a stressful situation with other people when a joke broke the ice. Humor therapy is even used in some medical institutions as an enhancement to medical treatment (Ziegler, 1995).

There are several techniques you can use to enhance humor in your life. Tell appropriate jokes and even keep a humor file. One of the most effective tools is to simply *smile* and laugh out loud more often. Look for humor in every situation you can, and don't be afraid to laugh at yourself. At the same time, always remember to take your study and work responsibilities seriously.

The next time you are on hold, or dealing with one of those frustrating automated telephone menus, or in a traffic jam and begin to tense up and stress out—force a big smile on your face. You will find out it is nearly impossible to feel bad when you are smiling. This will prevent something that is out of your control from ruining the rest of your day. Try it now in Exercise 1-6 to demonstrate its effectiveness.

Place a big smile on your face and try to be angry or think a bad thought. Write a description of how it worked for you.

EXERCISE 1-6
A Simple Method That Works Wonders

_____

_____

_____

Social Support.

Social support in the form of friends, family, loved ones, or clubs and organizations can all help with stress relief. Be careful because interactions with people can also cause bad stress. However, all you need to do is remain *aware* of your early stress signals, and when they alarm *do something positive* to get you back to your good stress zone.

Although social support can be very positive, it is always good to keep in good touch with *yourself.* Do Exercise 1-7, which helps you vent safely.

Is there something happening that you perceive as unfair? Do you have a friend with a personality trait that drives you crazy? Is an upcoming event stressing you out?

EXERCISE 1-7
Venting

Using your computer microphone, camcorder, or other recording device, talk to yourself about it. Make a recording of yourself talking about this problem as if you were venting to a trusted friend. Be honest, be brutal, or be ultrareasonable, but be yourself. Get it all out. Then let a few hours or a day go by, and listen to yourself. How does the problem sound to you now? Does it seem as important or "vent-worthy" as it did before? And how do *you* sound to yourself? Would you sympathize with yourself? Major leap of faith: Would you let someone you trust listen to this recording? Talking with a close friend and journal writing can be two additional and very effective ways to vent.

We don't see things as they are, we see things as we are.
—Anais Nin

Relaxation Techniques.

Practicing relaxation techniques will help to clear your mind and make you sharper. Many people will find a million excuses why they can't take the time to relax because of their demanding schedule. Do you see the problem this sets up? If they are that busy, then they *need* to take the time to relax and restore the body and mind or life will continue to be crazy. This time also allows you to listen to your body. Two types of effective relaxation techniques include breathing relaxation and meditation techniques, and these are demonstrated on your CD.

Slow and deep breathing serves several purposes. First, it increases oxygen to your brain and your body. It also slows your thinking to help clear your head and relax your muscles. Here is a breathing relaxation technique to try:

First, find an area with few or no distractions (insects, noise, interruptions, etc.). You can sit in a favorite chair (recliners work best) or even lie in your bed and use this technique before going to sleep if you can't find the time during the day. Sometimes, this may even make you fall asleep, which is good because you will get a much more restful and restorative sleep. Now that you have your area, get comfortable and do the following:

1. Close your eyes and have your palms face upward (this removes distracting sensory input).
2. Take a *slow* and *deep* breath in through your nose and out your mouth. When you breathe in, your stomach should slowly rise and it should then slowly fall when you breathe out. You can put one hand over your stomach to make sure you are doing this correctly until you get used to this.
3. Continue breathing slowly and deeply concentrating on your breathing and nothing else (thoughts will enter, but just go back to concentrating on your breathing).
4. Once you are comfortable doing this, add some visual imagery. For example, as you slowly breathe *out*, visualize all the tension in your body leaving with the exhaled breath.

This is a basic technique, and with practice you can eventually do one or two deep cleansing breaths when tension rises and feel immediate relief within 1 minute. This becomes important when your demanding schedule is causing stress and you need to take a quick refreshing pause. In addition, you'll see in an upcoming chapter how this 1-minute technique can help when you begin to "stress" while taking that big exam. However, try to do at least 10 breaths in the beginning until you get comfortable with the technique.

Strange But True Fact

Meditation is recommended by more and more physicians to prevent or slow the pain associated with chronic diseases such as cancer. New research with sophisticated imaging techniques is showing that meditation can train the mind and reshape the brain to prevent "traffic jams" within the brain that cause stress (Stein, 2003).

Meditation.

Meditation means basically slowing your mind down and clearing it of internal chatter. Techniques can vary greatly, but they all center around attempting to focus your mind on "one thing." This one thing can be your breathing, as you just learned. It can also be an object, chant, or phrase, or even a positive thought (Stein, 2003).

Examples of healthy interventions to bad stress.

Yoga deals with the study of meditation and has been around for centuries. Although many people think of yoga as all those twisted postures, this is really the lowest form of yoga in which the body is being conditioned, so it does not distract the mind. Think how hard it would be to concentrate on "one thing" or a positive thought with a "nagging" backache. It may be an interesting and relaxing experience to take a yoga or tai chi (meditation in movement) class.

KNOW YOUR SCHOOL

Your school will have support services to help you in many areas. Research and find what school resources can help you with stress management. One example would be counseling services. Others include student health services, resident advisers, and clergy. List the information here, and for quick reference place the information in a prominent place such as on your refrigerator.

Resource Name _____

Office Location _____

Phone Number _____

E-Mail Address _____

Now that you have developed *your* stress continuum and can recognize when you are entering your bad stress zone, use Exercise 1-8 to list a few interventions you can use to get you back into your good stress zone. It may be something from this chapter or it may be something unique to you. Pick interventions that work for you. It is also a good idea to pick interventions in different environments and situations. For example, you may pick a "walk in the woods." However, when the stress is mounting during an exam, this isn't feasible, and something like a single relaxing cleansing breath may be appropriate.

HEALTHY DECISION MAKING

Mary has been out of school for several years and is a single parent. She has decided to go back to school to better her life and has been accepted for the fall semester, which is 3 months away. She has been reading about how much her program stresses critical and creative thinking skills, and she is concerned that she gets too stressed out to think clearly at times. In addition, she has attempted several study schedules but gets overwhelmed and very anxious and is unable to complete them. What would you recommend Mary do prior to the start of school to give her a more hopeful outlook and maximize her chance of succeeding in school?

_____

_____

_____

_____

SUMMATION EXERCISE 1-8

List and describe several interventions, so you can have them ready in any given situation or environment.

An exercise choice:_____

A step you will take toward better nutrition:_____

A way to improve your sleep habits: _____

A hobby: _____

Your favorite relaxing music: _____

Your favorite type of humor or favorite comedian:_____

Your social and family supports:_____

A favorite relaxation technique: _____

At least one intervention for work or school:_____

At least one intervention at home: _____

Note: You may want to keep this list handy so you can pick out something that would help you at that "stressful" moment. Eventually, you won't need the list because you will automatically respond when your stress alarm goes off with a healthy and effective intervention.

Now that you have read this chapter and performed the assessments and exercises, please go to your CD for this chapter to reinforce these concepts. The CD will present you with a fun and interactive journey back through stress management and visually show you such things as how to develop your stress continuum, meditation, and relaxation techniques.

References

American Institute of Stress. (2007). Job stress. Retrieved April 14, 2007, from http://www.stress.org

American Medical Women's Association. (2007). How stress affects you & physical symptoms of stress. Retrieved April 17, 2007, from http://www.amwa-doc.org

Burt, V. L., Cutler, J. A., Roccella, E. J., Sorlie, P., & Hughes, J. (2004, August 23). Journal report. American Heart Association. Retrieved April 14, 2007, from http://www.americanheart.org

Gudka, P. (2002, December). Fight of festive stress. *The Express.* Retrieved from Beatstress.com

Laurence, L. (2004, April). How stress makes you sick. *Ladies Home Journal,* pp. 131–138.

National Institute for Occupational Safety and Health. (1999). Stress at work. Retrieved April 15, 2007, from http://www.cdc.gov/niosh/stresswk.html

Posen, D. B. (1995). Stress management for patient and physician. Retrieved April 17, 2002, from http://www.mentalhealth.com

Stein, J. (2003, August 4). Just say om. *Time* pp. 48–56.

Women's Heart Foundation. (2005). What is a heart attack? Retrieved March 23, 2007, from http://www.womensheartfoundation.org

Ziegler, J. (1995). Immune system may benefit from the ability to laugh. *Journal of the National Cancer Institute, 87*(5), 342–344.

For a listing of further suggested readings for this chapter, please visit the companion website for this textbook.

Positive Attitudes and Goals

Preparing the Mind for Success

OBJECTIVES

What you will discover by the end of this chapter:

- The power of your mind
- Methods to reframe your thinking
- How to foster and maintain a positive attitude
- Goal-setting strategies

WHY LEARN THIS SKILL?

Why does attitude matter? Simply put, attitude and self-motivation *directly* determine your academic and professional success. If you have a positive attitude and are motivated to learn, you have a head start on a productive career. One characteristic that successful people share is a positive attitude. In addition, people with positive attitudes have been shown to have a more responsive immune system (Segerstrom, quoted in Crawford, 2002).

Keeping a positive outlook can sometimes be tough because we are constantly bombarded by negative messages and thoughts (Just watch the news!). As you journey through life, outside messages and internal thoughts can begin, like seeds, to grow and thrive in our minds. Our minds represent a potentially fertile garden that can bear healthy fruit, if that garden is cared for properly. This chapter will show you how to cultivate your mind's garden and develop a *successful* attitude. In addition, this chapter will help you to set goals for personal and professional success.

Fantastic things happen—to the way we feel, to the way we make other people feel. All this simply by using positive words.

Leo Buscaglia

As you work through the exercises in this chapter, one goal will be to slow down your "mind talk" and make it positive and supportive. Let's begin with Exercise 2-1.

You have a way to go before we try specific techniques, so for now choose the statement that most closely describes your current mind talk:

EXERCISE 2-1
Describe Your Thoughts

_____ Frantic and gloomy

_____ Fast and furious

_____ Escapist and rambling

_____ Positive and supportive

or make up your own description:

_____

Now, describe a specific internal dialogue that supports your choice. For example, if you chose "frantic and gloomy," your description may be something like, "I'm never going to pass this test—there just aren't enough hours in the day." (Hopefully this isn't yours, but if it is, we will work together to change it.)

_____

_____

_____

There are no limitations to the mind except those we acknowledge.
—From a fortune cookie the author ate

People often stress the importance of a positive attitude. You probably have heard sayings such as "You are what you think" and "Your attitude determines your life." If this sounds like pop psychology, you may be skeptical and require proof. So, let's discuss exactly why a positive attitude is so important and actually *prove* just how powerful it can be. To understand this, we must begin with a basic understanding of that wonderful and mysterious thing we call our mind.

THE CONSCIOUS VERSUS THE SUBCONSCIOUS MIND

We can begin to understand the mind by considering it in two parts: the **conscious** and the **subconscious**. The conscious mind is what we are most familiar with. This involves our day-to-day thoughts about what to wear, how to pay the bills, and what our future holds. We spend most of our waking lives immersed in this part of the mind. In Chapter 1 on stress management, we started a journey to slow that conscious mind to a reasonable speed. In this chapter, we take that journey a bit further.

Operating just under the conscious mind is the subconscious, much like a submarine operates unseen under the surface of the water. This part of our mind is concerned with survival. Imagine if we had to consciously think about each heartbeat! We would be unable to think about anything else. We are less aware of the subconscious because it functions more in our sleep. During our waking hours, it also functions, but often at such a level we are not aware of its presence.

Strange But True Fact

In cave-dwelling days, people were more immersed in the subconscious because simply maintaining survival was a dominant concern. Mainly, people worried about how to get their next meal—and not *become* the next meal! They had to be in tune with their environment and *feel* danger when it was lurking behind a rock. In other words, they had a highly developed intuition, which many experts believe resides in the subconscious realm.

The Power of the Subconscious Mind

The subconscious can be a powerful ally in developing and maintaining a positive attitude and creativity. Let's learn more about the subconscious and illustrate its power.

Important Fact 1.

The thoughts or ideas you plant in your subconscious will grow there.

Proof. Have you ever had a problem weigh on your conscious mind? You think and worry about it all day. Then you go to sleep at night, and you dream about your concerns. This happens because the subconscious takes over while the conscious mind is asleep. Remember, the subconscious is the survival part of your mind. It will consider something you perceive as a threat as something it must deal with. Even if you consciously think you cannot deal with your problem, your subconscious is always on the job. While sleeping, you might have some crazy dream about the problem while the subconscious mind tries to sort it all out. The

you tell yourself you will never get organized, you won't—because that is the seed you are planting. In addition, you are wasting a lot of time telling yourself all the reasons why you can't get organized, time you could have spent actually getting organized!

Positive Self-Talk

You can use this same principle to your advantage by using *positive* self-talk. Talking to your-self does not mean you are crazy. In fact, talking is slower than thinking and therefore slows your racing mind, which helps you to be more focused. Self-talk can boost self-esteem if it is optimistic and positive. For example, replace negative internal messages such as "I'm not

---

TEST YOURSELF

Do You See the Glass as Half Empty or Half Full?

The following table contrasts characteristics of positive and negative attitudes. Put check marks by the statements that best describe you.

Contrasting Attitudes

Characteristics of Positive Attitudes	Characteristics of Negative Attitudes
_____ Think mostly positive thoughts	_____ Think mostly negative thoughts
_____ Willing to learn	_____ Resistant to learning
_____ Accepting of change	_____ Not accepting of change
_____ Upbeat	_____ Gloomy
_____ Calm and in control	_____ Out of control
_____ Open to other people and views	_____ Not open to other views
_____ Nonjudgmental	_____ Judgmental
_____ Accepts responsibility	_____ Blames others
_____ Shows sense of humor	_____ Shows little sense of humor

For each check mark on the negative side, develop a specific action plan to move it over to the positive column.

Characteristic:_____

Action Plan:_____

_____

_____

Characteristic:_____

Action Plan:_____

_____

_____

It may be interesting to have someone you trust check the list so you can learn how others see you.

TABLE 2-1	
Constructive Versus Destructive Approach	
Constructive	**Destructive**
Confronts a problem (appropriately)	Thinks problems will resolve themselves
Discusses things in calm manner	Fights or yells
Accepts responsibility	Blames others
Uses relaxation techniques	Uses alcohol or drugs
Accepts/learns from mistakes	Is a perfectionist
Practices good nutrition	Over- or undereats
Lives in the present	Agonizes over past or future
Helps others	Avoids people

smart enough to pass this course" with "If I study hard and develop an effective action plan, I *will* do well in this course."

In addition to positive self-talk, other strategies can get rid of the weeds that may grow in the mind. Don't dwell on past negative or unpleasant experiences, and don't carry grudges. Those thoughts only serve to deplete your energy and destroy your motivation.

Balance Your Attitude

We should all strive for balance in our lives, including in our attitudes and emotions. Many people view anger as a negative emotion, but just like stress, a little anger can be good. It can spur us on to do better or to right an injustice. However, prolonged anger can lead to destructive behavior and illness.

We all get sad when a tragedy strikes. This makes us human. But, it's important to differentiate depression from sadness. If someone is sad following a painful disappointment or the loss of a loved one, it is a normal part of the grieving process. However, if the sadness remains for a prolonged period of time and interferes with the ability to go about one's daily business, it becomes depression. Balance, again, is the key factor.

Look at Table 2-1, which contrasts a constructive versus destructive approach to life. Where do you fit in?

Now complete Exercise 2-4.

EXERCISE 2-4
Change Destructive Beliefs

Assess yourself and check any of the negative/irrational self-beliefs you have:

_____ I must be perfect in all things I do and say. (irrational)

_____ The place where I work owes me a job. (irrational)

_____ I never have enough time. (negative)

_____ I am responsible for other people's happiness. (irrational)

_____ I should be happy all the time. (irrational)

_____ Change is bad. (negative and irrational)

_____ So-and-so is out to get me. (negative and hopefully irrational!)

For any statements you checked, develop an action plan to change those beliefs to positive and rational ones. In one or two sentences, state actions you can take to turn your attitude around.

_____

_____

_____

_____

Change Worry into Concern

Mark Twain's quote was cleverly telling us that most of what we worry about never happens. We waste all that negative energy by worrying, and we do not experience a positive outcome. You may think we are telling you not to worry about your grades this semester, and you are right. The difference is that, rather than worry, you should be *concerned* about your grades this semester.

> *I'm an old man and have known a great many problems, but most of them never happened.*
> —Mark Twain

When you are worried, you wring your hands and your mind goes a million miles per hour with messages such as, "I'm never going to understand this," "I'm never going to pass this course," and "What if I fail?"

When you are concerned, you take *action* to maximize the positive outcome. For example, students should be concerned

Sobering Fact

People do not get you upset—you do! You are the only person who can make you angry or upset or feel bad. *You* feel the way *you* think.

about how well they will do in a difficult course. This example could illustrate their approach: "I know this is a tough course; however if I *do* the following, I *will* pass this course":

- Study for 45 minutes each day
- Keep up with assignments
- See my teacher at least once per week

Notice the difference? *Worry* is wasted negative energy with no action, and *concern* involves planning a course of action that will most likely lead to a positive outcome. In Exercise 2-5, you can try out this strategy. Remember this old saying: "Worrying is like sitting in a rocking chair; it gives you something to do, but it doesn't get you anywhere."

EXERCISE 2-5
Changing Worry into Concern

A. Write down something you worry about.

_____

B. Describe some things you will *do* about what you have just written. In other words, develop a specific action plan to create a positive outcome.

_____

_____

C. Now write down when you will start your action plan. (Hint: It should be a three-letter answer that rhymes with "cow"!)_____

METHOD 3: MEDITATION—GETTING IN TOUCH WITH YOUR SUBCONSCIOUS

Albert Einstein asked, "Why is it I get my best ideas in the morning while I'm shaving?" He came to realize that he did not have to think about shaving because he did it so often. The routine act of shaving allowed him to slow his mind down and let his subconscious bubble up toward the surface with ideas. We talked about meditation in the first chapter. Simply put, it is focusing on *one thing*. Now we can build on that idea by making that *one thing* a positive thought to plant in our minds. Please try Exercise 2-6.

EXERCISE 2-6
Meditating on Positive Thoughts

1. Eliminate the possibility of noise and other distractions.

2. Get comfortable in an easy chair or lie down with palms facing upward.

3. Slowly breathe in through your nose and out through your mouth. As you breathe in, your stomach—not your chest—should rise. The key is slow and steady breathing on inhalation and exhalation. It may take a while to get comfortable with this step.

4. After you feel yourself relaxing and are in a slow and steady rhythm, focus on your feet and relaxing those muscles. Progressively work upward with all your muscles until you reach your forehead.

5. As you exhale, picture in your mind the muscular tension flowing out of the area you are focusing on.

This activity was discussed in Chapter 1 and demonstrated on your CD. You can now take it a step further after you are relaxed. As you exhale, concentrate on one simple, positive thought, such as "I will take care of myself." With practice, you will plant the thought firmly in your mind.

This activity usually takes 5 to 10 minutes. However, if you feel you can't fit it in your hectic schedule, then try it before going to sleep. Do this for 1 week, and describe any observations or results you may have seen. Did you take better care of yourself that week?

_____

_____

_____

Meditation can be used to relax and recharge your mind.

METHOD 4: HUMOR THERAPY

Humor was briefly covered as a coping mechanism in Chapter 1 on stress management, but we can expand on this topic. Many scientists are researching the effects of humor on our physiological and psychological well-being. Some research suggests laughter improves the immune system's ability to ward off illness (Ziegler, 1995). This is not to say that humor therapy and positive emotions can replace medical treatment. They simply can enhance medical treatment and the body's positive response. Let's look at the process of laughter.

> ### Story with a Meaning
>
> In the children's story *Peter Pan*, Peter had the children "think happy thoughts" in order to fly. Although it won't really make you fly, thinking happy thoughts will help you get closer to reaching your higher goals in life.

Positive Effects of Humor

Humor can have many positive effects on your physical and mental health (Berk, quoted in "Therapeutic Benefits of Laughter," 2007). A good laugh increases the heart rate and improves blood circulation. *Epinephrine* levels in the blood also rise. Epinephrine is the body's arousal hormone and stimulates the release of endorphins and serotonin. *Endorphins* are the body's natural painkillers, and *serotonin* helps elevate our mood. Finally, with a good belly laugh, the entire respiratory system, internal organs, and diaphragm get a workout. These are some physiological outcomes of laughter, but what about the psychological effects?

Humor relieves stress and lessens anxiety. In addition, it can help combat depression. When appropriately used, humor can also stimulate one's self-image and creativity. In Chapter 5, you will be encouraged to use humor in making up silly stories to aid your learning. Some smoking cessation programs are now using humor therapy, substituting humor as a coping strategy versus addictive and dangerous nicotine. Use humor when you can, appreciate the benefits when someone is sharing humor with you, and remember that what is learned with humor is not readily forgotten.

So what are some techniques that can be used to enhance humor therapy? Here are some suggestions. Feel free to come up with some more.

- **Tell appropriate jokes.** Humor should never be used in a hurtful manner. Tell good jokes or stories, and avoid those that may offend others.
- **Keep a humor file.** File away good jokes or funny pictures in your computer or a desk drawer. Keep some things around that are funny to you. It's a long-standing tradition to decorate one's work area with wall posters, cartoons, or funny sayings. (What would be someone's first impression of your work area?)
- **Simply SMILE and laugh out loud more often.** This is probably one of the simplest and also most effective techniques. The average 4-year-old laughs many times during an hour. How often do you laugh in the course of your day? Laughter helps bring you back in perspective, and besides, it feels good. Don't forget to have a good laugh at least once a day.
- **Look for humor in every situation you can.** It really is all around you. For example, look at some of the humorous photos and signs that people pass everyday. Would you have taken the time to see and enjoy them?
- **Finally, remember to laugh at yourself.** People are more comfortable around individuals who can make fun of themselves instead of finding fault in others. Have fun at both work and school, but make sure you take your academic and professional responsibilities seriously.

Exercise 2-7 ties in with healthy habits, positive thinking, and a form of goal setting to get you ready for the next section.

SUCCESS STORY

During a workshop, a participant told me that he works in a customer complaint department, so 100% of his interactions with customers are negative. He went on to say that many times a caller will ruin his whole workday; his bad mood will then carry over when he goes home, and he will treat his family horribly, all because of that one bad call. I advised this person that the next time a caller was "getting to him," he should simply put a big smile on his face and continue the conversation. This would help prevent him from saying something that would get him fired. Also, it would be impossible for him to get worked up when he smiles. The participant later stated that this simple technique had a dramatic impact on the way he reacted to bad calls at work. It especially helped him to leave work in a positive frame of mind, which translated to more positive interactions when he got home.

Humor is all around us.

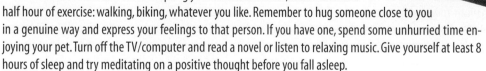

EXERCISE 2-7
"Your Day"

Think ahead about a week or two to a day that will be fairly normal for you: no un-usual events, just your regular schedule. Take this day and plan it as one com-pletely healthy day for yourself. Do not take any extraordinary measures. From what you know about proper nutrition and using what you might normally have in the house, plan three healthy meals and a few healthy snacks. Have a lot of fresh water on hand. Without interrupting your routine schedule, make time for a half hour of exercise: walking, biking, whatever you like. Remember to hug someone close to you in a genuine way and express your feelings to that person. If you have one, spend some unhurried time en-joying your pet. Turn off the TV/computer and read a novel or listen to relaxing music. Give yourself at least 8 hours of sleep and try meditating on a positive thought before you fall asleep.

Describe how you felt the next morning, physically and mentally:

_____

_____

GOAL SETTING

Why Set Goals?

If you can learn the best way to set goals, you can map out your personal and professional suc-cess. Having a well-charted map greatly increases the likelihood that you will arrive successfully

> *A dream is just a dream. A goal is a dream with a plan and a deadline.*
>
> —Harvey Mackay

at your chosen destination. The conclusion of this chapter will show you how to set achievable goals to map your academic, personal, and professional success. Research (Schunk, 2002) shows that people who effectively set goals:

- Concentrate better
- Show more self-confidence
- Feel more motivated
- Focus on tasks better

Can you see how concepts such as stress management, positive attitude, and goal setting are all interrelated? Goal setting builds on everything you've learned so far in these first chapters.

What Are Goals?

Goals are what we aim for, the things we want to achieve in our lives. Goals motivate us and help map our journey to success. You may have already chosen your educational goal and can use goal setting to help you achieve it. If you haven't yet chosen your educational program, you can use goal setting in the upcoming exercises to help you determine your career path.

Developing goals will help you to decide where you want to go and actually get you there. Later in this book you'll learn about using memory aids, such as *acronyms,* to understand concepts. We will introduce an acronym here to teach you how to set goals. Because setting goals is part of the journey to chart, or *map,* your way in life, remember the term *MAPS* in setting your goals:

M = measurable
A = attainable
P = positive
S = self-chosen

Let's look at each of these characteristics in a little more depth.

Measurable. Your goal must be specific and able to be measured. For example, let's say your goal is to "do well in your first semester." This is too vague. How well is well? If you say, "I want to get a B average or better in my first semester," you now have a measure of your success. You will know for sure if you achieved the goal or not when you receive your semester grades. A time period should be associated with the goal to know when to measure your success. All goals need a target time or deadline.

Attainable. You must be able to see yourself accomplishing this goal, and therefore it must be realistic. You must be able to believe you can do it and have the resources available to help you. Even though the desired goal may take a lot of work and time, you must "in your mind" be able to see yourself attaining it.

Positive. Always use *positive language* when stating a goal. For example, stating, "I will earn a B average or better in my first semester," is much better than "I will not get any D's or F's this semester." It is better to say what you *will* do than to focus on what you will *avoid* doing. Along with being positive, affirm your goal by stating it firmly ("I *will* earn a B average or better" rather than hedging by saying "I will *try* to earn a B average or better."

Self-chosen. Do you think you will better commit to a goal someone else set for you or one that you set? Several well-meaning people in your life may have your best interests at heart and attempt to set goals for you. Although you should consider their thoughts, your ultimate goals must be chosen by you. This gives you ownership and responsibility for your goals. Your goals should be something *you* desire and really want to accomplish.

Keep in mind that goals are something you should reach for. You need to set a goal that will challenge your ability. This is the way you grow. For example, in sports it is easier to play against weak competition and look really good. However, to improve, you should play against people who are actually better than you. Many coaches say, "You're only as good as your competition." Become your own competition by choosing a goal that will challenge you, and then enjoy the payoff in a big way once you achieve it.

It is also important to have goals that balance your personal and professional lives. If you have all professional goals and no personal development goals, you may soon burn out by not taking care of yourself. Your professional goals will then suffer. So develop a balance of goals that complement each other.

Time Frame

Note that goals can also be broken down according to the *time frame* in which they will be accomplished. You can have short-, medium-, or long-range goals.

- Short-range goal: tomorrow, next week, next month
- Medium-range goal: 1 to 6 months
- Long-term goal: 1 year or more

You may not be comfortable yet in writing down your long-term goal, so Exercise 2-8 will give you a fun but somewhat challenging way to accomplish a short-term goal and get your feet wet in this goal-setting process at a basic level.

TEST YOURSELF
Which Is a Better Goal?

1a. I will do better in my classes this semester and will try to participate more in class discussion.

1b. I will assess my study skills and class participation, and I will develop three specific action plans to improve them for the upcoming semester.

2a. I will exercise for 30 minutes a day at least three times a week.

2b. I will get in better shape so that I look better at the beach.

3a. I will successfully pass a course on cardiopulmonary resuscitation (CPR) by term's end.

3b. I may take a CPR course to improve my résumé, if it is not too hard.

4a. I will volunteer at least 5 hours per week for a local nonprofit organization that can help me improve my business skills and make potential contacts for the future.

4b. I will try to find some volunteer work that will increase my business. Hopefully, I will meet some people who can help me find a job later.

EXERCISE 2-8
You Can Run, But You Cannot Hide

Think of a short-term goal, one that your friends may think is uncharacteristic of you: getting on stage for karaoke, volunteering at the local animal shelter, writing a letter to the editor. It doesn't have to be "Fear Factor" material, but pick something you can do within the week. *Tell* someone that you trust about your goal. Ask that person to give you a realistic deadline for completing it. Be prepared to prove that you have achieved your short-term goal. If you don't, you must do something for that person, like treating him or her to a nice lunch! Revisit this exercise after you attempt your short-term goal. Did you have to buy lunch?

One problem with goal setting is that people set too many goals, get overwhelmed, and then fail. Therefore, this text focuses on goals that fall around the medium- and long-range period. This will give you a clear vision of where you want to be in the next 6 months to a year and will help you develop a successful plan to get there. Once you experience that initial success and see the power in goal setting, it will serve to motivate you to go even further.

One of the first rules is to *write down* your goals and keep them where you can refer to them. Exercise 2-9 will get you started.

EXERCISE 2-9
Setting Your Goals

Pick one personal and one professional goal you desire to achieve within the next 6 months to a year, and write them below. Be sure to use each of the characteristics in the MAPS system. Examples are given in Figure 2-2 as a guide. Remember these must be *your* goals. If you haven't chosen a career path, develop a goal that will help you as you explore academic programs and/or careers.

Educational/professional goal:

_____

_____

Personal goal:

_____

_____

Figure 2-2 lists some examples of educational and personal goals.

FIGURE 2-2
Example of educational and personal goal.

Educational goal/professional goal: *I will maintain a B average or above and make a positive impression on the faculty at my school in my first year.*

Personal Goal: *I will develop and begin an exercise program and commit to following it at least three times a week for my first semester in school.*

Objectives

Now that you have a clear picture of where you want to be in 6 months to a year from Exercise 2-9, just how do you plan on getting there? The plan is the development of objectives related to your goal. **Objectives** are actions you need to take to achieve your stated goal. You can also think about your objectives as the specific steps in your overall action plan or the blueprints leading you to successful completion of your long-range goal. Developing *specific* objectives, or action plans, will help you to reach your goal.

For example, your goal may be to graduate and start your own business. That's a wonderful goal, but you have to chart a plan of action with specific steps. Some of the objectives may include researching program requirements, talking to other business people, obtaining an internship to gain experience and contacts, and others. Let's continue with the goal-setting process by completing Exercise 2-10.

Now that you have written down your long-term goals, you have your vision. Naturally you are not going to achieve your goal overnight. You must take small steps, in the form of short- and medium-range objectives, in your journey. For your long-range educational goal, write at least three specific objectives that will move you toward your long-range goal. Please see Figure 2-3 for an example.

Rewrite your *educational goal* from Exercise 2-9.

_____

Describe why you chose this goal:

_____

Now develop a specific action plan.

Action plan (your specific objectives):

1. _____

2. _____

3. _____

List some resources that can help with your action plan:

_____

Notice in Figure 2-3 that both the action plan and resources mention *community*. We are all part of a community. This includes the community where you live and the community of your school. Getting involved in your community can help improve neighborhood conditions as well as give you valuable skills and experiences for the future. This is definitely a win/win situation: You win, or gain benefit, from this interaction, and your community wins by being improved. There are various ways to perform community service, including volunteer work with the homeless or senior citizens, coaching children in your community, or teaching illiterate adults to read.

FIGURE 2-3

The fully developed goal plan.

Educational goal/professional goal:
I will maintain a B average or above and make a positive impression on the faculty at my school in my first year.

The reason I chose this goal:
By maintaining a B average or better, I will make the requirements to be successful in my chosen career. Making a positive impression on the faculty will give me good future references to secure a good job. This will all lead to a good career and the financial security to do the things I want in my life, and the chance to give back to my community.

Action plan (specific objectives):
Use the methods in my students success course to manage stress and develop successful study habits and time management skills.
Use the learning resource center or group study sessions.
Come to class on time and get to know my teacher by being prepared and asking questions on the material.
Reevaluate my progress after the first semester.
Volunteer for special projects at school or in the community.

Some resources that can help me:
My teachers
Study Skills Center
This textbook/CD
Positive fellow students
Family and community resources

Now in Exercise 2-11, you'll use the same goal-setting system to work through the *personal* goal you named in Exercise 2-9. Remember that a personal goal can be anything important in your personal life, for example, learning to play a musical instrument, learning to paint, learning sign language, or improving a personal relationship.

**EXERCISE 2-11
Refining Your
Personal Goal**

Rewrite your personal goal from Exercise 2-9:

_____

Describe why you chose this goal:

_____

Now *map* out a specific action plan.
Action plan (your specific objectives):

1. _____

2. _____

3. _____

List some resources that can help with your action plan:

_____

_____

_____

Useful Hints on Goal Setting:

- When obstacles arise, be prepared to revise your objectives (or even your goals) to address changing conditions because *change* is a natural part of life.
- Don't get frustrated if your progress seems to stall. Many people work furiously toward a goal for a while and then trail off. This is also a natural occurrence. At first you may make rapid progress toward a goal and eventually reach a period where your progress is not as great. This **plateau period** is the crucial stage where you should not give up! Realize that everyone reaches a plateau and that it will pass.
- Don't set too many goals at one time and become overwhelmed. One educational/professional goal and one personal goal are adequate.
- Describe and visualize what it will be like when you achieve your goal. Visualization can also help you reach your goal. Imagine your success and feel all the good feelings. This will help you maintain your commitment.
- Learn from your past and from others. List anything that prevented you from reaching this goal in the past. Make a note of anyone else who has achieved your goal—don't reinvent the wheel. If you can, talk to other people who have achieved your desired goal, and find out what they did. Learn from their mistakes. They may also prove to be valuable contacts in the future.
- Consider keeping a goal-oriented journal and writing notes about your progress. This activity will help you stay focused.
- Be creative and have fun with this process. Most importantly, reward yourself when you reach a certain objective. Even small rewards will motivate you to go to the next step in your plan. Another reward, then, will lead you ever closer to your goal. The reward can be as simple as going out to eat, seeing a movie, or staying at home and watching your favorite TV program.

Not So Strange But True Fact

The U.S. Olympic Committee developed a training program to have their athletes "think" like winners. It includes these four components (Kabat-Zinn & Beall, 1987):

- Visualize yourself in the successful performance of your event.
- Set short- and long-term goals to achieve "the gold".
- Practice physical and mental relaxation techniques.
- Concentrate on positive thoughts.

From what you have learned so far, can you apply this strategy to your plans for academic success? How does it apply to your life and your future career?

In reading this text and doing the exercises, you will see how each element of your journey relates to the others. Try Exercise 2-12, which connects stress management to goal setting.

SUMMATION EXERCISE 2-12: RANKING THE STEPS

Of the following goal-setting strategies, evaluate them from your point of view as either "very stressful," "somewhat stressful," or "not very stressful." Compare your results with the class.

3 = very stressful   2 = somewhat stressful   1 = not very stressful

_____ Deciding on a goal

_____ Writing down your goal

_____ Setting a deadline

_____ Planning the steps necessary to achieving the goal

_____ Taking action on the first step toward the goal

_____ Following your plan through to completion

As we said in Chapter 1, a little bit of stress can be good, so a rating of "somewhat stressful" is acceptable because it might simply indicate a need to practice that strategy until you are comfortable with it. However, you might want to explore any "very stressful" strategies and consider ways to improve those elements of goal setting, including identifying resources to help you with your goal(s) or, possibly, even modifying your goal(s).

Resource Name _____

Office Location _____

Phone Number _____

E-mail Address _____

KNOW YOUR SCHOOL

Your school has support services in many areas. Identify school resources that can help you with positive attitudes and goal setting. Examples could include personal and career counseling services. List the information here and add it to the information about your school from Chapter 1. Remember, for quick reference, place the information in a prominent place, such as on your refrigerator.

Congratulations! You have now completed the chapter on positive attitude and goal setting. Coupled with your stress management system from Chapter 1, you now have the tools to set a positive course of action. The next three chapters on time management and study skills will complete our discussion of basic academic and professional success skills.

HEALTHY DECISION MAKING

Juan knows that his schooling is going to prepare him to do well in his chosen profession. However, Juan has a burning desire to start his own business within 2 years of graduation. He is concerned that he has no business courses or background in his current academic courses. He is a year from graduation. What decisions can Juan make now that can help him to realize his dream?

_____

_____

_____

Explain how the concepts from this chapter can help him succeed.

_____

_____

Now that you have read this chapter and performed the assessments and exercises, please go to your CD to reinforce the concepts. The CD will present you with a fun and interactive journey back through positive attitude and goal setting. It will show you methods to reframe your thinking and goal setting, along with additional assessments to help track your progress.

References

Crawford, N. (2002). Positivity pays off for winners of psychology's top monetary prize. *Monitor on Psychology, 33*(7), 98. Retrieved April 17, 2007, from http://www.apa.org/monitor/julaug02/positivity.html

Kabat-Zinn, J., & Beall, B. (1987). A systematic mental training program based on mindfulness meditation to optimize performance in collegiate and Olympic rowers. Paper presented to the Department of Athletics, Massachusetts Institute of Technology, Cambridge.

Posen, D. B. (1995). Stress management for patient and physician. Retrieved April 17, 2007, from http://www.mentalhealth.com

Schunk, D. H. (2002). Self-regulation through goal setting. *ERIC Digest.* Retrieved April 17, 2007, from http://www.ericdigest.org/2002-4

Therapeutic benefits of laughter. (2007). *Holistic Online.* Retrieved April 17, 2007, from http://www.holisticonline.com

Ziegler, J. (1995). Immune system may benefit from the ability to laugh. *Journal of the National Cancer Institute, 87*(5), 342–344. Retrieved April 17, 2007, from http://find.galegroup.com

For a listing of further suggested readings for this chapter, please visit the companion website for this textbook.

Managing Your Resources

Time and Money

OBJECTIVES

What you will discover by the end of this chapter:

- How to better organize your life
- How to use strategic planning in large projects
- How to become a better time manager
- How to maintain balance in your life
- How to develop a personal budget
- How to improve your financial health

WHY LEARN THIS SKILL?

When you realize that time is a not a renewable resource, you begin to see how truly valuable it is. Once a moment goes by, it is gone forever. Time truly is our most precious asset. Like any resource, you need to use it wisely. Effective time management skills will help you live your life to the fullest on both a personal and professional level.

Using effective time management techniques produces many benefits. It allows you to complete your academic work while providing *free* time for the personal activities that are also important in your life. Time management works hand in hand to facilitate stress management and maintain a positive "can-do" attitude in life.

This chapter also addresses the importance of managing your financial resources. Money can be used for many wonderful things, such as financing your education and providing for you and your family, but keep in mind that many people place too much value on material possessions. Your self-worth should not be based on how much money you make or the stuff you have. Consider the following statement:

"He or she is wealthy who is happy with what they have."

Paraphrase from the movie Yentl

You may have heard of the saying *carpe diem,* Latin for "seize the day," but to be a truly effective time and money manager who lives life to its fullest, you should "seize the moment." It's time to start learning these valuable concepts and techniques.

It has been said that time is life itself. Therefore, it may follow that if you waste time, you are actually wasting your life. However, be careful not to take this view too far. Taking a walk in the woods may be considered by some to be a waste of time, but it isn't necessarily. Taking that walk may give you time to clear your mind, recharge your batteries, or just enjoy the beauty of nature. This certainly is time well spent. However, you will learn in this chapter, as in life, that balance is the key. If you always walk in the woods and don't do the things you need to do in your life, the consequences can be serious.

The good news is that you have already begun to manage your time by reading this book. Learning to handle your day-to-day stress and having a more focused and positive mind allows you to be more productive. The goals and objectives you established in Chapter 2 will help you to utilize time management techniques in a productive manner. Your goals will tell you where it's best to focus your energy, and the objectives or action plans will give you the specific steps to accomplish those goals. Now let's begin to show you some time management techniques so you can, as the country comedian Larry the Cable Guy says, "Git R done!" Do Exercise 3-1 for a self-assessment.

Place the number that best reflects your feelings.

3 = Often   2 = Sometimes   1 = Rarely

_____ I feel or say there isn't enough time in the day.

_____ I put things off until the last minute.

_____ Deadlines stress me out.

_____ I am late for my appointments.

_____ I turn in my assignments late.

EXERCISE 3-1
Assess Yourself:
How Good a Time
Manager Are You?

_____ I get overwhelmed with a large task and don't know where to start.

_____ I jump from one task to another and never seem to fully complete any.

_____ I feel like I never accomplish very much.

_____ I stress out over tests.

_____ I pull all-nighters studying for an exam or writing a paper that is due.

_____ Total

Evaluation
10–15: You're a pretty good time manager and can just work on those areas rated 2 or above.
16–20: This chapter will definitely help you.
21–25: You need to work on improving your time management strategies and you will greatly benefit from this chapter.

Do you feel like you are barely holding on to time?

If you scored 26–30, well, let's put it this way: If you follow through with the suggestions and work in this chapter it will be a positive life-changing experience. Let's work on improving your number and improving your life!

USING TIME MANAGEMENT TECHNIQUES

To become an effective time manager, you must first assess and identify the time wasters in *your* life. Then you can use effective time management techniques to overcome them. In addition, you will learn to use time management as a powerful tool in strategic planning for large projects or assignments.

> ## Timely Fact
>
> Time is a fixed commodity. Time is the one resource equally available to every person regardless of education, sex, or social status. The best possible investment you can make is using your time wisely.

Assessing and Identifying Time Wasters

Have you ever heard someone say that there aren't enough hours in the day? Of course, the truth is that everyone has 24 hours in a day. If you know of a place that has more, everyone would probably want to move there! Seriously, we all have the same amount of time. How we use our given time is what makes the difference. One of the first assessment techniques is to identify and eliminate common time wasters that could free up valuable time for other pursuits. Following is a list of common time wasters, followed by techniques to combat them.

Lack of Organization.

How much time do you waste looking for your keys, books, or tools? When you sit down to study, does it take you more than 5 minutes to actually begin? Do you forget important dates, such as birthdays and anniversaries? Exercise 3-2 will help you evaluate your organizational skills. These are signs that lack of organization may be stealing 10 minutes here and 15 minutes there, which may add up to hours of wasted time during the course of an entire day. Not only do you lose precious time, but bad stress enters your life and detracts from a positive attitude.

Answer each question with either "yes" or "no."

EXERCISE 3-2
How Organized Are You?

_____ Do you often misplace your keys, glasses, or other personal items needed for the activities of daily living?

_____ Do you forget birthdays, anniversaries, or other important dates you want to acknowledge?

_____ Do you find crisis situations arising because you "forgot" to do or get something?

_____ Do you spend more than 10 minutes trying to locate an assignment, a bill, or study tools that you know "had to be right here"?

_____Have you ever "lost" something only to have it reappear after several months?

_____Do you have stacks of unanswered correspondence, unpaid bills, and unread magazines or books?

_____Are you frequently late for appointments, commitments, or other activities?

_____Do you have piles of items around the house or in your room waiting to be put away?

_____Do you feel that having more space is all that you really need to solve all of your storage problems?

_____Do you want to organize things but are turned off when you realize how much there is, and you do not know where to start?

_____Do you usually feel that you haven't accomplished as much as you had hoped to each day?

_____Do you have to clear things out of the way before you can sit down to relax, visit, or work?

Score 1 point for "yes" answers only.

My total score _____

1–2	You are in good shape and only have a few areas to work on.
3–5	Disorganization is causing bad stress and low productivity in your life.
6–9	Disorganization is greatly interfering with your life.
10–12	You need to take immediate action to get organized.

So now that you have an idea of how disorganization can affect your life, what will you do? The best way to combat organization problems is with your own specific action plan. One hint is to tackle only one issue at a time, moving to another when you see progress. If you try to tackle several issues at once, you may become overwhelmed and fail at all of them. Achieving success with one action plan will motivate you toward the next one, and so on. To get started, perform Exercise 3-3.

EXERCISE 3-3
Combating
Disorganization

Pick one item from Exercise 3-2 that you are motivated to overcome. Write it down and think about it for a while. Develop strategies and a specific action plan that will turn that "yes" into a "no." Refer to Chapter 2 on goal setting to review the basic components of an action plan. Don't be afraid to ask trusted family and friends for help. Two examples are given in Figure 3-1.

_____

_____

_____

_____

FIGURE 3-1

Sample action plans to combat disorganization.

Yes: Do you often misplace your keys, glasses, or other personal items needed for the activities of daily living?

Action Plan: I will now place my keys in the cabinet by the door as soon as I enter my house/room. In addition, if I have to remember to take anything to school the next day, I will put a note under my keys so when I grab them in the morning the note will remind me of what I need to take.

Yes: Have you forgotten birthdays, anniversaries, or some other important dates you wanted to acknowledge?

Action Plan: I will purchase a large desk calendar and fill in all the important dates in my life. I will keep this calender on my special study desk (more on this in Chapter 4) so it will serve as constant reminder of upcoming important dates or events.

Lack of Strategic Planning.

Do you dread major tasks like writing a research paper or doing a class presentation? These special projects usually require several steps to complete. A poor strategic planner is overwhelmed by these tasks and spends much time dreading the task but taking little

> **Fact to Ponder**
>
> Your misplaced keys or other misplaced items will always be in the *last* place you look!

action. Often poor planners do not even know where to begin. However, just by using a simple tool such as a large desk calendar strategically placed in your study area, you can become a highly effective strategic planner.

You can certainly use electronic tools or calendars to perform strategic planning. However, a large desk calendar in your study area seems to work best for a number of reasons. First, it is in a place you frequently visit. The calendar allows you to write all your important upcoming events and deadlines in one place, and at a glance you can see what your future holds. In addition, physically writing something seems to help your memory.

This type of planning gives you an overview of the entire picture even if an event takes place over several months. If you choose, you can even carry with you a written or electronic pocket planner to note things as they come up during the day and then transfer them to your desk calendar.

Now you have the important events and deadlines in your life all written in one place, but how does it help you in the strategic planning process? Let's say you have a large paper due toward the end of the semester. A poor strategic planner waits until a few days (or even the night before) and quickly throws together a poorly written project. Part of this student's issue is procrastination, but most of it is poor planning and can easily be rectified.

Let's use the example of a smaller paper (three to five pages) assigned at the first of the month that is due at the end of the month. If you use the following steps, not only will the project be much easier to complete, but the quality and resulting grade will be higher.

1. Place the due date on your calendar in bright red.
2. Break the paper down into specific steps that need to be done with approximate times for each step:

a. Choosing a topic (1 hour)
b. Researching and gathering information (3 hours)
c. Developing an outline (2 hours)
d. Writing a rough draft (4 hours)
e. Getting feedback (2 hours)
f. Rewriting and rechecking final paper (4 hours)

You now have a total of 16 hours over the month to devote to this project, and you can see from your calendar where you have the time for each of these tasks. Make sure you give yourself plenty of time before the deadline to complete your paper. This way, you will allow a buffer zone in case you underestimate the time needed for a certain task or if something unexpected comes up (like your printer breaking down).

You can write these tasks on your desk calendar in blocks of time. For example, you might break your research time into two days of 1.5 hours each (please see Figure 3-2). Remember, your first few attempts are learning experiences. Keep notes on areas that did not go as planned so you can improve in the future. Now that you have your major tasks planned, you can continue to update your calendar and repeat this process for each assignment. Exercise 3-4 gives you a chance to try this out.

FIGURE 3-2

Strategic plan for writing a paper.

AUGUST						YEAR 2008
Sun	**Mon**	**Tue**	**Wed**	**Thu**	**Fri**	**Sat**
					1 Choose Term Paper Topic and Title (1 hour)	**2** *Jill's Birthday*
3	**4** Research and gather info for term paper (1.5 hours)	**5** Continue to research and gather info for term paper (1.5 hours)	**6** *Movies with Joe*	**7** *Mom and Dad's Anniversary*	**8** Football camp 8 AM–3 PM	**9** Football camp 8 AM–3 PM Develop outline for term paper (1 hour)
10 Football camp 8 AM–3 PM Continue to develop outline for term paper (1 hour)	**11** Football camp 8 AM–3 PM *Phone Bill Due!*	**12** Football camp 8 AM–3 PM	**13** Begin to write rough draft for term paper (1.5 hours)	**14** Continue rough draft for term paer (1.5 hours)	**15** Football practice 1–3 PM	**16** Football practice 1–3 PM Finish rough draft for term paper (1 hour)
17 Football practice 1–3 PM	**18** Get feedback for term paper (1 hour)	**19** Football practice 1–3 PM	**20** Finish getting feedback for term paper (1 hour)	**21**	**22** Begin to rewrite and recheck final paper (1 hour)	**23** *Lunch with Josh*
24 Continue to rewrite and recheck final paper (1 hour)	**25** Continue to rewrite and recheck final paper (1/2 hour)	**26**	**27** Continue to rewrite and recheck final paper (1/2 hour)	**28**	**29**	**30** Finish final revisions of term paper (1 hour)
31 Term Paper Due 8 AM!						

This calendar-based system can be used for any task that requires multiple steps to complete. For example, using Figure 3-3, strategically plan a 30-minute oral presentation for class. Note that this assignment was given on the first of the month and that the due date is already listed on the calendar. First, pick the steps and time necessary, and then fill them in on the mock calendar.

EXERCISE 3-4
Strategic Planning

List steps needed with approximate times to complete:

_____

_____

_____

_____

Fill these steps in on the mock calendar in Figure 3-3.

FIGURE 3-3

Insert the steps from Exercise 3-4 to plan and complete the oral presentation.

JANUARY   YEAR 2008

Sun	Mon	Tue	Wed	Thu	Fri	Sat
		1	2 *Cheer Practice* *3–5 PM*	3 *Cheer Practice* *3–5 PM*	4 *Cheer Practice* *3–5 PM*	5
6 *Steph's 21st* *Birthday!*	7	8 *Cheer Practice* *3–5 PM*	9 *Cheer Practice* *3–5 PM*	10	11 *Cheer Practice* *3–5 PM*	12 *Cheer Practice* *3–5 PM*
13 *Cheer Practice* *3–5 PM*	14	15	16	17 *Cheerleading* *Competition!!*	18	19
20	21	22	23 *Get Card for* *Gram & Pap*	24	25	26 *Dentist* *Appointment* *2 PM*
27	28 *Gram & Pap's* *Surprise Party*	29	30	31 *Oral* *Presentation* *Due!*		

Personal Habits.

Do you have personal habits that waste your time? Worry and procrastination are two of the most common. In Chapter 2, we talked about how worry is wasted negative energy. If you find yourself worrying a lot, please go back and review the difference between worry and concern. **Procrastination** is another personal habit that can waste a large amount of time. Procrastination and worry are related. Procrastination robs you of time and power by causing stress in the form of guilt, embarrassment, and anxiety. The anxiety and fear of failure can cause worry. Both procrastination and worry are powerful enemies of time management and cause great stresses on your mind and body. Students who tend to procrastinate regularly tend to have higher stress levels and more health problems than those who consistently plan their time better (Tice & Baumeister, 1997).

Procrastination means you often put off doing something until the last possible minute. In addition to wasting time, procrastination causes the work you finally complete at the last minute to be less than the quality possible if you'd planned ahead. Causes of procrastination can include fear of failure, fear of success, and fear of losing, among others (Burka & Yuen, 1983). It can also result from not understanding the task. Think about other personal habits that could be classified as time wasters in your life.

Do you talk for hours on your phone or send numerous text messages throughout the day? Do you spend hours on the computer playing video games, aimlessly surfing the Net, or participating in chat rooms? The telephone and computer/Internet are among the most useful facilitators of communication ever invented. However, many people can let these devices completely control their lives, thus wasting a lot of time. To call someone you have just seen in school and gossip for hours or to text-message someone while you are sitting in class is certainly not a productive use of time. To play a video game for 3 hours when you have an important test the next day is certainly not wise. These behaviors also create problems outside of the classroom: Use of the telephone and/or computer for personal matters during work hours has been identified as a major reason for low productivity in the workforce. Rate your personal habits in Exercise 3-5.

EXERCISE 3-5
Rate Yourself on Your Personal Habits

3 = often   2 = sometimes   1 = rarely   0 = never

_____ I worry about many things in my life.

_____ I put off tasks until the last minute.

_____ I talk on the phone for long periods of time even when I have other tasks that need doing.

_____ I spend time on the computer or interactive games even when other priority tasks need to be accomplished.

_____ I get bored easily with a task.

_____ My total score

A score of 0–5 is very good. Even the best time managers have a rare occasion where they engage in some of these habits. However, if you only occasionally engage in these behaviors (1 point each), you have very good time management habits. A score of 6–10 ranges from fair to poor, and you could improve your habits with better time management strategies. A score of 11–15 is cause for concern, and you really need to work on your personal habits because they create a large amount of wasted time in your life.

Now that you have assessed your personal habits, you will develop the single most powerful tool to combat all the "yes" responses in Exercise 3-5, avoid procrastination, and become an effective time manager. This almost magical tool is called the *to-do list*. Be careful: Before you dismiss this as too simplistic or not very powerful, consider the following success story, which occurred in 1910.

SUCCESS STORY
A Simple Time Management Idea, Worth $25,000 in 1910!

When Charles M. Schwab was president of Bethlehem Steel, he confronted Ivy Lee, a management consultant, with an unusual challenge. "Show me a way to get more things done," he demanded. "If it works, I'll pay anything within reason." Lee handed Schwab a piece of paper. "Write down the things you have to do tomorrow," he said. Schwab did it. "Now number these items in the order of their real importance," Lee continued. Schwab did. "The first thing tomorrow morning," Lee added, "start working on number one and stay with it until it is completed. Next, take number two, and don't go any further until it is completed. Then proceed to number three and so on. If you can't complete everything on schedule, don't worry. At least you will have taken care of the most important things before getting distracted by items of lesser importance. The secret is to do this daily. Evaluate the relative importance of the things you have to get done, establish priorities, record your plan of action, and stick to it. Do this every working day. After you have convinced yourself of the value of this system, have your men try it. Test it as long as you like, and then send me a check for whatever you think the idea is worth." In a few weeks, Charles Schwab sent Ivy Lee a check for $25,000. Schwab later said that this lesson was the most profitable one he had ever learned in his business career. And $25,000 in 1910 dollars would be worth 25.5 million dollars by today's standards. (Pauk, 2000)

The problem with to-do lists, like anything else, is that they must be fully understood to make the most effective application and integration into your life. One of the biggest downfalls is that people make long, complicated lists that end up becoming negative motivators. Let's look at the proper way to develop this powerful time management tool.

The Daily To-Do List.

Do you start each day without a plan? If you have a plan, do you understand how to prioritize tasks that need to be accomplished first? Without a plan, you have no sense of direction and can wander aimlessly. Of course, it does take some time to plan, but the small amount of time invested will pay off by freeing up the tremendous amount of time you would waste without a plan. Part of the plan has to include priorities. One cautionary note: You can actually take planning and organizing to an extreme. Again, *you must find a balance*. A few minutes spent planning your day will help to save you time later. If you find yourself fretting over how many items to put on your to-do list or filling in three different calendars, then you've defeated the purpose of planning as a time-saver.

Like Charles Schwab, many successful leaders feel that making effective lists is the secret of their success. It allows them to plan and prioritize tasks, and it also helps them generate ideas and see better ways of combining tasks for a more efficient use of time.

There are several types of lists you can make and several places you can make them. The process of keeping different types of lists can become so confusing that you may get lost in all your lists. Therefore, this text recommends a somewhat simpler way to organize your life. The first step is to get the proper tools.

Your large desk calendar can complement the process of a daily to-do list. For consistency, create your to-do list in your study area with your calendar in front of you for reference because it will already have important events written down. To construct this list, do the following:

1. Write down or record electronically every activity, assignment, meeting, or promise that comes your way each day, and keep this list with you. (Complete Exercise 3-6 to practice prioritizing.)

2. Complete any activities you can as they occur, if time permits, and cross off or delete them from your list.

3. At the end of your day, prioritize the remaining items on your list. Place those tasks that need to be done the next day at the top of your list, and mark them with an asterisk. Then list other tasks that you hope to complete. It would be best to do all of this in your study area with your desk calendar as a reference. Now go to bed, secure in the knowledge that you don't have to "worry" about the next day.

4. Consult your list throughout the next day, and cross off any completed tasks. Crossing off the task should give you a sense of accomplishment and pride, which will reinforce your good behavior and keep you dedicated to your list. You should have all top-priority items crossed off at the end of the day, but if you don't that's all right. Just move any remaining high-priority items to the top of your list for the following day. Stress and worry will accomplish nothing.

5. At the end of that day, make a new list for the next day. Get in the habit of spending a few minutes each day to plan for the following day. This process will help you greatly and will eventually become automatic and take only minutes to complete.

Helpful Hints:

- Do not make your lists very long. Three to five items per day is usually sufficient. This number may seem small to very busy people. If you accomplish three to five items each day, though, you will be amazed at how much you can do. Writing down 10 things on your list and accomplishing none of them because you're overwhelmed by the number of items on your list accomplishes nothing. In other words, *keep it simple*!
- Set priorities so you are not jumping from one task to another.
- Find ways to make tasks interesting. Be happy and have a positive attitude.
- Do your most demanding work when you're fresh and alert.
- Reward yourself when you get a job done.
- Organize your desk so you are not wasting time trying to find pencils, dictionaries, and other supplies.
- Control interruptions.
- Commit to finishing what you start.

Imagine that you have reached your long-range career goal and are now a successful employee. You have the following tasks to do in addition to your daily work routine. You start work at 8 A.M. Prioritize this list by writing numbers 1 to 5 on the line to the left of the item to indicate which you would do first, second, and so on.

EXERCISE 3-6
Prioritizing Tasks

_____ Prepare for important meeting scheduled from 9 to 10 A.M.

_____ Begin research for a report due in 2 weeks.

_____ Reserve a conference room for an in-service meeting for your department by 11 o'clock.

_____ Call two clients to schedule appointments for next week.

_____ Meet with your staff members to assign their daily duties.

In summary, the combination of a daily to-do list with a large desk calendar at your study area can do much to improve your time management skills. See Table 3-1 for a listing of some of the major outcomes of this system.

Exercise 3-7 gives you the opportunity to make a daily to-do list.

**EXERCISE 3-7
Making a Daily
To-do List**

Using your desk calendar, make a daily to-do list for tomorrow. Keep it with you and derive pleasure from crossing off the items. Try this for at least 10 consecutive days, and then write about your results. Did it make you more productive? Did it help with your personal organization? You can get copies of this to do-list form on your CD.

Things To Do Today		**Date** _____
Priority	**Task**	
_____	_____	
_____	_____	
_____	_____	
_____	_____	
_____	_____	

TABLE 3-1

To-Do Lists and Calendars: What They Do for You

To-Do Lists

- Help you to begin your day with a written plan of action and prevent other people and distractions from dominating your time
- Combat procrastination
- Help you develop a prioritized list that prepares you for the next day and prevents you from jumping from task to task
- Allow you time to think and plan to increase efficiency
- Help to organize your life

Calendar

- Helps you see the *Big Picture* of what is coming up
- Assists in the strategic planning of getting large tasks accomplished
- Notes important appointments, events, and deadlines

ADDITIONAL TIME MANAGEMENT TECHNIQUES

A few additional time management techniques and concepts will add **synergy** to your time management skills. Synergy happens when $1 + 1 = 3$, an equation that may drive mathematicians crazy. It simply means that if you combine these new concepts with what you already know, it won't just have an additive effect and make your life a little better, but it will create an even greater than imagined increase in your effectiveness.

Make Time Your Friend

Waste Time Productively.

Do you know people who continually complain that "There aren't enough hours in the day" or they "just don't have any time to get anything done"? Remember the discussion in Chapter 2 on the power of the subconscious mind: If you continually plant the thought that you never have enough time, guess what? You won't!

So how do you turn time into a friend? One of the best methods is to learn to *waste time productively.* The best way this concept can be demonstrated is by revisiting the reframing concept.

> *"Someone once told me that time was a predator that stalked us all of our lives. I'd rather believe time is a companion that goes with us on a journey that reminds us to cherish every moment because they'll never come again. What we leave behind is not as important as how we lived. After all, number one, we're only mortal."*
> —Jean-Luc Picard, captain, USS *Enterprise*

Scenario 1. You have a doctor's appointment at 1 P.M. You also have some errands to run, a big test coming up in 2 days, and you want to do some studying this evening. The office is extremely busy; it is 1:30, and there are still several people ahead of you. You begin to feel angry, your blood pressure rises, your muscles tense, and you begin to worry about all the things you must do and how this is going to put you behind. By 2 o'clock you are ready to explode. Finally, at 2:45 you see the doctor and it is not a pleasant interaction because you are so mad. You even forget to tell your doctor some important information. You then run your errands, feeling upset the whole time, and when you get home, you have a pounding headache. You are unable to study effectively and have a rough time sleeping that night.

Scenario 2. You have a doctor's appointment at 1 P.M. You also have some errands to run, a big test coming up in 2 days and you want to do some studying this evening. The office is extremely busy; it is 1:30, and there are still several people ahead of you. You calmly pull out your note cards to study for the exam. You study until your name is called at 2:45. You then go in and have a pleasant interaction with your physician and remember all the important information you needed to pass on. You run your errands and then go home, and, now that you have already studied, decide to go out and see a movie. You come home refreshed and ready for a good night's sleep.

In scenario 2, you managed to reframe a bad situation into a good one. You made good use of *found time,* such as waiting in line or at the doctor's office. You probably know of other areas where you can apply this principle. This does not mean you constantly take your work with you, but even writing out your bills while waiting for an appointment will free up some time for something else that might be fun and relaxing.

Capitalize on Peak Periods.

We used Einstein's question in Chapter 2 on the power of the subconscious mind. But it also serves a purpose here. In the study skills chapter, you will learn why you should understand your *internal biological clock*—in other words, knowing the times of day when you are most effective. Most people are more productive in the morning, but we all differ. If you know what times of day are most productive for you, you may be able to schedule your more difficult tasks for these times. Maybe you come up with good ideas on your morning commute or walk to school. If so, it may be a good idea to carry a small tape recorder with you so you don't forget the idea. Today most cell phones offer voice mail capabilities. You can use this to substitute for the small tape recorder.

Conversely, there are times during the day when your mind may not be at its optimum level. For example, most people feel less productive and creative after they eat lunch. These are good times to sit back, relax a little, and read over your work versus trying to come up with new ideas.

All of us have an internal biological clock, and if we pay attention to it, we can optimize our performance. Have you ever noticed how you may feel sicker or more anxious at night? Even seasonal changes can alter your productivity or feeling of well-being. That is why a bright and cheery study room in the dark of winter can be more productive.

Plan for the Unexpected.

You've done a great job planning with your daily to-do list and desk calendar. However, life doesn't always go as planned. This is why you must be flexible and positive. If something unexpected comes up, don't panic or worry. This will accomplish nothing. Calm down, reorganize, and do the best you can to make the situation positive.

Also, know when you are overcommitted and learn to say "no." Saying "no" is difficult because we fear not being liked. However, if we say yes to everybody and take on too many tasks, none of them will get done well.

There are other ways to soften your commitment. For example, the next time someone asks you to do something, ask, "Can I have some time to think about it?" You can still say no later, but now you can assess whether you really have the time to do this task. If you still need to say no, you have time to prepare a thoughtful response.

Just as important as learning to say "no" is learning *how* to say "yes." Let's say someone asks you to help with a large project. If you simply say yes, you may get several tasks dumped on you. However, you can say yes in a way that forces the person to define your exact role. For example, you can respond, "With my limited time, can you identify one part of the project I can best support?" Such a statement defines exactly what is expected of you and gives you a chance to pick something you like or that matches your talents.

Finally, many unexpected things may occur that disrupt your well-planned lists. Remember, don't be a slave to your schedule or make large lists. Make sure they are reasonable and give you time for yourself each day. Keep your motivation sustained by periodically rewarding yourself for getting all your tasks done. If you have a large task (such as that research paper), reward yourself along the way for each little step accomplished. A small reward will help your motivation and move you on to the next step. But remember to save the biggest reward for when your large task is done.

LEARN TO MAINTAIN BALANCE

You may be tired of hearing the word *balance* by now, but it is a key concept in many of the topics in this text and on your CD. It is generally accepted that the happiest, most productive people combine work, family relationships, and leisure time into a satisfying whole. This type of person is a *balance expert*. They know if they exclusively take care of everyone else, there is little time or energy for themselves, and their stress will grow both physically and emotionally. See another connection between stress management and time management?

As with stress management, balance experts hear internal alarms when work demands intrude on family time or family responsibilities distract them at work. They also realize that time away from work or school is essential to recharge their batteries. Balance experts approach their commitments with well-defined goals and a positive attitude.

Table 3-2 shows you some of the signals that should alert you that you are drifting out of balance.

> ## Old Fact
>
> We think technology will save us time, but that doesn't always happen. A Harris Poll between 1973 and 1987 showed the average American's amount of free time had shrunk from 26.6 to 16.6 hours per week (Keyes, 1991). Do you want to guess where that average would be today?

Enjoy Your Time

Take your large desk calendar and write some fun things in and make them stand out. This way, instead of looking at your desk calendar with dread, you now have fun things interspersed between tasks. This makes your calendar much more user-friendly and reminds you to take some time for yourself.

Similarly, you need to recharge your batteries. When your cell phone battery is low, you need to recharge it or it will run down and be useless. You, too, must recharge your batteries, which can be done in several ways.

> ## Fact to Ponder
>
> Wherever you go on vacation, you must take *yourself*. Make sure you are good company. In other words, learn to enjoy your time no matter what you are doing or where you are.

Research has shown that peak performers alternate between intensive productive bursts followed by time to recuperate and brainstorm before a new task. Learning to take it easy is also good for productivity.

TABLE 3-2
How to Recognize When You Are Drifting Out of Balance

- Losing sense of humor, one of the first signs
- Lack of restful sleep (most people need 8 hours)
- Excessive yawning or fighting sleep in class or at a meeting
- Tasks piling up to an overwhelming level

Vacations are one way to recharge. However, some people cram everything into a stress-filled getaway and actually feel like they need a vacation when they return. The answer lies in the meaning of the word. *Vacation* means "to vacate, or get away." Vacations should be refreshing and invigorating to the mind and body. Only you know what kind of vacation works for you. For some it may be a couple of days at the beach, for others it may be mountain climbing, and for others it may be simply staying at home and leisurely getting some work done. Again, choose what works for you to recharge your batteries.

FINANCIAL WELLNESS: MONEY MATTERS

Too often in our society, money and the accumulation of material possessions equate to success. Although monetary success may be part of your long-term goals, try not to make it your sole focus. Many successful people in history had little or no money. Mahatma Gandhi is a good example of somebody who changed his entire country of India, as well as the world, yet he had only four worldly possessions (glasses, watch, sandals, and a homespun cloth robe). Think about your definition of success and views on money by doing Exercise 3-8.

EXERCISE 3-8
What Are Your Views on Success and Money?

What is your definition of success?

_____

_____

_____

List characteristics of people who you think have successful lives.

_____

_____

_____

What personal qualities enabled them to achieve success?

_____

_____

_____

What characteristics do you have that will contribute to your success in life?

_____

_____

_____

List two success goals you will accomplish within 1 year.

_____

_____

_____

List a success goal you wish to accomplish within 5 years.

_____

_____

_____Do you equate money with success?

_____Do you use money as a tool to improve your personal and professional
life as well as the lives of those around you?

> *"The use of money is all the advantage there is in having money."*
> —Ben Franklin

Money can be an effective tool to help you reach your goals. The more you understand money, the better you can manage it. Much like time management, your attitude toward money is important. If you continually tell yourself you will *never* have enough money, you *never* will. You must change negative attitudes, understand financial concepts, and learn to use money as a positive tool that can enrich your life and the lives of others.

For most of us, money is a limited resource that must be managed much like our time. Everyone's financial situation is unique, so each budget needs to be personalized. Keep in mind that the majority of people will always need to budget carefully no matter how much their income increases. This is because as your income grows so will your financial responsibilities and, often, your wants. Many people who have millions of dollars go broke and/or live very sad lives. Of course, the opposite is true of people who are considered poor but live very happy and successful lives.

Maintain balance in your financial attitude.

In Balance

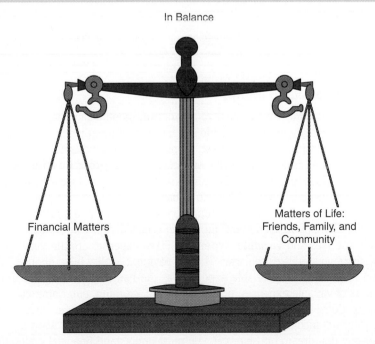

Financial Matters

Matters of Life:
Friends, Family, and
Community

**EXERCISE 3-9
Needing versus
Wanting**

Do you really *need* those $150 sneakers, or do you just *want* them? This is a question you must ask yourself if money is tight. Answer the following questions to help you distinguish between "wants" and "needs."

List all the things you spent money on this month, including all fixed and variable expenses:

Item	Was It a Need or Want?	Cost

Did you spend more money on things you wanted or you needed?

_____

Did you buy any of the items because someone made you feel you had to?

_____

Did you shop for the best deal?

_____

Explain the following statement: "It is best to live within or even beneath your means."

_____

Hint: If you are not sure if you want or need something, wait 24 hours and then decide.

Understand the Basics of Money

The money you have coming in is called your **income.** Income can come from a variety of sources such as your salary, allowance, child support, government payments such as welfare or social security, tax refunds, gifts, interest, money made on investments, and so on.

The total you have coming in from all these sources is your **gross income.** However, your employer will withhold some of your pay for reasons such as taxes, social security, insurance, union dues, parking, and other deductions. What you actually take home is called your **net income.**

Your income can be pretty easy to account for. Now for the hard question: "Where does your money go?" What you spend your money on is called your **expenses.** There are two types: **fixed expenses** and **variable expenses.** Fixed expenses are the same each month. Examples include your rent or mortgage (home) payment, utility bills (phone, TV, Internet service), and loan payments. Variable expenses, as the name suggests, differ from time to time. Examples of variable expenses include your food, clothing, entertainment, gas, car repairs, and educational expenses. Do Exercise 3-9 to see how to evaluate variable expenses.

Ideally, your net income is greater than your total expenses! If you want to pay for your education or buy that dream house or car, you must understand financial matters and come up with a successful money plan. Planning and controlling the use of your money is called **budgeting.** Its many benefits include:

- Giving you an idea of where your money is going
- Decreasing and (hopefully eliminating) your anxiety and money worries
- Focusing on your goals and priorities in your life
- Helping control your spending
- Allowing for resources for leisure and enjoyment

Steps to Budgeting

To keep things simple, here are two basic steps to budgeting. The first step is to gather all the facts by getting a very good picture of your income and expenses. This takes time and good record keeping. Once you have all the facts, the second step is to analyze your situation and to develop a budget. Of course, you will review your budget periodically and make modifications as necessary. Let's work on step 1 in Exercise 3-10.

Use this form or create your own to keep track of your income and expenses for 3 months. Your CD also has electronic monthly budget forms you can use.

EXERCISE 3-10
Getting a Good Picture of Your Income and Expenses

Month _____ **Year** _____

Total Income for Month

Wages/Salary (net pay) _____

Tips (if applicable) _____

Financial aid _____

Outside support (parents or others) _____

Other _____

Total income for month _____

Total Expenses for Month

Fixed Expenses (rent, utilities, loans, insurance, etc.)

Expense Type	When Due	Amount
_____	_____	_____
_____	_____	_____
_____	_____	_____
_____	_____	_____
_____	_____	_____
_____	_____	_____
_____	_____	_____

Total Fixed Expenses _____

Variable Expenses (This is the harder one. List everything, including food, transportation, entertainment, etc.)

Expense Type	Total Amount Spent
_____	_____
_____	_____
_____	_____
_____	_____
_____	_____
_____	_____
_____	_____
_____	_____

Total Variable Expenses _____

Total expenses for month (add fixed and variable) _____

If applicable, any money in savings for future expenses or in investments _____

You now have a good picture of your monthly income, expenses, and savings. Now is the time for step 2: Analyze your financial situation. There are several ways to do this. Some people like to break their expenses into larger categories and show the percentage of money spent in each. Figure 3-4 shows a sample.

Another method is to ask yourself several important questions, as in Exercise 3-11.

EXERCISE 3-11
Analyzing Your Income and Expenses

Answer the following questions:

Did you have enough income to meet expenses?

_____

Are you spending too much money in one area?

_____

Were you able to save money for one of your goals (vacation, tuition, future large expense such as annual insurance premium)? Remember you need to set aside a certain amount to pay those large but occasional expenses that will crop up during the year, such as car insurance.

Take heart. If you are like most people, you may think you will never have enough money to reach your goals. However, with a consistent plan, you can achieve your goals. The key is consistency. If you came up short when you compared your income versus expenses, there are many things you can do. First, consider areas you can trim. We aren't talking about living off of instant noodles here or even giving up basic cable. Most of us can easily trim $100 a month and much more by making simple changes. Here are some

---

FIGURE 3-4

Example of expense chart.

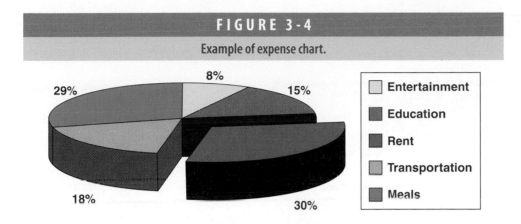

suggestions that can add up to save you a lot of money. After you've read the list, do Exercise 3-12.

- Is there anything you can do to reduce your utilities? Turn off lights when not in use, turn the thermostat down 1 or 2 degrees, or get a programmable thermostat so the temperature will be reduced while you are sleeping. Take shorter showers. Look at a cheaper phone plan. Even a few changes could mean substantial savings.
- Share living expenses/space, if possible, with a trusted roommate.
- Pack your lunch a few times per week. Just taking your lunch three times a week can save you $12 to $15 per week, or $60 per month.
- Walk, ride a bike, or carpool to save transportation costs. Cut down on driving and perform regular car maintenance to prevent costly repairs. Checking fluid levels and changing oil every 3,000 miles is the single most important way to increase your engine's longevity.
- Don't pay for purchases with a credit card. Use a debit card, which will help you track your variable expenses and encourage you to spend only what you have.
- Save on food and clothing expenses. Buy food in bulk, shop for clothes at discount and secondhand stores, compare prices, and look for items on sale. Find and use discount coupons. Eat out less frequently, so that when you do it is a special treat.

Select one idea from the preceding list—or create your own—to save money, and track it for a month or two. Calculate how much money you saved. When this behavior becomes automatic, pick another idea.

Write your idea here:

EXERCISE 3-12
Pick One Idea

- Find free or cheap ways to have fun. Examples include hiking a trail, reading a book, or joining a club. Rent or borrow movies. Look for student discounts on entertainment.
- Use generic products when possible. Use e-mail and direct pay versus stamps when possible.

> ## Health and Wealth Fact
>
> Reviewing the list, look at the examples that also relate to your physical health such as walking, exercise, and eating healthy. Your physical and financial health are interrelated. Little things add up. For example, taking healthy lunches, walking more, and/or cutting an unhealthy habit such as smoking, excessive drinking/gambling, or eating too much candy could benefit your health *and* wealth. If you saved just $10 a week, that would be $520 a year toward an emergency fund or an entertainment treat.

- Don't try to impress anybody, especially friends who have more money. Someone will always have more money than you.
- Write down your financial goals. If you want a vacation, plan a year in advance by budgeting a little each month, and it will happen. Also you can save money if you vacation with friends and share expenses. If your goal is very important (such as getting your education), a few years of frugal living will pay off.

See if you can now use the budgeting principles from this text to develop your personal budget in Exercise 3-13.

SUMMATION EXERCISE 3-13: CONSTRUCT YOUR BUDGET

Use the information you have gained so far, along with your data from Exercise 3-12 to construct a budget for next month. List your goal amount for the variable categories such as clothing, food, and so on.

Month _____   **Year** _____

Total Monthly Income   _____

Expense Type	**Budgeted Amount**
Rent/mortgage	_____
Utilities	_____
Telephone	_____
TV/Internet	_____
Loans	_____
Insurances	_____
Transportation/repairs	_____

Food   _____

Clothing   _____

Entertainment   _____

Medical/dental/eye care   _____

Education (tuition, books, loans)   _____

Emergency fund (future expenses)   _____

Savings toward long-term goals (house, vacation)   _____

Other: _____

Total Expense   _____

Your total expenses should equal—or, even better, be less than—your income.

Remember that things can change or you may forget an expense. Your income may increase or your goals may change. Don't worry. Just review and readjust your budget. Even on a small scale, budgets are powerful. If your parents are supporting you, in addition to being very thankful you should still budget and help out.

CHOOSING YOUR FINANCIAL INSTITUTION

Here are some basics on finding a suitable financial institution:

- You need to find a financial institution that offers the types of services you require. You can go to a commercial bank, savings and loan, or credit union. It is best to make sure that the institution is federally insured (FDIC), which means it is backed up by the government in case anything happens.
- Make sure the services include what you need, such as a checking account, debit cards, money market CDs, and/or opportunity for loans. Free checking and overdraft protection are also nice to have.
- Shop around for interest rates. Ideally you want the highest on your investments and the lowest on your loans.
- Convenience is also a factor, one that can include the location and hours of the financial institution and services such as direct deposit of your paychecks.
- Remember that a debit card is a great way to track your variable spending costs.

A Word About Credit Cards

It may seem like you get hundreds of credit card offers in the mail. When used properly, credit cards can be good, but the temptation of *easy* money can be dangerous. "Buy now, pay later" sounds good, but often you pay now and pay many more times later. See the CD for a graphic example.

You certainly need loans to pay for school, home, car, and emergencies, but be careful of falling into the credit card trap. You are borrowing someone else's money, but you must pay it back over time plus a charge for the money you are borrowing. This charge is **interest,** determined by the annual percentage rate (APR). Sometimes there are additional finance charges and fees. Be careful of charging items you want. Don't sign any credit card agreements unless you fully understand all the terms. Find a trusted person to explain if you are unsure.

Credit cards are helpful for:

- Travel when you don't want to carry large amounts of cash
- Emergencies
- Purchases over the phone, Internet, or by mail

The bottom line question is, "Would I buy it if I had to pay in cash?"

It is better to use a debit card for purchases because you only can spend what you have. If you must use a credit card, get one with a low credit limit and that requires you pay the entire balance off in full each month.

Educational Grants and Loans

Unlike a loan, a **grant** is a form of monetary aid that does *not* need to be repaid. Obviously, you should go after every possible grant you can find. Most are based on your financial need.

Scholarships are also free money that does not need to be paid back. Some are based on your need; others can be based on your achievements, community service, or your ability to write an essay.

Subsidized student loans are available to finance your education. Their interest rate is low because they are subsidized (assisted) by the federal government. Student loans are often not required to be paid back until after graduation. Requirements change from year to year, but here are some basic tips:

- Meet *early* with a financial aid officer to find out about all the loans, grants, and scholarships your school and government (state and federal) have to offer. This is your best source of updated information and requirements. Find out the deadlines and apply early.
- Search your community for grants and scholarships.
- Search the Internet for grants and scholarships, but be skeptical of companies that offer scholarship and grant services for a fee. You can find the same information with good detective work.
- Loans and gifts of money can come from relatives and friends. Borrowing money from friends or relatives can be uncomfortable. You should have a contract to define the terms of the loan and prevent future hard feelings. Understand that loans must be repaid or your credit will be ruined.

Remember that eligibility for financial aid, including grants and loans, is often tied to academic performance. If you do not maintain the required grade point average for satisfactory progress, however your institution defines it, you may lose your financial aid.

Maintaining a Good Credit Record

Having a good credit history is important in your ability to get credit and in getting better loans with lower interest rates. Your credit history is a permanent record of every bill you have paid or failed to pay on time. The higher your rating, the more money you can borrow for a house or car.

To maintain a good credit history, consider the following:

- Pay your bills on time and do not default (fail to complete payments) on your loans.
- Use a credit card that requires you to pay off the entire balance each month. Find a card with no annual fee and the lowest interest rate.
- Try not to charge for monthly expenses, but if you must, don't go over your credit limit.
- If you do not pay a credit card balance in full each month, at least pay more than the minimum amount due.
- Don't accept an increase in your credit card limit.

A Word About Identity Theft

You can be the victim of identity theft and not even be aware of it. All someone has to do is gain access to your social security number, and your credit rating can be virtually destroyed due to another person accruing credit in your name. To avoid being a victim, take the following measures:

- Never give out your social security number. There are few exceptions: You need to give your social security number when opening a bank or credit card account, applying for a job, and filing taxes, among others.
- Likewise, be cautious of giving out your credit card numbers. And don't throw away any credit card statements or mail items with credit and/or social security information. Shred them first.
- Do not carry your social security card in your wallet. If you have a safe deposit box, keep your social security card there. At minimum, keep it in a fire-safe box in a secure place in your home. With either option, you'll have access to your card if you need to produce it for a legitimate reason.
- Check your credit rating often. Make sure it is free of errors. Even the savviest consumers can have errors on their credit report or be the targets of identity theft. You can get a free credit report once a year from major credit bureaus.
- Regarding "spam" e-mails: There are many scams, some designed to entice you ("Register now to claim your cash prize") and others designed to scare you ("Regarding your past due account"). Do not respond to junk e-mails. If one looks legitimate (e.g., it appears to be from your bank or your place of employment) contact customer service or human resources to find out if the message is legitimate.

Resource Name _____

Office Location _____

Phone Number _____

E-mail Address _____

KNOW YOUR SCHOOL

Your school will have support services to help with financial matters. Research school resources that can help you. Examples include personal counseling services and financial aid offices. List the information here, and for quick reference place the information in a prominent place such as on your refrigerator.

HEALTHY DECISION MAKING

Sharlene has a test on Monday and some research she wants to do on a paper due in several weeks. She has scheduled time this weekend on her calendar to go to the library to gather some articles for her paper and meet with her study group before the test. Her friend Melissa has asked her to help out with a volunteer community event this weekend on teaching children about personal safety. Sharlene wants to help but is fearful of having a lot of work passed on to her. She also does not want to lose her library time. Can you give her some suggestions on how to say yes to Melissa without losing time for her academic work?

_____

_____

_____

_____

Can you suggest some tasks she could do before the weekend to help Melissa so she would still be free to go to the library and have some weekend time for herself? One hint would be making posters to advertise the event. Can you list others?

_____

_____

Congratulations! You have completed the chapter on time and money management. Combined with stress management, a positive attitude, and good goals, you are well on your way to a successful academic experience and life. The next two chapters will help you to develop your study and test-taking skills to complete the basic skills needed for academic and professional success.

Now that you have read this chapter and performed the assessments and exercises, go to your CD for this chapter to reinforce these concepts. The CD will present you with a fun and interactive journey through time management and visually show you such techniques as making a daily to-do list, strategies for effective planning, ways to capitalize on your peak periods of productivity, and much more. In addition, it will help you to prepare your personal budget and manage your financial resources.

References

Burka, J. B., & Yuen, L. M. (1983). *Procrastination: Why you do it, what to do about it.* Cambridge, MA: Perseus.

Keyes, R. (1991, October). How to unlock time. *Reader's Digest,* pp. 111–114.

Pauk, W. (2000). *How to study in college* (7th ed.). Boston: Houghton Mifflin.

Tice, D. M., & Baumeister, R. F. (1997). Longitudinal study of procrastination, performance, stress, and health: The costs and benefits of dawdling. *Psychological Science, 118* (6), 454–458.

Active Study Strategies

Learning "How to Learn"

WHY LEARN THIS SKILL?

The establishment of good study skills is one of the top reasons for student academic success. Even if you have had study strategies course work in the past, this chapter will help you to brush up. After all, many employers offer time management and stress management for employees who have long since earned their degrees or certifications, so we can all benefit from improving our skills and expanding our strategies.

Also, the strategies that worked in the past may need to be modified or changed altogether for success in your current course work. If you've changed majors or career paths, you may need to learn different strategies.

Keep in mind that study strategies apply to your life even after you complete your academic program. We are sure you have heard of the importance of being a lifelong learner. You may not have to worry about your teacher's grading policies once you are established in your career, but colleagues and supervisors will evaluate your work and your work habits. Creating an organized space to study will transfer into your work environment. Reading strategies will yield results for textbook reading as well as reading you have to do on the job. Notetaking skills will help you at work as well as in the classroom. We could go on, but you get the idea: All of these skills are transferable.

This chapter covers several important ways to develop stronger study skills. These will include organizing your study area and revisiting study schedules and time management techniques. In addition, you will learn new methods for reading text material and taking good lecture notes. Let's begin by covering some strategies that will help you manage your study load more effectively. Exercise 4-1 will help you assess your current study skills.

Check the answers that apply to you:

_____ I have a quiet area for study.

_____ I have developed an organized system for studying.

_____ There are few distractions where and when I study.

_____ Friends and family support my efforts and don't interrupt my study.

_____ I avoid reading and studying school materials when I'm in bed.

_____ My books and notebooks are organized.

_____ I have no trouble finding my study materials when I need them.

_____ I never forget to bring homework to class.

_____ I keep a calendar with due dates for projects and exams.

_____ I maintain a study schedule that helps me stay up to date on homework and other responsibilities.

_____ Total number of items checked

EXERCISE 4-1
Assess Yourself:
How Organized
Are You?

If you checked eight or more items, you're a pretty organized student and only need to work on one or two issues. Checking six to seven items indicates that this chapter could help you to refine your organizational strategies. Four to five checked items indicates that you would benefit from becoming more organized, and three or fewer items indicates that you have some work to do and need to read the following ideas without delay.

ORGANIZING STUDY MATERIALS

How to Organize

A number of textbooks will tell you the so-called right way to organize, and retail stores will offer to sell you the latest notebooks, calendars, electronic planners, and countless other organizers.

If you're like a lot of students, you may have gone to your bookstore or the nearest discount store to buy the latest organizational gadgets—perhaps you have a PDA or a software program to schedule your commitments. However, after a few weeks, many students' good intentions fall by the wayside.

Although we give you many ideas on organization, there is no one way to organize. You simply have to create a system that works for *you*. The key is to keep it *simple, consistent,* and *systematic.*

Notebooks and Other Materials.

Not submitting an assignment because "I left it in another notebook" doesn't cut it. Keep your materials organized in such a way that you can access them with little stress and confusion. One recommendation is to keep a notebook for every class. For many classes, three-ring binders are simplest because you can easily keep everything in order and three-hole-punch handouts, exams, and such. If you're a full-time student, it is often easiest to have separate notebooks for each class so you don't have to cart all of your materials to each class. Finally, many students find they need to have a different color notebook for each class to minimize the chances of taking the wrong one to class.

Calendars.

In Chapter 3, we discussed time management and maintaining a semester, weekly, and daily calendar. A calendar with room for writing to-do lists will be helpful. In addition, the calendar can assist in identifying deadlines and in strategic planning of large tasks, as described earlier.

Study Area.

Where you study is also very important. Ideally, your study area should be the same place each time so you mentally connect this place to studying. It should have minimal distractions and good lighting. The table or desk should have the necessary study tools such as pen, paper, calculator, computer, and so on. Please see Figure 4-1.

If You Live on Campus. Begin by thinking about how you study best. Do you concentrate best in total quiet, without interruption? Depending on your residence hall situation, you might find yourself having to leave the environment to do your best studying. Perhaps there is a quiet space in a library or an empty classroom.

FIGURE 4-1

Which person is getting the most out of study time?

If You Commute. For the commuter, it is equally important to maintain an organized study space. You may not have to deal with the typical residence hall distractions, but you still need to create a study area of your own. If you have to use your bedroom, remember to avoid studying in bed. Use a desk or table in a well-lit area. Also, sit in a desk chair, which will force you to sit up straight (and will aid in concentration). If you study in a living room or dining area, try to avoid distractions such as the TV, MP3 player, or radio. Also, see if your school has designated commuter study areas.

SCIENTIFIC APPLICATION
Classical Conditioning

Throughout the textbook you will notice instances of the mind–body connection. The psychological term **classical conditioning** illustrates this concept and actually relates to study skills. The term came from an experiment performed on dogs by the Russian scientist Ivan Pavlov. In this experiment, a bell was rung and dogs were then fed meat. The meat stimulated the dogs to salivate in anticipation of the digestive process. Again and again, experimenters would ring a bell and feed the dogs. After repeated exposure to this procedure, the dogs connected the ringing of the bell to the meat. All the scientists had to do was

ring a bell, and the dogs would salivate like crazy, even if they weren't given meat (Huffman, 2005). So what's the purpose of telling you this story other than making you hungry or grossing you out?

When you repeatedly study in bed and then go to sleep, you soon connect studying to sleeping. Every time you begin to study (even in midafternoon), you may begin to yawn and lose focus. You are conditioning yourself to connect studying to sleeping. Avoid studying in bed because you will not be as focused and therefore as effective in retaining the material. Besides, studying in bed will interfere with your ability to get a good night's sleep.

Now do Exercise 4-2.

EXERCISE 4-2
What's Wrong With This Picture?

Looking at Figure 4-1, identify three things the student in the poor study area can do to improve.

1. _____

2. _____

3. _____

DEVELOPING A STUDY SCHEDULE

There are several ideas to consider when developing your personal study schedule. These include utilizing time management techniques and strategies for maximum gain.

The Importance of Time Management

As with any journey you are about to undertake, there is *no* substitute for good planning and preparation. The same can be said for your successful academic journey. Successful preparation includes developing a daily schedule that includes proper study time. Don't be discouraged if your first few schedules don't work well and be sure to build in some flexibility. Don't forget to schedule relaxation and recreational time because these are also important to academic success (and to general well-being).

Scheduling Study Sessions

In creating a study schedule, many students look for blocks of several hours during which they can study. Do not underestimate the value of finding small pockets of otherwise "wasted" time, as we discussed in Chapter 3. A few minutes here and there will add up. For example, commuting students can tape record vocabulary terms and definitions and listen to them during their drive or bus ride to campus. If you have an appointment and the person you're meeting is running late, be prepared by having your math homework with you. If you complete one or two problems while you're waiting, it's time well spent.

Alternating Subjects

As we said in Chapter 3, studying notes and other course materials over shorter periods of time in more frequent intervals is more effective than long cramming sessions. If you have several hours blocked off as study time, remember to take a short break every 30 to 50 minutes or so (whatever works best for you). Listen to a couple of songs on your iPod, throw in a load of laundry, or check your e-mail—anything that will only take a couple of minutes and allow you to clear your head a bit. Then move on to another subject. A good way to see if you are studying efficiently is to ask yourself questions periodically about what you have just read. If you can't answer these questions, you probably are losing interest and need to take a short break to become more focused.

Time of Day

The actual time of day that you choose to study can be very important. It may not be the same time for everyone. Some people are so-called morning people; others are not. An interactive CD exercise for this chapter will help you to determine your best study time. We all have different biological clocks, and becoming aware of your personal biological clock can help you to be a more effective and efficient learner (Ammons, Booker, & Killmon, 1995). The message for now is to schedule as much of your study time as possible when you are most alert and focused. (Note: It is not always up to you, though, when you get to study: Following our scheduling tips will help you to make the most of your study time, whatever the time of day.) In Exercise 4-3, you'll have the opportunity to revisit the time management principles from Chapter 3.

Use the weekly grid in Figure 4-2 to block out your class time along with dedicated study times that work best for your schedule. You can also include any other fixed obligations such as work or school activities. In addition, your CD will allow you to enter your schedule electronically and print it out.

EXERCISE 4-3
Creating a Study
Schedule

FIGURE 4-2
Study grid.

	MON	TUE	WED	THU	FRI	SAT	SUN
6–8 AM							
8–10 AM							
10–12 AM							
12–2 PM							
2–4 PM							
4–6 PM							
6–8 PM							
8–10 PM							
10–12 AM							
12–2 AM							
2–4 AM							
4–6 AM							

Write in your schedule of classes and include study time and free time as you see fit.

Note: Remember to switch subjects periodically (every 30 to 50 minutes or so).

Some Additional Words of Wisdom:

- Don't forget your large personal desk planning calendar for the quarter or semester, which can include due dates for assignments, test dates, meetings, and important events to augment your weekly schedule.

- Leave some open blocks of time. Your week will seldom go exactly as planned, and you will need flexibility. If you find that you frequently depart from your schedule, you may not be in control of your time, and a review of the time management chapter is in order.

- Remember the daily to-do list principles. Establish the habit of holding your own personal planning session each day. Take a few minutes in the morning or at the end of the preceding day to list what you need to accomplish; then prioritize your tasks.

Use Exercise 4-4 to assess your current study skills.

EXERCISE 4-4
Assess Your Current
Study Skills

Answer the following questions. Be critical and honest in circling the response that best answers the question.

Do you have an organized place to study?
Sometimes   Always   Rarely

Is it quiet where you study?
Sometimes   Always   Rarely

Are the conditions and lighting comfortable?
Sometimes   Always   Rarely

Do you have all the tools (pencils, paper, electronic tools, etc.) you need to study at this place?
Sometimes   Always   Rarely

Do you know when major exams, papers, and assignments are due?
Sometimes   Always   Rarely

Do you make the most of short time periods throughout the day?
Sometimes   Always   Rarely

What were your results? For now, it doesn't matter as long as you were honest. Remember this is an assessment of where you are now. Your eventual goal should be to have all your responses be "Always." If they are now, great! If not, you need to develop an action plan to change all the responses to "Always" in the near future.

Map out a plan: In creating your action plan, remember to follow the MAPS model from Chapter 2.

_____

_____

_____

_____

_____

READING TEXT MATERIALS

You can also develop effective strategies to get the most from assigned readings. These strategies are powerful and will make studying for exams much easier and less stressful.

First, assess your skills in Exercise 4-5.

Check the ones that apply to you:

_____ I preview my texts before classes begin to get a sense of the material.

_____ I schedule time each day to complete reading assignments.

_____ I stay up to date on reading assignments, rarely falling behind the schedule outlined on the syllabus.

_____ I preview the assigned reading, taking note of subject headings and subheadings and carefully reviewing the introduction and conclusion.

_____ I ask questions of or argue with the text.

_____ I check my comprehension of text material, noting areas where I do not understand material.

_____ I review the chapter after completing the reading assignment, making note of concepts I may still not understand.

_____ I underline and/or write notes in the margins of my text.

_____ I write supplemental notes on assigned readings in outline or some other organized form.

_____ I take advantage of supplemental material in the text, including end-of-chapter questions and summary material (when available).

_____ Total number of items checked

If you checked nine or more items, you use good reading strategies for assignments. You can work on the unchecked areas, but you're in pretty good shape. A total of seven or eight checked items indicates that your strategies could be better, and you will benefit from this chapter. A total of five or six checked areas means you need to improve your reading strategies; four or fewer checked items indicate that you *really* need to improve your retention of reading material.

Regardless of age, academic background, major, or confidence level, students are universally surprised by the challenges of reading assignments—both in content and in volume. Students generally improve managing their reading by (1) managing time for reading assignments and (2) using active rather than passive reading strategies.

Managing Time for Reading Assignments

Let's take an example. You have to read a difficult chapter of 50 pages this week, and you feel overwhelmed by the amount of material. Fifty pages can seem like a lot for only one course, especially if you have the same amount—or more—for some or all of your other courses. However, if you commit to reading 10 pages a day for a week, it seems more manageable. Further, if you break a 10-page assignment into two daily sessions of 5 pages each, it's even more manageable (Van Blerkom, 2006, p. 172). The key is to use the time management strategies from Chapter 3 to manage your reading load.

Reading Strategies

We've given you a number of strategies that will help you to keep up with your reading. However, you want to do more than simply read the material. You want to (1) understand it and (2) remember it. Students who read *passively* merely decode the words on a page, not pausing to check for comprehension, mark unfamiliar terms, or ask questions of the text. Students who read *actively* use a variety of strategies to monitor their understanding (Irwin & Baker, 1989, p. 18). Although (initially) active reading takes more time than passive reading, it actually saves you time because you better understand the material and need less review time for the exam.

Active reading typically includes writing, both in marking the text and in taking text notes. Most active text-reading strategies have the following features:

Previewing.

Preview the assignment by skimming the chapter headings and subheadings and carefully reading introductions and conclusions. Attend to key points written in italics or bold print. Some text chapters have summaries and discussion questions at the end. Many students like to read those materials first rather than last. Why? Because then they will know what they are reading for.

Highlighting and/or Underlining.

Read a section, and then highlight or underline the key points. Marking your text keeps you involved in the reading and forces you to attend to the key points. Generally, it is best to read a section and then go back over the material and mark it. If you mark as you read, you will very likely mark too much material, which will defeat the purpose of marking the most significant information.

Fact or Fiction?

If you want to sell a textbook, you shouldn't mark in it.

Many students want to sell back their books and thus hesitate to write in them. Your purchase of textbooks is truly part of your investment in your education. Students who mark in their textbooks tend to learn the material better, and isn't that why you bought the book in the first place? If you buy the book, keep it unmarked and in near-perfect condition, and then earn a poor grade in the class, have you gotten as much from your investment? Besides, keeping your books in pristine condition doesn't help much if you sell texts back to buyers on campus. You can refer to the Nebraska Book Company (2007) *Buyer's Guide* for many buy-back prices.

Marginal Notes.

In addition to highlighting or underlining key information, it is a good idea to write notes in the margins. Such notes can include questions you have of the text, important terminology, or very brief paraphrasing of important points. These notes can help you to prepare for exams, and the very act of writing these notes can aid in your retention of the material. See Figure 4-3.

Using Support Materials.

Does your text have review questions at the end of the chapter? Try to answer them. Does your instructor post study guides and other materials on her or his website? Use them. Does your text come with a study guide or CD? Use it to aid in your comprehension of the material.

FIGURE 4-3

Sample textbook page with text marking and marginal notes.

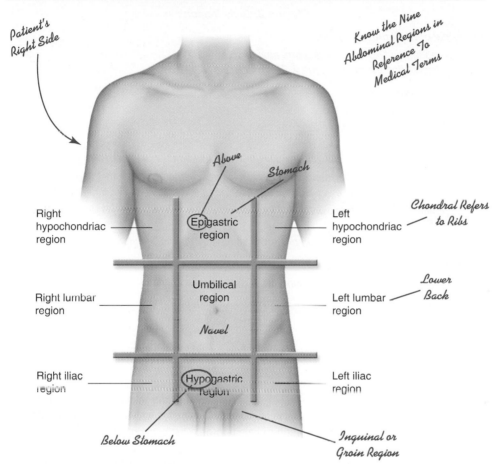

Know the Nine Abdominal Regions in Reference To Medical Terms

Patient's Right Side

Above

Stomach

Right hypochondriac region

Epigastric region

Left hypochondriac region

Chondral Refers to Ribs

Right lumbar region

Umbilical region

Left lumbar region

Lower Back

Navel

Right iliac region

Hypogastric region

Left iliac region

Below Stomach

Inguinal or Groin Region

Source: Colbert, Bruce J.; Ankney, Jeff; and Lee, Karen. *Anatomy and Physiology for Health Professionals: An Interactive Journey,* First Edition. Copyright © 2007. Electronically reproduced by permission of Pearson Education, Inc., Upper Saddle River, New Jersey.

Text Notes.

Take good, accurate, legible notes. Remember that the purpose of taking notes is to get key points from textbooks and lectures and not to write every word that is said or written. In addition to highlighting, outline your chapters so you can make the connection from your brain to the pencil. This is what you'll need to do on the test.

Outlining can be done in a number of ways. Many of us are familiar with the structure of formal outlines, with alternating Roman

Flashback to Flash or Note Cards

In Chapter 3 on time management, we spoke about wasting time productively. Carrying your flash/note cards with you, say to a doctor's appointment or any appointment where you may have to wait, can save you valuable study time.

FIGURE 4-4

Samples of text notes.

Chapter 2: Body Regions

Overview of Abdominal Regions

1. *The abdominal region is divided into nine regions*
2. *Understanding the medical term will help to locate*

The Actual Regions:

Epigastric Region—*located above (epi) stomach (gastric). Region above the "belly button"*

Right and **Left Hypochondriac Regions** *are located to the right and left of the patient's epigastric region.*

The centrally located region houses the belly button or navel and is called the **Umbilical Region.**

The **Right** *and* **Left Lumbar Regions** *are located to the patient's right and left of the Umbilical Region. Lumbar refers to your lower back and these regions are at level of lumber vertebrae of the spine.*

The **Hypogastric Region** *lies below (hypo) the stomach and is flanked on each side by the* **Right** *and* **Left Iliac Regions.**

The inguinal region is where the thigh meets the body; AKA the groin region.

Questions and Concepts to Know:

What are the nine regions of the abdominal area and where are they located?

Study tools:

Use figure 4-3.
Learn regions in reference to medical terms to help locate.
Do CD drag-and-drop exercise for additional practice.

---

numerals and letters. Outlines can also take the shapes of lists, diagrams, pictures, and flashcards. The more you can see it, as it were, the better you can understand relationships or how it all fits together. See Figure 4-4 for some examples. In addition, please see the companion CD with this textbook to create more visualization to help reinforce the concepts in your mind's eye.

Test your knowledge in Exercise 4-6.

EXERCISE 4-6
Test Your Knowledge on Text Reading

Do you schedule time each day to read text material?
    Sometimes   Always   Rarely

Do you mark important points in your text?
    Sometimes   Always   Rarely

Do you outline the important points in your text?
    Sometimes   Always   Rarely

In your text notes, do you write in your own words?
    Sometimes   Always   Rarely

If you answered *always* to these questions, that's great! For each one you answered sometimes and rarely, develop an action plan for improvement, remembering to follow the MAPS model.

Map out a plan:

_____

_____

_____

_____

TAKING EFFECTIVE LECTURE NOTES

You may be tired of hearing the word *strategy* by now. However, it is an important concept to achieve success and, yes, there are note-taking strategies that will help you take effective lecture notes. First, assess yourself in Exercise 4-7.

_____

Check each item that applies to you:

EXERCISE 4-7
Assess Yourself: How Good Are Your Note-Taking and Classroom Strategies?

_____ I am able to concentrate during lectures.

_____ I have strategies for coping with or minimizing distractions.

_____ I prepare for lectures by keeping up with my reading and other assignments.

_____ When given the choice, I sit where I am least likely to become distracted (near the teacher, away from the window or exit, etc.).

_____ My lecture notes are legible and easy to follow.

_____ I review my notes before the next class to check for needed clarification, missing information, or inconsistencies.

_____ My notes are organized so I can find information right away.

_____ I mark my notes by underlining or highlighting important information.

_____ I am willing to ask questions during the lecture or go to my teacher's office for assistance if I do not understand some of the lecture material.

_____ I volunteer to answer questions in class.

_____ Total number of items checked

If you checked nine or more items, you're a pretty good note taker and can just work on the checked areas. A total of seven to eight items means you're a fair note taker, but there's room for improvement. If you checked five to six items, you should work on improving your strategies. Finally, four or fewer checked items means you need a drastic overhaul of your note taking strategies.

Pick an item you did not check and develop a specific action plan that will have you checking it in the near future.

Action plans:

_____

_____

_____

_____

Note-Taking Tips

Listening.

To become a good note taker, you may need to sharpen your listening skills. You want your notes to be accurate, legible, and understandable; to capture main points, ideas and relationships; and to identify questions. You need to be able to stay tuned in and manage distractions, day-dreaming, and fatigue. Here are some methods for increasing your concentration during lectures:

- Sitting in the front of the classroom: If you can choose where you sit during a lecture, try to sit at or near the front of the class. Students who sit in front are less likely to become distracted during lectures. You will also be less likely to engage in side conversations with other students.
- Prepare for the lecture: Read the material, review your notes, and identify questions before class.
- Ask questions—of yourself and of the instructor: How can I use this? How does this relate? Listen for answers, or raise questions with the instructor, either during or after class.
- Handle distracting thoughts: As thoughts intrude, you may need to write a quick note to yourself about the distraction and set it aside until after class.
- Answer questions: Volunteer when the instructor poses a question to the class.

Organization.

There are a number of good ways to organize your notes. As we told you at the beginning of the chapter about study space, the key is to find a system that works for you without making it too complicated. Here are some suggestions:

- **Use the Cornell method:** The **Cornell method,** developed by Walter Pauk (2000), provides a unique way to organize your material and to check your retention of material. Draw a vertical line down each page about 2 inches in from the margin. Write your notes on the right side of the line. Use the left side for brief comments, key words, questions you may want to ask, and for other notations that add emphasis or clarity. See Figure 4-5.
- **Organize your notebooks:** Keep your notes in a three-ring binder with dividers to separate the various subjects. Better yet, keep a separate notebook for each course. If you do this, make sure you label the notebooks or perhaps have different colored notebooks for each class, so you are less likely to take the wrong notebook when you leave for class.
- **Analyze your notes:** Review your notes right after class whenever possible or at least within a day of the class. If you review your notes shortly after class, then you will be able to fix most errors and gaps yourself. You might also want to compare your notes with those of another student. If you're still missing essential points, you might want to ask your instructor to review your notes with you and make suggestions.

FIGURE 4-5

Example of Cornell method side by side with disorganized notes.

Disorganized Text Notes

Sentences

A complete sentence has two parts, a subject and predicate. Both can be more than one word. Subject includes noun or pronoun. Noun–person, place, or thing. Pronoun–substitute word for noun. Pronouns: personal, demonstrative, indefinite, possessive.

Verbs are action words. Forms change–person, number, tense. Person is first, second, third. Number is singular or plural. Tense is present, past, future, present perfect, past perfect, future perfect. Verbs are regular and irregular. Regular–add the correct ending to the base form. Irregular–change the entire spelling of the word. Some verbs need auxiliary (helping) words.

Cornell Method of Text Notes

Simple Sentences: Subjects and Predicates

What are the two parts of a sentence?	*A complete sentence has two parts: a subject and a predicate*
What is a subject?	*Subject–a noun or pronoun.*
What is a noun?	*Noun–person, place, or thing.*
What is a pronoun?	*Pronoun–substitute word for noun.*
What are the types of pronouns?	*personal pronouns (he, she, it, they, we, etc.)* *demonstrative pronouns (this, these, that, those)* *indefinite pronouns (each, either, neither, anyone, somebody, etc.)* *possessive pronouns (mine, its, his, hers, theirs, ours)*
What is a predicate?	*Predicate–includes a verb, the action of a sentence.*
What are verbs?	*Verbs–action words. The form depends on person, number, and tense:*
Identify the components of verb forms	*Person: first (I, me, we, etc.), second (you), third (he, she, it, they, etc.)* *Number: singular or plural* *Tense: present, past, future, present perfect, past perfect, future perfect*
Define regular and irregular forms.	*Verb forms are regular and irregular.* *Regular–add the correct ending to the base form.* *Irregular–change the entire spelling of the word. Some verbs need auxiliary (helping) words, such as "have" in "have helped" (present perfect), "will" as in "will walk" (future), and "had" as in "had gone" (past perfect).*

Summary: Simple sentences are composed of subjects (nouns/pronouns, which indicate person, place, or thing) and predicates (verbs). There are four types of pronouns. Irregular and regular verb forms depend on person, number, and tense.

- **Mark your notes:** As you should with a textbook, underline or highlight key information or questions.

  Try out a new note-taking method in Exercise 4-8.

A WORD ABOUT ATTENDING CLASS

The importance of attending your classes cannot be overstressed. Beyond the fact that skipping class is a waste of your tuition money, there are several other reasons. When you skip class, you miss class discussions when instructors tend to highlight what they consider most important and what is likely to show up on the exam. Skipping class is not a very smart time management technique. It will take you twice as long to find out what you miss and copy someone else's notes than if you just had attended the class. Being on time and attending class tells the instructor you value what they have to say and shows respect.

EXERCISE 4-8
Revising Lecture Notes

Take notes from one lecture period and convert them by using the previous method (leaving room in the left margin for notes, questions, summary, etc.) Compare the new with the original, and see which system you prefer. Answer the questions below:

Which version of your notes do you prefer?

_____

What are the strengths of your original set of notes?

_____

What are the weaknesses in your original notes?

_____

Map out a plan: Write a brief action plan for how you will change your note-taking strategies for the rest of the semester:

_____

_____

_____

_____

Classroom Etiquette

In later chapters, we discuss the importance of making a good impression at job interviews. It is equally important to consider the image you communicate in class. Being on time and attending class is not the only way to communicate maturity and a positive attitude. You must also communicate respect for your peers and instructors (and yourself!) by remembering the following:

- Avoid side conversations. If you like to sit with your friends, either sit apart during class or sit up front so you're less tempted to talk to each other instead of attending to class material. (Your notes will be better, too.)

Resource Name _____

Office Location _____

Phone Number _____

E-mail Address _____

KNOW YOUR SCHOOL

Your school will have support services to help you with your study skills. Research what school resources can help you, such as peer tutors, learning skill centers, math centers, and so on. List the information here, and for quick reference place the information in a prominent place such as on your refrigerator.

- Text messaging: As well as person-to-person side conversations, also avoid electronic side conversations in the form of text messaging.
- Cell phones: Get in the habit of turning your cell phone off before entering a classroom. This habit will help you in the future as well.

HEALTHY DECISION MAKING

Read the following case about a student who has difficulty keeping up with her classes. What advice would you give to Alison?

Alison is taking 12 credits her first semester, and she is struggling academically. At midterm, most of her grades are either C— or D. She made B's throughout high school with minimal effort. She attends her classes and generally completes assignments on time, although just barely. She's never had to take notes before, at least not as much as she does now. Also, she doesn't understand why she does poorly on quizzes and tests because she does all the reading. Outside of the classroom, she is having a good experience: She's making friends and trying to get involved. Sometimes there are distractions in the residence hall, but she still tries to get her work done.

Your advice:

_____

_____

_____

_____

Congratulations! You have now completed the chapter on active study skills. By using the advice in this chapter in conjunction with time and stress management concepts from previous chapters, you are on your way to further academic success.

 Please go to your CD and see the chapter on study skills. Several activities on the CD will help you with getting organized, scheduling time to study, reading, note taking, and test taking. Additional assessments and activities will help you develop your own personal action plan for academic success.

References

Ammons, T. L., Booker, J. L. & Killmon, C. P. (1995). *The effects of time of day on student attention and achievement.* (ERIC Document Reproduction Service No. ED 384592)

Huffman, K. (2005). *Psychology in action* (8th ed.). Hoboken, NJ: Wiley.

Irwin, J. W., & Baker, I. (1989). *Promoting active reading comprehension strategies: A resource book for teachers.* Englewood Cliffs, NJ: Prentice Hall.

Nebraska Book Company. (2007). *Buyer's guide.* Lincoln: Author.

Pauk, W. (2000). *How to study in college* (7th ed.). Boston: Houghton Mifflin.

Van Blerkom, D. (2006). *College study skills: Becoming a strategic learner.* Boston: Thomson-Wadsworth.

5

Learning Styles, Memory, and Test Taking

Getting the Grade

OBJECTIVES

What you will discover by the end of this chapter:

- Your preferred learning style(s)
- Memorization techniques
- Test-taking strategies or how to "ace" those exams
- More strategies to create a positive impression in class

Students often begin their postsecondary education without strong academic strategies (Upcraft, Gardner, & Associates, 1989, pp. 108–109) including, but not limited to, minimal memory and test-taking skills and little awareness of their preferred learning styles. Soon, they realize that they need to improve their skills, particularly in the area of test-taking. Exams now are often more challenging: Instructors cover more material in less time, and they ask higher-level questions than many of us experienced in high school. Also, in some classes, your entire grade may be based on only two or three exams.

As we said at the beginning of Chapter 4, developing the skills and knowledge explored in this chapter will help you not only at school but in your career. Once you graduate, learning—and testing—does not end. You will have to learn (and sometimes memorize) new information and techniques for your work. To do so, it is important to gain a new level of self-awareness, particularly with how you best learn and remember new information.

To begin the chapter, we discuss learning styles. Once you better understand your preferred ways of learning, you can develop memory and test-taking techniques that work best for you. After exploring learning styles and memory techniques, we'll conclude with effective test-taking strategies.

LEARNING STYLES

Have you ever thought about how you learn? Each of us has preferred styles of learning. Understanding this preference can help make us even better learners. Let's begin by exploring your preference in Exercise 5-1.

Answer the following questions regarding your preferences. Remember, there are no right or wrong answers. These questions are designed to evaluate your preferred methods for learning and studying. (Note: If you're a new student and haven't spent much time in a classroom recently, you may have difficulty answering some of these questions. Just put the answer that you think would most closely apply to you.)

EXERCISE 5-1
What Is Your
Learning Style?

1. I prefer classes with
    a. Lectures
    b. Visual aids, such as PowerPoint, overheads, etc.
    c. Lab and other hands-on components

2. I like to learn from teachers who
    a. Lecture for most of the classes
    b. Are organized with material and provide handouts, write on the board, and use other visual cues
    c. Interact with the class and promote group work

3. When I read, I tend to
    a. Read out loud or start to move my lips as I read
    b. Highlight or underline main points, often using different colors
    c. Get bored or become restless easily

4. When taking notes, I benefit from
    a. Tape-recording the class so I can listen to any lecture material again
    b. Organizing the material in a visually clear and appealing way
    c. Sitting near the front of the class so I don't get distracted

5. To memorize material, it is best if I
    a. Recite it out loud a number of times
    b. See it in written form repeatedly
    c. Use mnemonics or write it out

6. I concentrate best in an environment that is
    a. Quiet
    b. Organized and neat
    c. Has limited activity around me

7. When studying for a test, I benefit from
    a. Discussing the material
    b. Organizing the material in outline or chart form
    c. Practicing concepts in a hands-on way

8. To learn something, I need to
    a. Hear it
    b. See it
    c. Practice it

9. I understand instructions best
    a. When someone explains them to me out loud
    b. When they're written clearly, perhaps with diagrams or charts
    c. If I can do it myself

10. In class, I like to sit
    a. Anywhere—it really doesn't matter, as long as I can listen to what's going on
    b. Near the front, where I can see the board or slides
    c. Near an exit, so I can get up if I need to

Assessment

There are three primarily learning modalities:

- **Auditory:** If most of your responses were "a," your dominant learning style is auditory. **Auditory learners** understand material best by listening. They tend to like lecture classes. If they need directions to get somewhere, they prefer oral directions to maps or written directions. Sometimes they like to tape-record classes. (Be careful. Sometimes, tape recording can make students less attentive during class, if they think they can just listen to the tape "later.")

- **Visual:** A majority of "b" answers indicates that you are a visual learner. **Visual learners** understand material best by seeing it. They tend to be organized readers and note takers, and they like to highlight or write notes in different colors. These strategies can help them to remember material better. If you're a visual learner, you might get frustrated if a teacher doesn't write on the board much or provide written directions. You benefit from sitting near the front of the class so you don't miss any visual cues, such as board work.

- **Kinesthetic:** If you answered "c" most of the time, you are a tactile, or **kinesthetic,** learner. In other words, you like to learn in a hands-on setting. You might find yourself getting restless during lectures, and you may tend to prefer classes with lab work, group activities, and fieldwork.

"Which learning styles are represented?"

Working with Your Learning Style

Although it is likely that you have one dominant learning modality, you probably had answers in all three (or at least two) of the areas. That's because most of us use a combination of learning modalities, and rightly so. Just as there are many types of learning styles, there are many types of teaching styles, and students have to be able to adapt to all of them. You will use similar adaptation strategies in the workplace (and probably have already) when you have supervisors or colleagues with different approaches to working and learning.

So what do you do with this knowledge of your learning style? You can use it to adapt to challenging classroom situations.

Auditory Learners.

In addition to using visual materials, perhaps you can tape-record material. Caution: Be selective about tape-recording class lectures. Many students tape record lectures, and, because they know they'll have a recording to go back to later, they zone out during the lectures: "I'm tired, and I don't have to pay attention—I can just go back and listen to the tape later." Unfortunately, "later" may never arrive. Also, it is a good idea to ask permission of your instructor to tape class.

A better idea might be to tape-record your own study materials. For example, if you have to learn some new vocabulary terms, record them and listen to the tape on your commute to school (or while going to class or while on the treadmill at the gym). Also, studying in groups and discussing material with fellow students can be helpful as well.

Visual Learners.

You might have difficulty with a lecture class that provides few visual cues, such as board work, overhead slides, or diagrams. In addition, you might struggle a bit to organize your notes. Find creative ways to write and organize your notes, such as visual concept maps. It can be helpful to rewrite your notes within a day of the lecture, so you get additional visual reinforcement.

Kinesthetic Learners.

With your preference for movement and hands-on learning, you should incorporate movement into your studying. Sometimes moving a bit while you study, as well as taking regular breaks, can be helpful. You might want to alternate active study tasks (writing a paper, doing math homework, completing a lab assignment) with your reading assignments.

Remember, you might have one dominant learning preference (or possibly two), but you have the capacity to use all three. Most successful students do.

Multiple Intelligences

Do you have a preference between following a map and following written directions to get to a new destination? Do you enjoy math and science classes more than English and literature, or vice versa? Are you praised as a good listener, or do you tend to shy away from groups?

Your responses to these questions provide insight into the various intelligences you possess. That's right—intelligenc*es*, in the plural. Howard Gardner (1993, 2006), a university professor, developed a theory of **multiple intelligences.** Basically, he argued that we have different types of intelligences and, within each person, some intelligences are better developed than others. If you are a student who prefers math and science classes over English, you have a well-developed logic/math intelligence. If you communicate well with others, your interpersonal intelligence is better developed.

Please do *not* take any of this to mean that if you struggle in an area, you cannot do it because of your innate intelligence. We have heard countless students say things like, "I don't have a mind for math" or "I'll just never understand chemistry." Rather than give up, most students need to work in these areas and take steps to develop these skills, perhaps by drawing on strengths in other areas of Gardner's framework.

A WORD ABOUT STUDY GROUPS AND ACTIVE LEARNING

We Learn:

10% of what we read
20% of what we hear
30% of what we see
50% of what we both see and hear
70% of what is discussed with others
80% of what we experience
95% of what we TEACH to someone else

—Edgar Dale's (1963) Cone of Experience

Although some may argue the percentages, the general concepts are true to what the research on learning has shown. The more senses you can get involved in the learning process, the more internalized the learning becomes. Therefore, text illustrations, CD and website animations, and videos enhance the learning process. Lab experiences and interactive games and exercises will also increase learning.

Group or study discussions are highly beneficial. Effective study groups can help you in achieving academic success. An excellent method to learn material is to explain concepts to each other. If you have to teach the group a concept, you will really learn what it is all about. *You'll soon learn that there is no better way to learn something than to teach it to someone else*.

Howard Gardner's Multiple Intelligences

1. **Linguistic Intelligence:** Someone with strong linguistic intelligence has an aptitude for using and understanding language. Writers, speakers, and lawyers typically have great linguistic intelligence.

2. **Logical/Mathematical Intelligence:** Someone with logical/mathematical intelligence can understand how systems work and can work well with numbers. Scientists, accountants, computer programmers, and mathematicians rely on this type of intelligence.

3. **Musical/Rhythmic Intelligence:** Someone with musical/rhythmic intelligence can recognize patterns and rhythms with relative ease. Musical performers/composers are the most obvious example of people who embody this type of intelligence.

4. **Bodily/Kinesthetic Intelligence:** Someone with bodily/kinesthetic intelligence often does something physical to solve a problem or to learn. Examples include athletes, firefighters, and performing artists.

5. **Spatial Intelligence:** Someone with spatial intelligence can imagine and understand the three-dimensional world in their own minds. Airplane pilots and engineers rely on spatial intelligence in their work.

6. **Naturalist Intelligence:** Someone with naturalist intelligence understands the features of and differences among living things and the natural world. Farmers, foresters, and others who work on the land and with animals demonstrate naturalist intelligence.

7. **Intrapersonal Intelligence:** Someone with intrapersonal intelligence has strong self-awareness. Those with intrapersonal intelligence are very aware of their strengths as well as any limitations and often work at self improvement. Researchers and philosophers demonstrate this intelligence.

8. **Interpersonal Intelligence:** Someone with interpersonal intelligence is able to understand and relate to other people. Educators, politicians, counselors, health care professionals, and salespeople demonstrate interpersonal intelligence.

Applying Gardner's concept means using as many intelligences as possible when learning or teaching a new concept. For example, when learning about interest and principal in loans, you could read about it (linguistics), do mathematical problems (logical/mathematical), construct graphs (spatial), make up a song (musical), relate it to your personal finances (intrapersonal), discuss it with a group (interpersonal), and physically demonstrate with real money (kinesthetic). You don't have to learn a concept in all eight applications, but the more intelligences you use, the better you will understand the material. Find out where you are strong in Exercise 5-2.

EXERCISE 5-2
Test Your
Intelligences

Put a check mark by those words or phrases that most closely describe you.

Linguistic/Verbal Intelligence　　　**Total** _____

_____ Verbally inclined.

_____ Enjoy reading.

_____ Enjoy writing.

_____ Like word games.

_____ Like learning new words.

Logical/Mathematical Intelligence　　　**Total** _____

_____ Logical

_____ Mathematically inclined.

_____ Like science classes.

_____ Enjoy logic puzzles.

_____ Like to understand how things and systems work.

Musical/Rhythmic Intelligence   **Total** _____

_____ Musically inclined.

_____ Keep time with music.

_____ Create rhymes to remember things.

_____ Play music in my head.

_____ Notice when someone sings or plays off key.

Bodily/Kinesthetic Intelligence   **Total** _____

_____ Athletically inclined.

_____ Hands-on in approach to learning.

_____ Enjoy lab classes.

_____ Learn by doing.

_____ Get restless easily.

Spatial Intelligence   **Total** _____

_____ Can draw things to scale.

_____ Understand how parts fit into a whole.

_____ Understand charts and diagrams.

_____ Understand cause and effect.

_____ Enjoy figuring out "how things work."

Naturalist Intelligence   **Total** _____

_____ Outdoors oriented.

_____ Realistic

_____ Enjoy nature.

_____ Learn well in "real-world" settings.

_____ Prefer not to be indoors.

Intrapersonal Intelligence   **Total** _____

_____ Need privacy.

_____ Strong self-awareness.

_____ Reflective.

_____ Questioning.

_____ Selective about friendships.

Interpersonal Intelligence   **Total** _____

_____ Communicative.

_____ Understanding.

_____ People oriented.

_____ Cooperative.

_____ Enjoy talking things over with friends.

What are three of your preferred intelligences?

1. _____

2. _____

3. _____

Now identify your most challenging course this semester: _____

Name three ways you can use your preferred intelligences to achieve success in this course:

1. _____

2. _____

3. _____

AIDING YOUR MEMORY

Although the purpose of education is to encourage thinking skills rather than memorization, you will recognize that memory is vital. Memory is used as an index of success because most techniques used to measure learning rely on it. Therefore, a good memory is a definite asset. Test your memory in Exercise 5-3.

EXERCISE 5-3
Testing your Memory

Time yourself for 1 minute and memorize the following food items. Then, try to recite them from memory.

Meat loaf

Grapefruit

Burrito

Eggplant parmesan

Kiwi

Frankfurters

Jam

Lemonade

Diet soda

Iced tea

Hummus

Cherries

Were you able to finish and recite them all? _____

If not, don't worry. This seemingly random list of food items would be hard to memorize, in large part because of its length. Another difficulty would be your familiarity with each item. Depending on the foods that were available in your home, you would be more familiar with some items than with others. Your lack of context, or connections (McPherson, 2000), would make these items harder to remember.

At times, we do have to memorize information. The key is to have a system for memorizing and, even more importantly, to make your learning meaningful. Take the food items in the previous exercise, but this time, place them in alphabetical order and in groups of three:

burritos, cherries, diet soda

eggplant parmesan, frankfurters, grapefruit

hummus, iced tea, jam

kiwi, lemonade, meat loaf

This memorization technique is called clustering, or grouping (Ferrett, 2006).

Grouping

There's a reason that our phone numbers are interrupted with a hyphen between the third and fourth number in the sequence. This technique makes it easier for us to remember the sequence. Rather than remembering a long sequence, we can more easily remember two shorter groups of numbers.

In the case of our food list, we first grouped the items in alphabetical order and in clusters of three. We can also group the items by type of food:

Entrees: burrito, eggplant parmesan, frankfurters, meat loaf

Fruits: cherries, grapefruit, kiwi

Drinks: diet soda, iced tea, lemonade

Spreads: hummus, jam

Mnemonics

Another effective memorization technique is the use of **mnemonics,** which are words, rhymes, or formulas that aid your memory. For example, did you have to memorize the names of the nine planets in order (Mercury, Venus, Earth, Mars, Jupiter, Saturn, Uranus, Neptune, and Pluto)? Perhaps, then, you heard this mnemonic (or a similar one):

My very educated mother just served us nine pizzas.

FIGURE 5-1

An acronym and visualization of what to do during a building fire: RACE.

Remove

Activate

Contain

Extinguish or

Evacuate

Wacky Mnemonics Fact

Now that Pluto has been taken off the list of planets, the mnemonic has changed: "My very educated mother just served us noodles"—or nachos, if you prefer. Another one found on the Web: "My vicious earthworm might just swallow us now" (Downs, "Ordering the Planets," 2007 www.teachingideas.co.uk).

This mnemonic is known as an **acrostic:** You take the first letter of every item to be memorized and form a sentence that will help you to remember vocabulary, terms, or concepts.

Another mnemonic device is an **acronym,** which is similar to an acrostic. Acronyms are words formed from the first letters of the terms you need to memorize. For example, the ABCs of CPR remind you that A = establish **A**irway, B = rescue **B**reathing, and C = establish **C**irculation. This mnemonic helps you to remember the steps and their proper order in a critical situation. Another classic mnemonic is the word HOMES to memorize the names of the Great Lakes (Huron, Ontario, Michigan, Erie, and Superior). Please see Figure 5-1 for an acronym to help you remember what to do in a building fire. Can you think of any others?

Rhymes or formulas are also helpful mnemonic devices. "In 1492, Columbus sailed the ocean blue." Many students in the United States are familiar with this age-old mnemonic. Formulas that appeal to your sense of logic can also help memory. For example, "Spring forward, Fall back" helps us adjust our clocks accordingly for daylight savings time. You can also make up silly stories to help remember facts. In fact, often the sillier the story, the easier it is to remember. Try your hand at mnemonics in Exercise 5-4.

Take the following list of colors: white, evergreen, gray, purple, white, red, black, indigo, and orange. Create mnemonics to remember the items on the list. Use at least two of the strategies described under the mnemonic section.

EXERCISE 5-4
Working with
Mnemonics

_____

_____

_____

TAKING EXAMS

Certainly one area that concerns most students is how to do well on exams. Developing your personalized test-taking strategies will improve your end results. However, let's first start with an initial assessment in Exercise 5-5.

Check all that apply to you:

EXERCISE 5-5
Assess Yourself: How
Good a Test Taker Are
You?

_____ I feel prepared when I go to take an exam.

_____ I study at least 4 or 5 days in advance for an exam.

_____ I use hands-on strategies such as writing answers from study guides and predicting and answering test questions.

_____ I feel calm, if not confident, when I take an exam.

_____ I finish exams without feeling "rushed."

_____ I rarely get an exam back only to see that I missed questions I actually knew the answer to.

_____ I use my own strategies for taking exams.

_____ I have strategies for taking multiple-choice and other objective exams.

_____ I have strategies for taking essay and short-answer exams.

_____ I keep old exams (when I have the option) to use as study tools later.

_____ Total number of items checked

Evaluation:

If you checked nine or ten items, you're a pretty good test taker and can just work on areas that you didn't check. A total of seven or eight items means you're a fair test taker but this chapter will definitely help you. A total of five to six items indicates you would greatly benefit from the techniques in this chapter. A score of four or fewer checked items shows that you have a lot of work to do. Regardless of your score, most of us can improve our test-taking strategies.

Active Test-Taking Strategies

Just as there are active reading, listening, and study strategies, there are also active test-taking strategies. Do Exercise 5-6 to assess your current strategies.

In which class have you most recently had an exam?

_____

Identify the strategy(-ies) you used to prepare for the exam:

_____

_____

_____

_____

For Exercise 5-6, most students might provide the following answers: "I looked over the notes" or "I read over the chapter." These strategies will only get you so far, even if you feel they worked for you in high school. It's better to use active strategies, which require you to do more than just "look at" or "read over" materials.

Active study strategies, as opposed to passive strategies, require you to write and rehearse materials, such as construct flash cards, rather than merely "look at" notes and other materials (Van Blerkom, 2006, p. 3). The following is a list of some examples of active strategies:

- Creating flash cards, problem/solution cards, or vocabulary cards (see Figure 5-2)
- Developing your own study guide
- Studying in small groups
- Outlining your chapters
- Drawing concept maps (see Figure 5-2)
- Producing charts or tables concerning the material
- Developing your own practice questions or mock exam

Developing these study materials and reviewing them at least a week before the exam will help your performance on an exam—and can also help your stress levels because you will have a greater sense of control. Use three or more different active strategies, preferably a week or so in advance, to prepare for your next exam. Now do Exercise 5-7 on page 102.

FIGURE 5-2

Example of a concept map and vocabulary card.

VOCABULARY CARDS

FRONT

RATIONAL
NUMBERS

FRONT

IRRATIONAL NUMBERS

BACK

- INTEGERS
- DO NOT EQUAL 0
- DECIMALS END OR REPEAT

BACK

- NOT RATIONAL
- DECIMALS DO NOT TERMINATE OR REPEAT

CONCEPT MAP

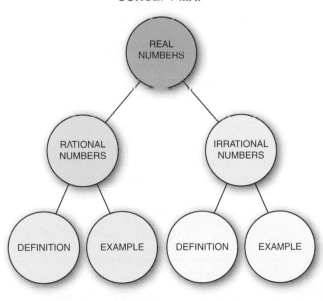

**EXERCISE 5-7
Exam Action Plan**

In the previous exercise, we asked you to reflect on a recent exam. Now we ask you to look to the future. Name a course in which you will have an exam soon:

Course: _____

If you know the date of the exam, write it here: _____.

Which strategies are best in preparing for an exam? The answer depends on you. For example, some students like to use flash cards, while others prefer outlines. The key is to use active rather than passive strategies and to use more than one strategy. For this next exam, commit to using three active strategies. Write them here:

Exam Preparation Strategies

1. _____

2. _____

3. _____

Before an Exam

Preparing properly and using good study habits should greatly reduce the anxiety you may feel on test day. However, it is normal to have some anxiety about taking an exam, no matter how much you have prepared.

To reduce anxiety, there is no substitute for simply being prepared. Begin to study at least a week in advance of an exam, and schedule study time for each day. Make sure you study all of the material. Sometimes it is tempting to focus on the material you already know well. It is important to study material you already "know" because overlearning will make it less likely that you will miss the material on the test. However, students sometimes avoid material they don't know as well, which is a mistake. Don't avoid areas that present difficulty, frustration, or confusion. Seek assistance from your teacher, tutors, and/or classmates.

Use the time management strategies discussed in the Chapter 3 to prepare for your exam. Set aside time each day on your weekly and daily schedules to prepare for an exam. If you're a full-time student, you may notice that exams seem to come in clusters. Each week, it is not uncommon to have either no exams or to have several exams. Time management is key. Use Exercise 5-8 to help you.

**EXERCISE 5-8
Prepare a Time
Schedule to Study for
an Exam**

Write down a subject for which you have an upcoming exam: _____.

How many days do you have to prepare for the exam? _____.

In the space provided, write down tasks you will complete each day leading up to the exam. These tasks can include studying particular materials, re-marking information in your text, completing practice tests, and so on.

Name and date of exam _____

Date:	Task(s):
_____	_____
_____	_____
_____	_____
_____	_____
_____	_____
_____	_____
_____	_____

Now review the tasks in the right column. Have you covered all of the exam material? Have you missed anything that may be on the exam? Have you allotted enough time for more difficult material without overlooking the easier concepts?

During an Exam

Your strategies do not end once you begin taking your exam. Several strategies can be used during an exam to maximize your chance of success. These strategies include time management and understanding the type of exam.

Time Management Revisited.

Pace yourself. Allow enough time to complete each section. Arrive at the exam a few minutes early so you don't feel rushed. If you complete the exam early, use the extra time to review your answers. Caution: It is usually a bad idea to change answers unless you know with 100 percent certainty that your original response was a mistake. More often than not, when students change answers, it turns out they had the right answer to begin with.

Where to Start.

Some people develop their own test-taking strategies. For example, they may do all the easy questions first and then return to the more difficult ones. Make sure you mark the questions you skipped or you may forget to return to them. Finally, do not destroy your old exams: Keep them and learn from them!

Hints for Objective Exams.

With an objective exam (multiple choice, true/false, matching), be sure you understand all directions first. Usually your first idea about the answer is your best. Here's one good technique for multiple-choice questions: Read the question, but cover the options with your hand or a piece of paper. Answer the question in your head before looking at the options; then select the option that most closely matches the answer you came up with.

Hints for Essay and Short-Answer Exams.

Survey the questions, plan your time, and give time to questions in proportion to their value. Believe it or not, it almost always helps to take a few minutes and do some *prewriting*: Sketch out information you need to include, perhaps in informal outline form. Then, you can concentrate on writing without worrying that you'll forget important information. Organization is important in writing for exams: Look to the question for clues as to format. For example, a common essay question involves comparison and contrast (see Exercise 5-9). For this type of essay question, first compare (citing similarities between the concepts) and then contrast (citing differences). Here are some other key words that you will find in exam questions:

- **Explain:** Demonstrate your understanding
- **Define:** Provide definition and explanation for a concept
- **Discuss:** Consider possible points of view on a topic
- **Summarize:** Present the main points of a topic
- **Argue:** Present an opinion in an informed way

EXERCISE 5-9
Planning an Essay
During an Exam

In this exercise, you'll practice writing informal outlines for essay questions. Compare your outlines with those written by a classmate. Would this material satisfy the requirements of the essay?

Example from an introduction to literature course: Compare and contrast the modern and postmodern periods of American literature.

Introduction

↓

Similarities between modern
and postmodern periods. (Comparison)

↓

Differences between modern
and postmodern periods. (Contrast)

↓

Concluding thoughts.

Now provide your own essay exam outlines for possible exam questions from this textbook:

1. Define and describe the types of mnemonics discussed in this textbook.

2. Explain the meaning of the acronym MAPS, and provide three or more examples to illustrate how this acronym applies to goal setting for students.

3. Compare and contrast techniques preferred by kinesthetic and visual learners.

Which question(s) asks you to consider differences and similarities? Which question(s) asks you to provide definitions? Which question(s) asks for specific scenarios to illustrate your point? The same structure will not work for each essay. You have to consider the kind of question being asked.

After an Exam

After an exam, some students eagerly look up the answers to questions they think they might have missed. Others avoid doing this not wanting to face the facts. Regardless, though, many students do not take advantage of post-exam strategies they can use to enhance their learning over the long term.

Whether or not you did well on an exam, you should note the items you answered easily as well as those you struggled with or missed. This information will help if you have a comprehensive final or if the material comes up in other courses.

Right after an exam, evaluate the strategies you used. Did you spend enough time studying? Did you study everything you needed? Are there particular content areas where you were stronger (or weaker) than others?

> ### Stress and Tests
>
> Remember from Chapter 1 that a little bit of stress is good to get you up for the test. However, if during the test, you start to feel yourself losing it, take a moment to refresh, recharge, and refocus. Simply close your eyes and take a slow, deep, cleansing breath and visualize the bad stress leaving as you exhale. This relaxation technique can calm your mind enough to refocus on the task at hand.

If You Did Poorly On an Exam

When one of your instructors returns an exam, take note of the types of questions you got right and those you missed. If you struggled with particular types of questions, your instructor may be able to give you some suggestions for studying next time. Look at the areas where you did poorly. Were there particular ideas or sections that you missed? Were there specific areas where you could have studied harder?

In addition, look at the types of questions you missed. Psychologist Benjamin Bloom identified six types of test questions. **Bloom's taxonomy** (Santrock & Halonen, 2007, p. 160) provides a helpful framework for many students as tests become more advanced and complex. After you read about the method, do Exercise 5-10 to practice it.

BLOOM'S TAXONOMY

Knowledge: These questions typically only require you to recognize information, perhaps on a multiple-choice test.

Ex: CPR stands for

a. Cardiopulmonary relaxation
b. Cardiopulmonary resuscitation
c. Cardiopulmonary reaction

Comprehension: Similar to knowledge, comprehension questions require you to remember information, even if paraphrased.

Ex: People with emotional intelligence

a. manage their emotions well
b. have high IQs
c. are overwhelmed by their feelings

Application: This type of question requires that you apply what you have learned to a new situation, perhaps a hypothetical scenario.

Ex: A preschool child sees two glasses with an equal amount of water. One glass is tall and slender; the other glass is short and wide. She thinks the tall, thin glass has more water. Which stage of development is she in, according to Jean Piaget?

Analysis: Analysis questions require you to break a complex system or process into its parts.

Ex: Identify and explain the events that led to the Civil War in the United States.

Synthesis: Synthesis questions, like analysis, are often found in essay questions. Here you bring information and ideas together from different sources.

Ex: Identify the characteristics of modernist literature, using the works of three authors as examples.

Evaluation: An evaluation is an informed opinion, informed being the key word. You have to explain your opinion by backing it with information from the course.

Ex: When purchasing a desktop computer, which factors need to be assessed, relative to one's technical needs and purchasing power?

You might see all six of these types of questions on exams, although some courses and professors may favor one or two types of questions. As you take an exam, try to note the types of questions being asked.

Take another look at a course in which you will soon have an exam. Write a question for each area of Bloom's taxonomy. You'll gain a better understanding of the types of test questions, and you'll have the beginnings of a study guide:

**EXERCISE 5-10
Applying Bloom's
Taxonomy**

Course: _____

Knowledge Question:

Comprehension Question:

Application Question:

Analysis Question:

Synthesis Question:

Evaluation Question:

Finally, if you do poorly on an exam, take the time to meet with your teacher. Reviewing the exam with your instructor may help you to improve in the future. Most instructors have office hours when they are available to meet with students. Many students do not take advantage of this opportunity. Showing concern about your performance on the exam will show that you care about your academics, as long as you make a good impression.

Faculty and Student Interaction

Positive communication with your instructor has been shown to be a key to academic success. You can facilitate a positive interaction in a number of ways. For example, sitting near the front of the room, showing a genuine interest in class, and actively participating in classroom discussion will go a long way toward establishing a positive relationship. Instructors are willing to help, but most expect you to initiate the request for assistance. Don't be afraid to make an appointment or meet with faculty during office hours to discuss your concerns. Be sure to be prepared with specific questions. Top-10 lists have become popular, so here are our 10 most desirable classroom attributes:

1. Positive attitude
2. Active classroom participation
3. Willingness to learn and work hard
4. Responsibility for their behavior and their learning
5. Creative problem-solving abilities
6. Dependability and good attendance
7. Respect

A positive faculty and student interaction will enhance the learning process
and your academic performance.

8. Ability to work well with others
9. Good communication skills
10. Education as a priority

How many would your instructor check off about you?

HEALTHY DECISION-MAKING BOX

Mary knows she has a strong preference for visual learning and scored high on her musical intelligence area. However, one of her classes is all lecture with no slides and very little written on the blackboard. Mary feels there is a lot of information to know in this course but is finding it difficult to retain it. What suggestions would you have to improve Mary's performance?

_____

_____

_____

_____

Congratulations! By completing this chapter, you have gained a stronger awareness of how you learn and developed better memorization and test-taking strategies. Please see the CD for more activities to practice your new knowledge.

References

Dale, E. (1963). *Audiovisual methods in teaching.* Austin, TX: Holt, Rinehart & Winston.

Downs, C. E. Primary school. Ordering the planets. Retrieved April 11, 2007, from www.teachingideas.co.uk

Ferrett, S. K. (2006). Memory skills. *Peak performance: Success in college and beyond* (pp. 6.12–6.13). New York: McGraw-Hill.

Gardner, H. (2006). *Multiple intelligences: New horizons.* New York: Basic.

Howard Gardner's multiple intelligences theory. (1993). *Great performances.* PBS. New York: WNET. Retrieved April 9, 2007, from www.pbs.org/wnet/gperf/education/ed_mi_overview.html

McPherson, F. (2000). *The memory key: Unlock the secrets to remembering.* Franklin Lakes, NJ: Career Press.

Santrock, J. W., & Halonen, J. S. (2007). *Your guide to college success: Strategies for achieving your goals* (4th Concise ed.) Boston: Thomson-Wadsworth.

Upcraft, M. L., Gardner, J. N., & Associates (1989). *The freshman year experience: Helping students survive and succeed in college.* San Francisco: Jossey-Bass.

Van Blerkom, D. (2006). *College study skills: Becoming a strategic learner.* (5th ed.). Boston: Thomson-Wadsworth.

Your preferred learning style. (2007). *How to study.com: A study skills resource site.* Retrieved April 9, 2007, from www.howtostudy.com

Creative Thinking and Decision-Making Skills

Making Good Choices

OBJECTIVES

What you will discover by the end of this chapter:

- Ways to improve your critical and creative thinking skills
- How to become an effective thinker
- How to become a better problem solver and decision maker

"I think, therefore I am."

Descartes

Thinking is something we all do every day. We make decisions each day that require **analytical thinking** skills. Often we need to come up with new ideas or new ways to look at a situation, which requires **creative thinking** skills. It goes without saying (but we will) that thinking is a vital tool we must use daily in life and, most certainly, in school.

However, most people pay little attention to how they think. Ask yourself the weird-sounding yet deep question: "Have I ever really *thought* about how I *think*?"

Some people are **reactive** thinkers, waiting for a crisis to occur, whereas others are **proactive** and think ahead to avoid the crisis. Some people are positive thinkers full of creative ideas. Some people have a difficult time generating ideas or being creative; others "can't make a decision to save their lives."

Thinking, like any other process, can be assessed and improved to increase your academic and professional success. This chapter shows you how to improve your thinking skills in many areas to include critical and creative thinking, decision making, and problem solving.

Psychologists specialize in studying *how* humans think. They have coined several terms to describe the many complex mental activities that comprise thinking. These mental activities can include speaking and interpreting language, reasoning, conceptualizing, remembering, imagining, learning, and the list can go on.

Several different types of thinking have been also classified. These may include logical, deductive, critical, creative, directed, undirected, proactive, and reactive thinking, to name a few. This chapter focuses on *how* to become an overall *effective* thinker. As an effective thinker, you will be able to maximize your creative thinking, decision making, and problem-solving skills. The development of these skills will, in turn, make you an excellent student, and the practice of these skills will make you a valued professional.

THE INTEGRATED THINKING PROCESS

Although a common theme in this project is to get to the heart of the matter without numerous steps to a process, integrated thinking does require us to go through several steps. However, as we discuss the steps, the entire process will become much clearer. In fact, by the time we finish, much of this process will become automatic and a way of life for you.

To prove this theory, we will go through a *very simple* example of the integrated thinking process illustrated in Figure 6-1. This example will show you that you already use these steps without even being aware of them.

Now for that *very simple* example. Let's say you notice your stomach is rumbling, and you have an empty feeling. You could interpret this Opportunity for Positive Change (step 1) as "I'm hungry and would like a satisfying meal." You would then Generate Ideas (step 2) on what it is you would like to eat. After reviewing the ideas by looking in your food pantry, refrigerator, or on the restaurant menu, you would then turn on your analytical thinking and Make a Decision (step 3). Next, you would Implement and Evaluate your decision by grabbing, making, or ordering the food and then eating it (step 4). After you've eaten, you would evaluate the meal and your level of hunger, which would give you Feedback (step 5). The

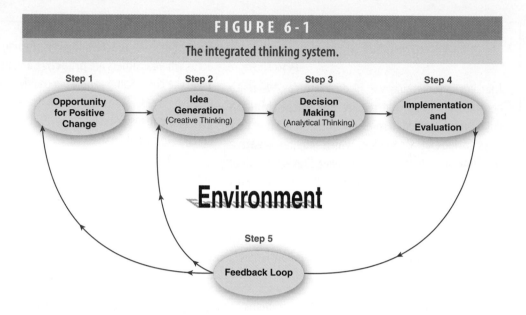

FIGURE 6-1

The integrated thinking system.

feedback from your evaluation could take you back to either another opportunity that deserves your attention, such as "I'm still hungry," or to more creative thinking like "Now what should I have for dessert?"

Notice we haven't yet mentioned the term "Environment" (shown in big bold letters in Figure 6-1) that pervades the entire thinking process. This is a powerful concept because often we do not assess the environment when evaluating thinking. The environment affects the entire thinking process, so that is where we will begin. Just think what would happen if we didn't assess the environment where we ate, and it was on a ship on rocky seas, or in the middle of a winter snowstorm, or in a tense stressful environment. The meal would not be very pleasant, and the process of digestion would be greatly impaired. This is why the atmosphere, or *ambiance,* is so important. Likewise, if the *environment of your mind* is not conducive to critical or creative thinking, all the subsequent steps will have a poor outcome.

Environmental Assessment

One very important concept to keep in mind is that what is implemented in a poor environment will most likely have a poor outcome. Therefore, before we begin going through each specific step in the integrated thinking process, we need to assess your internal environment.

Fortunately, you have already done much of this work in Chapters 1 and 2 where we focused on managing stress, maintaining a positive attitude, and keeping a positive internal mind dialogue. All of these strategies are critical in developing a

Food for Thought

If you are stressed out with your mind going a zillion miles per hour and you have a negative outlook, what type of decisions do you think you will make? How good a creative thinker will you be?

mind that can think effectively and make good decisions. Now, let's extend this environmental assessment by exploring your ability to think creatively.

One of the more difficult steps in the integrated thinking process is in the area of creative thinking (step 2; see Figure 6-1). Many people have barriers to the creative process that need to be identified and then broken down to free their creative juices. In Exercise 6-1, you will explore some of these barriers.

The following list represents the top four barriers to the creative process. After the discussion of each barrier, perform the assessment to see if this area is an issue with you. Mark the ones you need to work on.

**EXERCISE 6-1
Assessing Creative
Thinking Barriers**

Fear of Voicing Ideas

_____ Are you afraid to speak up when you have an idea?

If you answered yes, you need to determine the root cause. For the creative process to work, everyone must be free to share their ideas and perspectives because we all have different ways of viewing any given situation. Now write why you feel you are afraid to voice your ideas and what actions you can take to overcome this fear.

_____

_____

Action Plan: _____

_____

Fear of Losing Control

_____ Do you fear losing control if you are in an environment where ideas can freely flow? Are you threatened by allowing others to give ideas because you feel you may not be in charge?

Sometimes people in authority consciously or subconsciously send signals to others that they really don't want other ideas and will do it *their* way. Excessive control can act as a barrier to the creative process and coming up with new ways to do things. This stifling of creativity can cause companies to become outdated because they haven't found new and better ways of doing the things. If you fear giving up control or have been in a controlling environment that stifled your creativity, write your thoughts about it and an action plan to correct it.

_____

_____

Action Plan: _____

_____

Premature Criticism

_____ Have you ever heard someone say something derogatory such as "That's a stupid idea"? It doesn't even have to be that blatant. It can be a heavy sigh or eye rolling after someone presents an idea. You'll soon learn that it is important not to make instant judgments, good or bad, about someone else's idea in the creative process. Premature criticism stifles creativity in the person who was criticized, and anyone else who witnessed it, because they do not want to go through the same situation. Describe how you can avoid giving premature criticism to others.

_____

_____

_____

Resistance to Change

_____ When change is proposed, do you resist by thinking, "This is the way it always has been done; why should we look for a better way?"

Change is potentially a huge barrier to the creative process. New ideas on how to improve a technique, process, or situation that you have become comfortable with can be unsettling. Learning to embrace change with a positive outlook might be difficult. However, consider that change is needed for our very existence. In any basic biology class you will learn that for a species to survive, it must adapt and change. Change is part of life. Give your thoughts on change and any action plan if you personally resist change.

_____

_____

_____

Action Plan: _____

_____

External Barriers to the Creative Process

Having assessed some of your *internal* barriers to the creative process, you must also recognize that *external* barriers can interfere with both the creative and analytical thinking processes. For example, if you are trying to think or make a decision in a room that has several distractions such as a high level of noise or constant interruptions, it becomes very difficult.

Even how the room is arranged can affect the creative thinking process. In *The Tale of King Arthur,* we learned about the Knights of the Round Table. The table was round so that all could feel equal in status, and therefore equally welcome in sharing their ideas. Toward the end of this text, we discuss group creativity and brainstorming where the arrangement of the room, level of distractions, and, some may even argue, color, all become important factors. Now that you have put some "thought" into assessing *your* environment, let's move on to the first step.

STEP 1: STATE THE OPPORTUNITY FOR POSITIVE CHANGE

The traditional decision-making process often involves problem solving, but this makes it seem like *everything* is a problem to be solved. That is not always the case. Sometimes you are looking at maximizing an opportunity, choosing the right path, creating a new opportunity, or yes, solving a problem. With this fact in mind, rather than asking you to "define the problem" we challenge you to "state the opportunity for positive change." As we emphasized before, how you present something to your mind will greatly influence the outcome. By looking at each major decision, or perhaps problem, as an opportunity for positive change, you are already on your way to a great solution (see Figure 6-2).

The first step is very important because in any process, the quality of the early steps greatly influences the final outcome. In other words, if you start with a good foundation in step 1, it is more likely that the final steps will have a very positive outcome.

Using this positive approach for the first step also increases our *proactive* versus *reactive* thinking. You're using reactive thinking when you wait for a problem to exist and then react and try to solve it. This type of thinking is not very effective because now you may be dealing with a crisis situation in which emotions and tensions make it difficult to find the best solution. Proactive thinking is "looking ahead" and preventing problems from occurring. Now you can assess and optimize your environment with calm thinking and prevent or reduce many crisis situations.

Remember to clearly restate the problem into an opportunity that shows a positive outcome: How we state the problem *greatly* influences the rest of the process! Get rid of any negativity and have a clear outcome in the statement.

For example, here is a common problem some students may either think or say aloud.

Problem: *"I'm never going to pass this semester. What can I do?"*

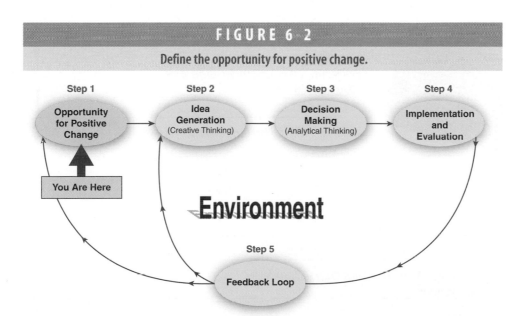

FIGURE 6-2

Define the opportunity for positive change.

Although a question is asked here, things seem to have ended before they've even begun. The statement does not clearly specify what the opportunity is or show any positive outcome. In fact, the word *never* can lead to a self-fulfilling prophecy of failure. A problem stated in this manner is unlikely to be solved; the person will only become more frustrated in time, feel like a failure, and take no action to solve the problem. However, this challenge can be restated:

Restated as an Opportunity for Positive Change: *"What actions can I take to be successful this semester?"*

Notice how the statement now presents an opportunity to develop positive actions toward a successful outcome. This statement now will facilitate the next step (Creative Thinking) in which you will come up with ideas concerning possible actions. This statement will also force you to look at the way things were done in the past to find a better way.

Let's see one more example of this critical step:

Problem: *"I'm too busy; there just aren't enough hours in the day!"*

This problem statement does not clearly tell us what the opportunity is; nor does it show any positive outcome. A problem stated in this manner is unlikely to be solved, and the person will only become more frustrated in time. However, this problem can be restated:

Restated as an Opportunity for Positive Change: *"What actions can I take to improve my time management skills to allow for more free time and academic success?"*

Notice how the phrasing now presents an opportunity for a reward of "free time" while keeping in mind the goal of doing well academically. When you go to the next step, you are more likely to generate positive ideas that will make the desired outcome happen. Now do Exercise 6-2.

EXERCISE 6-2
Restate the Problem into an Opportunity

Restate the following:

Problem 1: *"(fill in name) never listens to me!"*
Restatement: _____

Problem 2: *Why do I feel so tired and lack energy?*
Restatement: _____

Problem 3: *I'm so afraid of math, and it impacts many of my courses.*
Restatement: _____

_____

Problem 4: *Why can't I commit to my study schedule?*
Restatement: _____

Problem 5: *I can't figure out what program/career is right for me.*
Restatement: _____

_____

_____

After clearly stating the opportunity for positive change, you are ready to move on to the next step and generate possible solutions. Take some time to clearly state the opportunity with a positive outcome and plant it within your mind. This step may take some time, but it will lay a solid foundation for success in decision making. Practice this technique in Exercise 6-3.

State an "opportunity for positive change" (formerly known as "a problem") that you would like to work on as we continue our journey onto the next steps. If you haven't chosen your career path, this could be a good topic for this exercise. Keep your chosen opportunity in mind as we visit the next steps.

EXERCISE 6-3
Your
Opportunity

_____

_____

STEP 2: GENERATE IDEAS CONCERNING THE OPPORTUNITY

Step 2 requires you to use creative thinking and come up with many ideas concerning the opportunity. Please see Figure 6-3. One of the keys to this step is coming up with a *quantity* of ideas and not concerning yourself with the *quality* of the ideas. Remember that premature criticism is a barrier to the creative process; therefore, do not judge any of these ideas as good or bad. Even an idea that may seem to be far out should be encouraged at this step. It may be combined with another idea later to become a powerful solution.

Let's go back to our *very simple* example of satisfying your hunger. What if you picked the first thing you came to in your food pantry or on the menu you thought you might like? You would have missed the opportunity to see many more selections that may have been much more scrumptious and satisfying. You may have even found some unique combinations that you never tried before. Therefore, the purpose of this stage is to get out all the ideas. You might even consider combining some, but now is the time to lay all of your ideas and options out on the table.

Background Information on Creative Thinking

Step 2 seems to give many people problems. We focus on a later step, analytical/decision making, throughout our lives and in our early education. For some reason, we do not focus as much attention on the creative or generative side of thinking. So, let's begin to explore this step.

How good are you at creative thinking? If you don't rank yourself highly, you are not alone. Many people feel they are not creative, but the truth is we are all creative and we can enhance our creativity. You were being creative when you were hungry and came up

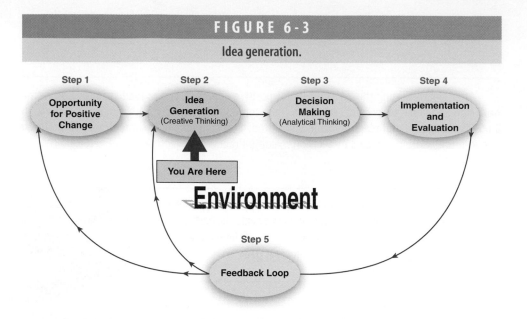

FIGURE 6-3

Idea generation.

with all of those unique food combinations or ideas for what to cook or order. Too many people believe creativity is only reserved for artists or those who have "Eureka!" break-through ideas. This attitude is unfortunate because it distances many people from their creative side. If we simply define creative thinking as "the generation of ideas that results in the improvement of the efficiency or the effectiveness of the system," we can see that creativity relates to all of us. A worker who develops a better way to do the job, a parent who helps a child to learn a new skill or overcome a problem, or even someone who finds a better route on a map are all being creative. We use creative thinking every day of our lives without being fully aware of it.

Learning to enhance your creativity also benefits you in other areas. For example, increasing creativity also increases your self-confidence and motivation. Creative thinking will also improve the quality of both your academic and professional work. If you feel free to contribute ideas, you will have a sense of belonging. This sense of belonging is one of the most important ingredients for employee morale and performance. Finally, creativity rejuvenates enthusiasm as you see the success of your efforts.

Much research in the past centered on the left and right sides of our brain. The left side of our brain is more analytical, whereas the right side is more intuitive and creative. Therefore, some scientists contended that creative individuals think mainly with the right side of the brain, whereas more logical or analytical thinkers are controlled by the

Fact Left-Handed People Will Love

The left hemisphere of the brain controls the right side of the body, and the right hemisphere controls the left side. Then it may logically follow that "If the right hand is controlled by the left brain and the left hand is controlled by the right brain, only left-handed people are in their *right* mind." Okay, all of you left-handed people, quit cheering!

left side of the brain. This was shown to be an oversimplification as to what was actually occurring.

During positron emission testing (using a device that can locate and measure brain activity) of individuals performing creative tasks, the brain's electrical activity flickered between both hemispheres. This demonstrated the need, even while performing creative tasks, of connecting the right and left brain hemispheres. Therefore, it is important to make these *cross connections* to enhance our creative thinking. Several techniques enhance this process, and they will be discussed shortly.

Creative Thinking Theories

Edward de Bono (1970), an expert on thinking, has extensively studied and written about the creative process. De Bono coined the terms **vertical thinking** and **lateral thinking** to contrast critical and creative thinking.

Vertical thinking relies on logic, and each idea relates to the next. Vertical thinking allows us to make assumptions based on past experiences and relies on logical thinking, which includes deductive and inductive reasoning. (We discuss this type of thinking further in the next step on decision making.)

Lateral thinking creates new ideas by making connections with no set pathway. Lateral thinking takes information stored in our brains and connects it in a previously unrelated manner. It generates the ideas that will later be evaluated by vertical or logical thinking modes. Some people consider this "sideways thinking," where you make cross connections with other thoughts in contrast with the vertical "step-by-step" thinking.

De Bono, in his book *Lateral Thinking* (1970), describes it with the following technical definition:

> Lateral Thinking views the brain as a self-organizing information system which forms patterns from informational flows. Insight and humor is developed when we disrupt the habitual storing process and form conscious links between previously unrelated patterns of informational storage units.

To simplify the understanding, and to use a creative learning technique, see Figure 6-4 on the next page, which demonstrates a nontechnical visualization of lateral thinking.

You may be scratching your head, wondering how that cartoon relates to lateral thinking. Picture your brain as a file cabinet. Somewhere you have a storage file that contains "The Reason You Believe Dinosaurs Are Extinct." Is this by itself funny? Of course not. A whole species was lost forever. In another section of your brain you have a storage file telling you that "Abusive Drinking and Smoking Kills"; this also by itself is not funny. However, when we connect these two previously unrelated storage files, we get humor. Now reread de Bono's explanation and see if it makes more sense.

The concept of cross-connecting previously unrelated bits of information is the power behind lateral thinking. When two or more people are sitting around discussing ideas (brainstorming), lateral connections are being made from one idea to another. When you are sitting alone thinking of ideas, your brain is literally *storming* back and forth between the hemispheres (as shown by positron emission), making those lateral connections between ideas and thoughts.

FIGURE 6-4

The alternate theory of dinosaur extinction.

We just used the creative learning technique of analogies to simplify the concept of lateral thinking. We cross-connected the two files in your brain about dinosaurs and smoking to get humor and made sense of the very technical definition.

Creative Thinking Techniques

Associative Thinking and Visualization.

One method to force cross connections or lateral thinking is through *visualization*. For example, you can draw your opportunity for positive change in the center of your paper. Now, write key words and ideas all around the opportunity for change, and connect them all together. Be creative and use different colors and/or symbols to emphasize certain

FIGURE 6-5

Example of a visual association related to finding a career.

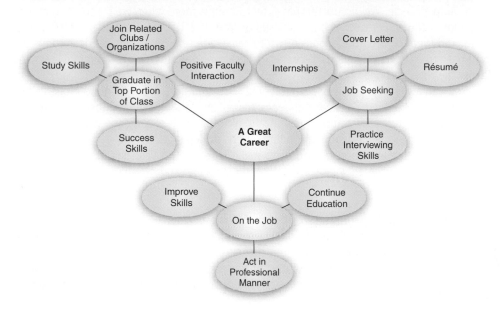

points. Study this visual picture and see if you can find new relationships, patterns, or ideas. It may take time, but the more ideas you develop, the better your chance for a successful solution. Please see Figure 6-5 for a sample visual creative map. Draw your opportunity in Exercise 6-4.

Now take your "opportunity for positive change" in Exercise 6-3 and draw a visual map. Generate at least five cross connections. More is better.

EXERCISE 6-4
Drawing Your
Opportunity

Personal Brainstorming.

Brainstorming is a powerful way to enhance creativity. Traditionally this is a process in which a small group of five to eight people get together and come up with ideas concerning an opportunity or issue. We discuss this powerful technique more when we get to Chapter 8 on group interactions. For now, the focus is still on you. It is helpful to meditate or slow your mind, and then focus on the opportunity for change you selected. Then, as ideas come into your head (the cross connections discussed earlier), simply write them without judgment and follow the rules described here.

You can also discuss your opportunity with a trusted person and, if done properly, you can utilize another brain that has different experiences, knowledge, and insights to greatly enhance the creative power. It is a good idea to pick the brain of someone who is successful in the area you selected as your opportunity for positive change.

The following are important rules to make sure this process is effective. Although mentioned previously, they are critical to the process and therefore deserve further discussion.

- **Rule 1: Withhold premature criticisms.** Don't tell yourself, "That's a stupid idea; I'm not going to write it." Premature criticism will kill the creative process and should be avoided at all costs. Consider any idea, no matter how farfetched. Remember, the goal is not to come up with the best solution at this time. The goal here is to list all kinds of ideas to analyze and evaluate in the next step. You might even combine some ideas at this stage.
- **Rule 2: The quantity, not the quality, of ideas is important at this stage.** The more ideas generated, the better the odds are that a quality idea will emerge. Although it may be true in math, there are no "right" or "wrong" ideas in creative thinking.
- **Rule 3: Get rid of distractions.** A nonthreatening atmosphere free of distractions provides the best environment for creative thinking. Distractions can include noise, poor lighting, squeaky chairs, telephone or pagers ringing, and so on.

Other Hints on Enhancing Personal Creativity

Allow your subconscious to work for you. Calming your mind by meditating and gaining focus allows creativity to flourish. Sometimes it is important to get away from the issue for a while and let it incubate in your subconscious mind. Remember the times when an answer to an issue came suddenly to you, seemingly out of nowhere? This is called the *incubation period.* Eugene Raudsepp (1983), past president of Princeton Creative Research, says it best: "Often when the conscious forcing of a problem to a solution has failed, the incubational process succeeds."

When is your best incubation period? Try to recognize and capitalize on your peak periods of creativity. Albert Einstein's was in the morning while he was *lost* in shaving. Some people are more creative in the evening or in certain rooms or environments. Again, using the principles discussed, you are the best judge as to where and when you are most creative. In Exercise 6-5, you will list ideas related to your stated opportunity.

Take your opportunity for change, and by using the concepts in our discussion, come up with a list of ideas related to your stated opportunity. This may take some time and several sessions. Use ideas from the visual exercise to come up with at least 10 ideas. (Remember to withhold judgment!)

EXERCISE 6-5
Generate Ideas

_____

_____

_____

_____

_____

_____

_____

_____

_____

_____

Analogies

Before leaving this section, a brief discussion of *analogies* is in order. An analogy also forces cross connections between two unlike things. This can be helpful in generating ideas that would otherwise have been missed. Many inventions came about as a result of analogies. Velcro was discovered during a walk through the woods, where an inventor got a bunch of sticky burrs on his pants. Analyzing the burrs, he developed Velcro, which has hundreds of uses. Using analogies can be both fun and creative in developing unique solutions.

Analogies are also a powerful learning tool. For example, when learning how the body regulates temperature, an analogy of the thermostat and heating/cooling system in your house can make the technical process of "homeostatic thermal regulation" much easier to learn.

STEP 3: DECISION MAKING OR ANALYTICAL THINKING

In this step, you shift to your logical or analytical thinking to evaluate each idea or combination of ideas for a successful outcome. Basically, you weigh the pros and cons of each idea in order to choose the best. See Figure 6-6.

> *"Ideas are one thing, what happens is another."*
> —John Cage, American composer and author

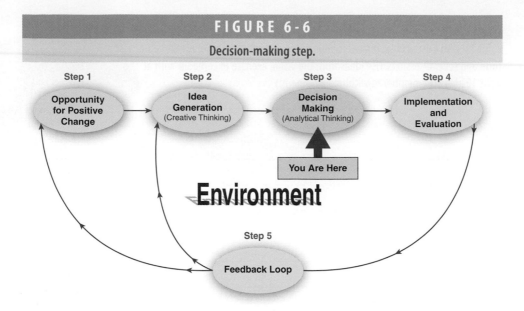

FIGURE 6-6

Decision-making step.

Critical Thinking

The catchphrase in education for some time has been *developing critical thinking skills*. However, the many definitions and views about critical thinking can make this concept quite confusing. In his book *Critical Thinking*, Robert Ennis (1995) explains, "Critical thinking is a process, the goal of which is to make reasonable decisions about what to believe and what to do" (p. xvii). Diane Romain (1996), in her book *Thinking Things Through: Critical Thinking for Decisions You Can Live With,* argues, "Critical thinking consists of those activities of the mind that are indispensable to making decisions we can live with. The processes involved in critical thinking include becoming aware of our emotions and reflecting on them, identifying our values, assessing information and the authorities who provide it, analyzing and clarifying language, imagining solutions to problems, evaluating alternative solutions, and assessing and producing arguments" (p.1).

There are many definitions of critical thinking in addition to the examples just cited. However, these definitions all include several thinking skills, such as the ability to develop a hypothesis, test and rate possible solutions, and maintain an objective viewpoint. Critical thinking skills relate to analytical thinking or your ability to analyze a situation or set of facts or ideas objectively. Note that critical thinking skills (like all thinking skills) can be developed and improved through practice.

Critical thinking relies on *logical* thinking. We use logic several times each day. Any time we evaluate, make judgments, or make decisions, we must rely on our logical thinking. Just what is logic? It is your ability to reason

Word Fact

The word *critical* came from the Greek word *krinein,* which means "to separate in order to select." This step requires you to separate and evaluate your ideas and facts to select the optimal choice.

in a given situation. If you are cold, you will figure out a way to become warm. Your logic might tell you to get a coat, go inside, build a fire, or turn up the thermostat. You will choose what you think is the best response given the situation and your previous knowledge. For example, if you didn't know what a thermostat was, adjusting it could not be one of your options. So one part of logic relies on your past experience and knowledge. Another part of logical thinking relies on your ability to reason deductively and inductively.

Deductive reasoning is a form of logical thinking in which you reach a conclusion based on true facts called *premises*. For example, you may have the following premises:

Premise: Students who develop good study skills improve their grades.

Premise: Mary has worked on her study skills with this project and her learning resource center.

Conclusion: Mary's grades will improve.

In this example, you used deductive reasoning to reach a true conclusion. The conclusion in deductive reasoning is always true if the premises are true. Thanks to deductive reasoning, Mary now has improved her study skills, which will continue to pay dividends by good grades in the future.

In this example, Mary took action that could prevent a potential crisis such as failing her first semester. As previously discussed, this represents *proactive thinking,* or thinking ahead, so you are not in a crisis situation. In contrast, many people wait for the problem to occur and then react to the crisis. This is called *reactive thinking.* Which do you think is better?

Another type of logical thinking is **inductive reasoning.** Here you make your *best guess* based on the premises or facts. Your conclusion has a high probability of being true but is not guaranteed to be true. Here's an example of inductive reasoning:

Premise: People who smoke have an increased risk of getting lung cancer.

Premise: Bill smoked two packs of cigarettes a day for 20 years.

Conclusion: Bill will get lung cancer.

Although the risk to Bill is much greater than someone who has not smoked, and it is quite possible that Bill might get lung cancer, the conclusion may not be true. He might never develop lung cancer in his lifetime. However, his best decision would be to stop smoking (proactive thinking) to prevent the potential for the future health crisis of lung cancer.

Decision Making

So how do you now proceed to make a good decision? First, begin by reviewing your list of ideas and gather any information that you have learned from past experience or from others to help choose the best solution. Use your logical thinking to analyze your ideas.

Most texts suggest listing the pros and cons for each idea, a very good place to start. However, consider adding a time element to encourage proactive thinking. Many times people jump at the first good solution, which may not always be the best in the long run. For example, in the business world, the short-term solution to making employees happier may be to give them all big raises, which certainly will result in a short-term positive effect. However, because of the raise, the company may go bankrupt or have to lay off some or all employees. This certainly would be a long-term negative effect. In Exercise 6-6 you will analyze the positive and negative effects of your ideas.

EXERCISE 6-6
Choosing the Best
Idea or Set of Ideas

You now need to choose from the ideas you generated in Exercise 6-5. Of course you want to choose the one idea or group of ideas that will provide the greatest chance for success. You can test each of them visually by imagining that each has already been put into effect. Consider the short- and long-term positive and negative effects of each of your ideas. Evaluate their merit, and then make your choice and write it here.

Your Chosen Idea or Group of Ideas

_____

_____

Short-Term Positive Effects

_____

Short-Term Negative Effects

_____

Long-Term Positive Effects

_____

Long-Term Negative Effects

_____

Note: You may have "none" for some of the above.

STEP 4: IMPLEMENT AND EVALUATE YOUR CHOSEN STRATEGY

> *"To think too long about doing a thing often becomes its undoing."*
> —Eva Young

Wow, it seems like we took a long time to get to the point where we will actually implement our ideas! However, consider that, with practice, these steps become so automatic that you will go through the process rather quickly depending on the size of the opportunity. If the opportunity for positive change is choosing the right meal, this process only takes a few minutes. If it is making a major change in your life such as choosing a major and school to attend, it will take some more time. The end result will be worth the effort. See Figure 6-7.

Now is the time to put your idea into action. There are several questions you can ask to make sure this process goes smoothly. Which factors should be considered when implementing

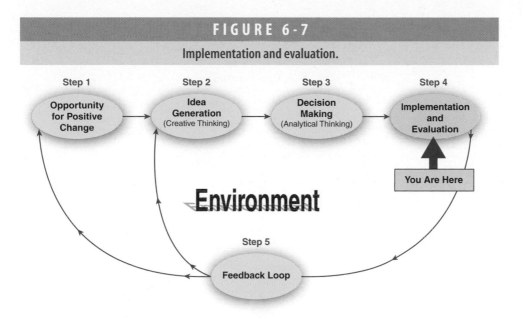

FIGURE 6-7

Implementation and evaluation.

your chosen idea? Do you need to communicate this idea and to whom? One of the most important questions is what is the best way to evaluate your chosen solution? This is important, not only to chart your progress, but also to modify your plan accordingly. Exercise 6-7 helps direct you through some questions to help make your idea become reality.

Answer the following questions concerning your chosen idea(s) in Exercise 6-6.

_____Does your chosen idea create the positive opportunity you desire?

Who do I need to communicate with, and how, when implementing my ideas?

EXERCISE 6-7
Implementing and
Evaluating Your Idea

_____

What resources can assist me with implementing and evaluating my ideas(s)?

_____

_____

How and when will I evaluate and measure my progress toward my opportunity for positive change?

_____

_____

When will I implement my idea?

_____

_____

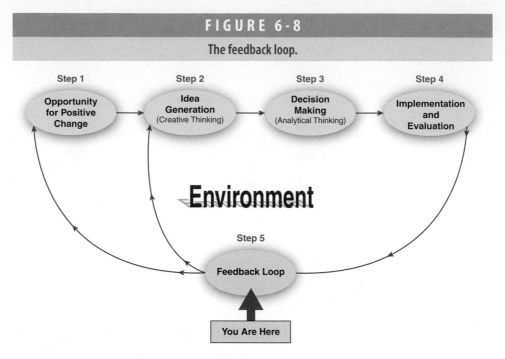

FIGURE 6-8

The feedback loop.

Almost the Final Step: Feedback

Notice that the feedback loop in Figure 6-8 can either lead back to another opportunity for positive change or to more idea generation. Once you implement your ideas, you may open up new doors or opportunities that may take you back to step 1. This is a good thing and begins a positive and expanding cycle of change concerning the opportunity.

Another possibility is that once you implement your idea(s) and gain some feedback, you might need to modify your plan. This might lead you back to step 2 and the need to generate more ideas. This process forms a continuous loop that keeps assessing and improving your plan. Of course, another outcome is when you reach a point where you have attained the level of positive change or completely solved the problem. Remember to get feedback from as many sources as possible to determine if your idea is having a positive impact. The more feedback you receive, the better your ability to evaluate and modify the outcomes.

Although the five steps to the decision-making process may seem like a lot, it is well worth the effort. With practice, these steps will become second nature and be performed almost effortlessly. Besides, aren't you worth the best effort in making the truly important decisions in your life?

Final Thoughts

Just the process of going through these steps will help you to understand and therefore improve your thinking processes. For most small issues, this formal process is done within the confines of your mind. However, it can be very powerful to take one opportunity related to your professional life and one opportunity related to your personal life, and then work through the steps. The results will amaze you! However, choose only one issue in each area to maintain a sharp focus and to avoid becoming overwhelmed.

In Exercise 6-8, ponder an opportunity for change in your personal and professional life.

SUMMATION EXERCISE 6-8

List a major opportunity for positive change you would like to address in your personal life.

_____

_____

_____

List a major opportunity for positive change you would like to address in your professional/academic life.

_____

_____

_____

HEALTHY DECISION MAKING

Jerome is a senior in high school and unsure about which postsecondary program he wants to enter. Therefore, he is having a difficult time selecting his school. He has taken inventory tests to try to find the types of programs that might be a good match for his skills and interests. However, he still has many options and is getting anxious about making a choice. What would you do to help Jerome if he asked for your advice?

_____

_____

_____

_____

Congratulations! You have completed Chapter 6 on Critical and Creative Thinking. Chapters 1 to 6 have focused on *you*. These chapters helped you develop the internal skills you need for academic and professional success. You are ready to move on to Part Two and the chapters that will develop your external skills for communicating with others, effective group interaction, leadership development, and workplace readiness.

Now that you have read this chapter and performed the assessments and exercises, please go to your CD for this chapter to reinforce these concepts. The CD will present you with a fun and interactive journey back through the various types of thinking and go through the steps of the integrated thinking process visually along with additional assessments to help track your progress.

References

De Bono, E. (1970). *Lateral thinking: Creativity step by step.* New York: Harper & Row.

Ennis, R. H. (1995). *Critical thinking.* Englewood Cliffs, NJ: Prentice Hall.

Raudsepp, E. (1983). Profile of the creative individual. *Creative Computing, 9*(10). Retrieved April 17, 2007, from www.atarimagazines.com

Romain, D. (1996). *Thinking things through: Critical thinking for decisions you can live with.* Boston: McGraw-Hill.

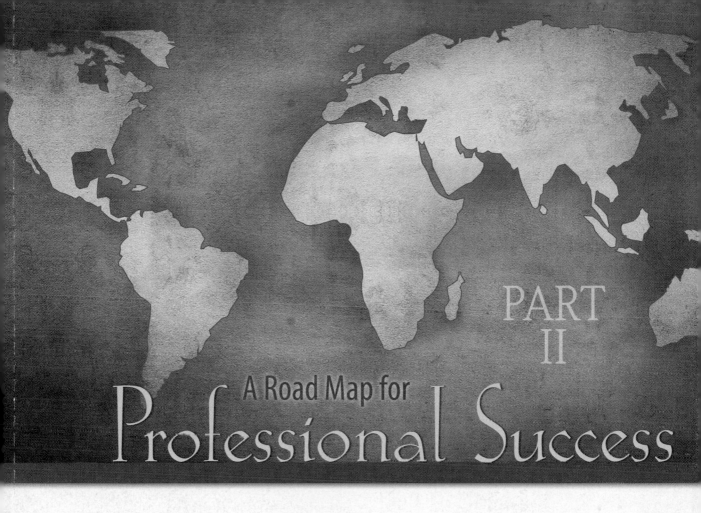

A Road Map for
Professional Success

PART II

Communication in Action

Presenting Yourself to Others

OBJECTIVES

What you will discover by the end of this chapter:

- How to assess and improve your current communication skills
- How to become a better listener
- How to become a better speaker
- How to write effectively
- How to communicate a professional image

Chapters 1 to 6 focused mainly on your internal or intrapersonal communication skills. In essence, they dealt with getting to know yourself better. We now begin the journey outward, by developing action plans to enhance and improve your communication with others.

Communicating is not just something we do every day; it is a skill that we can hone and develop just like all the other skills discussed in this book. Have you ever sensed when you are losing someone in a conversation, or have you become lost and drifted away while someone was communicating with you? Have you ever received a written communication that you just didn't understand or gotten feedback that revealed you had been completely misunderstood? Lack of communication can cause big and small problems in both our personal and professional lives.

If you want to be successful, a key ingredient is good communication skills. These skills should never be taken for granted; they are the means by which you present yourself to the world.

Before we begin to put communication into action, as promised by the chapter title, we begin with the basic concepts. Communication has long been studied (and undoubtedly will continue to be studied), and Figure 7-1 illustrates a simplistic communication model.

THE COMMUNICATION MODEL

As you can see from Figure 7-1, for any communication to work, you must have someone (transmitter) who is sending the communication (message) to another person or persons (receiver). The receiver can return a message (feedback). In all cases, the message and feedback passes through some type of filtering mechanism.

For example, a teacher transmits his or her message in class to (hopefully) eager receivers or students. This message can be transmitted in a number of ways, including lectures, videos, demonstrations, and PowerPoint slides. The filter it must pass through can include the noise and distractions in the room or even in the student's mind. The feedback can be in the form of student questions, class discussions, and, of course, those dreaded exams. In an ideal situation, the teacher transmits a clear message that passes to the student with little filtration, and the student then gives feedback in the form of a great grade on the exam. Do Exercise 7-1 to help you understand the communication model.

Give examples for the following:

Describe a situation in which you were the transmitter of a message._____
_____
_____

Who was the intended receiver(s)?_____
What filters were involved?_____
_____

EXERCISE 7-1
Understanding the Model

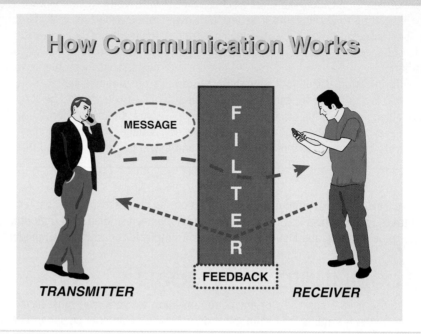

FIGURE 7-1

The communication model.

What type of feedback did you receive?_____

_____

How could you have improved this communication?_____

_____

Modes of Communication

On the surface, communication might appear complex. However, as you read through this chapter and complete the exercises, you will see common concepts and principles in all forms of communication.

The three broad categories of communication include **verbal, nonverbal,** and **written communication.** Verbal communication includes all communication forms that produce sound. This can include conversations, lectures, songs, stories, animal sounds, grunts, and the list goes on. Nonverbal communication is communication without the use of sound. This can include a handshake, smile, wink, or people rolling their eyes in disgust. Nonverbal communication is very powerful—and much underestimated. The third broad category is written communication. This includes communication in the visual realm and can be letters, memos, reports, e-mails, charts, and pictures, among many others. We begin by assessing and developing each of these communication categories separately and then take a look at specific examples. In Exercise 7-2 you will identify the three broad categories of communication.

Choose the type or types of communication (verbal, nonverbal, or written) in the following examples. For some, there is more than one answer. As you will see as we further develop these topics, there is much crossover.

EXERCISE 7-2
What Is the Type of Communication?

_____ cheerleading

_____ a mean look

_____ an advertisement

_____ laughter

_____ a deep sigh

_____ a dog snarling and barking

_____ a letter

_____ a speech

_____ grunting

_____ a to-do list

_____ a phone message

_____ teaching a class

_____ job interview

_____ musical audition

_____ taking a test

The Relationship Between Verbal and Nonverbal Communication

Studies show that although of course the spoken word is important in communication, we rely even more on nonverbal communication when interacting with others (Hecht, DeVito, & Guerrero, 1999). (Please see Figure 7-2.) So, we can conclude that *how* you say something is

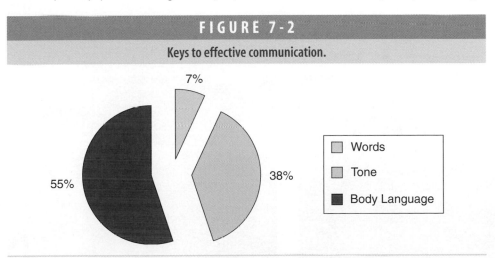

FIGURE 7-2

Keys to effective communication.

7%

55%

38%

☐ Words
☐ Tone
■ Body Language

often more important than *what* you say. This might seem like a pretty dramatic statement, but this chapter will show you how this idea works. See how well you interpret nonverbal communication in Exercise 7-3.

**EXERCISE 7-3
Body Language**

Pair up with a partner and take turns trying to convey a feeling without using any verbal communication. See if you can guess accurately the nonverbal message.

Describe the nonverbal communication you think your partner is conveying in two separate instances.

Nonverbal communication 1 _____

Nonverbal communication 2 _____

Were you able to identify the nonverbal message correctly?

From the exercise, was it easy to communicate a nonverbal message? Now start to put communication principles into action. Let's explore how verbal and nonverbal communication styles are interwoven.

Informal Communication

Let's begin with a common experience that we all frequently encounter: meeting someone for the first time. From what you have learned so far, your nonverbal gestures have a great impact, followed by your tone of voice and, finally, the words you speak. A positive approach would include a friendly smile, good eye contact, and (usually) a firm handshake (see Figure 7-3). Your tone should be positive and friendly. Your verbal communication should be clear, and you should introduce yourself by the name you wish to be called. This sounds pretty simple, but

FIGURE 7-3
Who is making the better first impression?

this first encounter often sets the tone for any future relationship, so it is critical. There is no better way to learn than with practice. Please spend some time with Exercise 7-4.

Pair up with a partner and practice meeting each other for the first time. Keep practicing until your partner feels you have all the following items checked.

_____ friendly smile

_____ good eye contact

_____ good handshake

_____ positive clear tone of voice

_____ well-spoken introduction

EXERCISE 7-4
You Never Get a Second Chance to Make a Good First Impression

Just to reinforce this concept, repeat the introductions but change one element according to each scenario below. Describe how it makes you feel.

Scenario 1: No eye contact
How this made you feel:

_____

_____

Scenario 2: No smile
How this made you feel:

_____

_____

Scenario 3: Weak or poor handshake
How this made you feel:

_____

_____

Of course, you have to continue the conversation after the initial meeting. Here is one helpful hint: "*People like to hear genuinely nice things about themselves.*" You will see the evidence in their subtle physical reactions: in the glance of their eyes, or a quick smile, or a more relaxed posture. They respond with appreciation. When meeting people for the first time, it is often helpful to repeat their names back to them in greeting. This well-known memory aid will help you remember names for future meetings.

LISTENING: THE OFTEN FORGOTTEN COMMUNICATION SKILL

An often neglected communication skill is listening. Many of us are too busy thinking of what we are going to say back or what we have to do that day to *truly* listen to somebody. There is a difference between *hearing* and *listening*. Your ear is able to process sound waves, and the brain can interpret them for the sense of hearing. However, listening takes more work. For example, have you ever been in class or in a conversation and could hear the words but got lost in other thoughts and didn't really know what the speaker was saying? You were hearing the speaker, but you were *not* listening.

Listening seems like a passive process, but in reality it is very active. **Active listening** means to pay close attention to what the speaker is saying and feeling. These are the key points to active listening:

- Face the individual who is speaking, and maintain good eye contact.
- Maintain an open posture and even lean slightly toward the individual(s) to convey interest in what they are saying.
- Be relaxed and confident.
- Think about what they are saying, and ask clarification questions. Even restate what you think they are saying in your own words to make sure you understand the message.
- Do not interrupt.

The benefits of active listening read like a recipe for world peace:

- Shows concern for others (speaker)
- Leads to better exchange of information
- Improves relationships
- Leads to better understanding and cooperation
- Can calm another person(s) in a heated, tense situation

If you can listen well to other people's words and body language, you can convey you understand their message, that they have gotten through to you. The payoff to listening well is that usually the other person will be more receptive to listening to *you*.

Consider this idea from another angle: What can you do to improve someone's ability to listen to you? Try to maintain good posture (which will help you breathe better) while you are speaking,

A Friendly and Powerful Fact

"You can make more friends in two months by becoming genuinely interested in other people than you can in two years by trying to get other people interested in you."

—Dale Carnegie

and pronounce your words clearly. If you slouch or your voice fades, you imply that your message is not that important, which virtually asks a listener to tune you out. An open posture (i.e., not crossing your arms) indicates a willingness to listen as well. Maintain eye contact to show you are attending to what the person is saying, and nod to show you are interested (Denney, 2002). Put the principles of active listening to work in Exercise 7-5.

Active listening.

EXERCISE 7-5
Active Listening

Work in pairs or small groups to use the principles on active listening. Make up a skit that shows all the "wrong" things to do concerning active listening. It can be someone discussing a problem with a course or a funny incident that happened at work. Have fun with the skit, and see if the class can identify all the "wrong" things to do. Then follow up with the same skit. Only now show all the right things to do concerning active listening.

List of wrong things skit 1:_____

_____

_____

List of right things skit 2 :_____

_____

_____

_____

SPEECHES AND PRESENTATIONS

Now let's build on your knowledge of communication with a discussion of public speaking. Although public speaking takes training and experience, it can be done well with an understanding of basic communication principles.

> *You can observe a lot by watching.*
> —Yogi Berra

Types of Speeches

There are several different types of speeches. You can give an **informative speech** in which you explain something to a person or group of people. Examples include teaching a class, giving a workshop, or demonstrating a technique such as CPR. A **persuasive speech** attempts to convince or influence an audience about your topic. Examples could be a political speech or sales pitch. An

evocative speech is meant to evoke, or create, certain feelings. Evocative speeches can entertain, inspire, or commemorate a person or event. Examples can include a sermon, testimonial dinner, or a comedy sketch. Most comedy acts are actually well-rehearsed speeches that look impromptu. **Impromptu speeches** are off the cuff and unrehearsed, such as the impromptu comedy of Robin Williams. If you were asked to stand up in class and give a speech on world economics, it would be an example of an impromptu—and probably pretty scary—speech.

Some speeches fall under more than one category. For example, a political speech may be mainly persuasive (vote for me) but can also tell about issues (informative) and stir up certain feelings (evocative) in the crowd.

So how do you go about preparing *your* speech, which you will undoubtedly have to do during the course of your program? Keep in mind that the steps and principles in public speaking, or formal verbal communication, discussed next, are almost identical to the ones in formal written communication that follow this section.

Prespeech Preparation

First and foremost, select and analyze your speech topic, purpose, and type. Think about the audience for your speech. What are their backgrounds, and what will most appeal to them? Are there any special considerations, such as a presentation for preschool students that would require unique strategies for keeping their attention? Do Exercise 7-6 to practice prespeech preparation.

**EXERCISE 7-6
Prespeech
Preparation**

Answer the following:

What is the topic of your chosen speech?_____

What type of speech are you presenting?_____

(Note: you can have more than one type)

Who is the audience?_____

Are there any special considerations given the audience composition?_____

Where and how will you research material for your speech?_____

What types of sources will you use?_____

Next, you need to research your topic by looking in the library, periodical indexes, search engines, and databases. You could even conduct personal interviews. Citing your sources during your speech gives you credibility as a speaker.

Composing the Speech

There are three parts to a good speech—or a good paper, for that matter: an **introduction, body,** and a **conclusion.**

The Introduction.

The main purpose of the introduction is to state your purpose and get the audience's attention. The goal is to have them *want* to hear what you have to say. This sets the tone for everything that follows. Keep it short but powerful. One example is a rhetorical question (one you really don't want the audience to answer, just think about).

For example, "Do you think smoking just kills people who smoke?" could be an opener for a talk on the hazards of passive smoking. A startling statistic can be used. For example, if giving a talk on breast cancer you can start out with, "Without early detection, it is estimated that 1 out of 5 women will die of breast cancer. That means 4 people in this room of 20. Who will it be? Hopefully, nobody, if you follow the recommendations I will be presenting in my talk."

The introduction can also contain a related personal story or even a joke, but be careful because the joke could bomb or even offend someone. A brief demonstration could also be used, depending on the topic. The introduction should be well rehearsed, and the speaker should have direct eye contact with the audience to make that good first impression. In Exercise 7-7 you'll brainstorm ideas about a compelling introduction.

Working in pairs or small groups, brainstorm ideas about an attention-getting introduction for the speech you chose in Exercise 7-6. Write or explain it here.

EXERCISE 7-7
Coming Up with a Great Introduction

_____

_____

_____

Rehearse in front of your group and have *them* answer the following questions.

Does it grab the audience's attention?_____

Is the purpose and relevance of the speech clearly stated?_____

You now have the audience sitting on the edge of their seats (or at least curious) from your great introduction. Now what? You need to support what your introduction said you were going to do with well-organized facts and information. This is the body of your speech.

The Body.

The body usually represents about 75 percent of your speech and should cover three to five main points, depending on the time allotted for the speech. Trying to cover too much will lose your audience's attention, and so, in most cases, we would suggest

Funny Fact to Think About

Someone once said there were three rules to good public speaking: Be genuine, be brief and, most importantly, be seated.

limiting yourself to three main points. Support these points with facts, theories, statistics, or expert testimony. Use analogies or visual imagery to make the material more familiar and personal. Cover each point fully before going on, and use a transition, or bridge,

between each point for a smoother speech. During the body of your presentation, aim for keeping the audience on their toes with an unexpected viewpoint or analysis and vivid language. Whenever you can, help your audience *visualize* your content, perhaps by using metaphors or topical images. Short sentences, vivid language, personal stories, unusual statistics, balanced humor, rhetorical questions—all of these will make your presentation pop. Different speeches require different rhetorical strategies. The key is to keep it interesting. Exercise 7-8 will give you some practice.

EXERCISE 7-8
The Body of Your Speech

Research and list the three to five main points you want to cover in your chosen speech, along with one startling fact, statistic, interesting story, and so on, for each. Finally add a transition sentence between the main points.

Point 1:_____

Interesting fact, story, etc._____

_____

Transition sentence to Point 2:_____

_____

_____

Point 2:_____

Interesting fact, story, etc._____

_____

Transition sentence to Point 3:_____

_____

_____

Point 3:_____

Interesting fact, story, etc._____

_____

Transition sentence to Point 4 or to conclusion:_____

_____

_____

_____

Now that you have completed the body of your speech, you need to end with the conclusion. Often, it is a good idea to review the main points briefly. If possible, restate them in a different context instead of simply reading them again to your audience. Be creative. Provide closure with a strong final statement that will leave a lasting impression. Sometimes a powerful quote or story will work. If you are doing a persuasive speech, your ending statement should be a call to action. Do Exercise 7-9 now.

Write or describe your conclusion of your chosen speech:

_____

_____

_____

EXERCISE 7-9
Your Conclusion

Now practice your conclusion in front of your group, and have them answer the following questions:

Did your conclusion summarize your main points?_____

Was the summary interesting/creative?_____

Was there a strong final statement that brought closure to the speech?_____

What will you take away from this speech?_____

It's Show Time: Delivering Your Speech

Now that you have prepared your speech, you must decide on your delivery style. Although you can try to memorize a speech word for word, this is not recommended because it usually ends up in disaster (forgetting parts) or is painfully boring because it has no spontaneity. Use the *extemporaneous* style with a brief outline, note cards, or electronic guide such as a PowerPoint presentation to keep you organized. Of course, you rehearse this style of speech, but the main points are just keys to jog your memory and your elaboration will be more spontaneous. With this style, you can more easily maintain good eye contact and have a more dynamic presentation.

Another style is the *manuscript* speech in which you read words from a script or off a teleprompter. This style is needed when precise accuracy is important, such as a presidential speech in which a change in wording can have global effects. This type of speech can be dynamic if it looks extemporaneous. Certain techniques, such as weaving personal stories or humorous comments throughout the speech, give it a more off-the-cuff feel.

Vocal Delivery Skills

Practice your speech by paying close attention to the following vocal skills:

Volume: Is the volume of your voice loud enough so everyone can hear you (without being too loud)?

Rate: Is your rate of speech so fast you are hard to follow? This is a common first-time mistake. Is your rate so slow that you put your audience to sleep? A good speaker watches the audience and varies the rate to maintain interest.

Pitch: Pitch represents the highness or lowness of your voice. Sometimes nervousness will cause your pitch to get very high as your vocal cords vibrate faster. Too high or too low a pitch can be distracting.

Rhythm: This is a combination of your pace and the pauses you use to emphasize main points or new ideas. Use pauses that vary in length and frequency, which allows the listener to think about an emphasized point. It takes practice to become skillful at maintaining a good rhythm throughout your speech.

Word emphasis: Just like you can highlight a written word in boldface type to emphasize it, you can highlight a spoken word or key point by changing your volume or varying your rate or pitch.

Dynamic speakers hone their vocal skills through practice. They use variety in volume, rates, and pitch along with establishing the appropriate rhythm for the type and content of the speech.

Physical Delivery

There is more to your speech than your vocal skills. Remember the importance of nonverbal communication. Your appearance will speak volumes about you and your topic. Decide the kind of message you want to send to your audience via your dress, hairstyle, and accessories because your appearance directly affects your credibility. Think of someone giving a talk on investment strategies with frayed jeans, tennis shoes with holes, greasy hair, and T-shirt stains versus the same speech given by someone in a nice suit and tie or business outfit.

You don't always have to dress like a Fortune 500 president, of course. Again, your presentation depends on your topic. If you are talking about ethnic customs, you might want to dress in an ethnic costume for your speech.

Movement during your speech is also important. Formal speeches usually take place behind a podium. However, if you are teaching a class or workshop, always staying behind a podium may create a barrier between you and your audience.

Facial expressions are critical. If you know your material well and you are connected to it emotionally, your facial expressions should occur naturally. This is similar to smiling while talking on the phone. The *smile* comes through on the other end. Make sure your expressions agree with your speech because smiling while you are talking about the stages of death and dying may seem insensitive. Gestures and hand movements can also aid in emphasizing points and keeping the speech interesting. Be careful not to overuse gestures, as they could become distracting to your audience.

Some Other Pointers:

- When trying to explain a difficult concept, start off with the simple parts and use analogies the audience can understand.
- Avoid overloading the audience with too much information.
- Stagger examples, motivators, humor, stories, and so on, throughout your speech to keep it interesting.
- Use presentation aids to help with visual imagery and keep you organized.

- Visuals should be large and uncluttered. These can include flip charts, PowerPoint slides, or posters. Make sure you have good color contrast.
- Know how to use your technical equipment, and have backups of all your electronic presentations. I always load my presentation on a laptop and have two separate backups kept in two separate places when I speak. Imagine going to do a speech, and your Power-Point crashes with no backup.

Final Words of Wisdom

There are three important concepts in presenting a good speech:

1. Practice
2. Practice
3. Practice

Get the point? Practice in front of helpful and trusted reviewers such as family and friends (or even dogs because they will usually wag their tail supportively). The importance of rehearsing in front of a mirror or camera cannot be stressed enough. If you can film yourself, you will get more of a feel for being in your own audience, and you might surprise yourself: "Like, I had no idea I said 'like' so much!"

Keep in mind that being nervous about your speech is normal. To reduce your fears, know your topic well and practice daily. Use the relaxation techniques from the stress chapter, and remember that a little stress to get you up for your speech is good. Replace any negative self-fulfilling thoughts, such as "I'm going to mess up my speech and forget what to say," with "I know my material well and have practiced it out loud several times." If during your speech you start to get worked up (and hopefully you won't), you can use a technique called *redirection*. This turns your fear into power. For example, an increase in heart rate and nervous energy can be used to project your voice and create a dynamic impression, as opposed to panicking to a point where you run away. In Exercise 7-10, you'll have a chance to identify and tackle your greatest challenge in preparing a presentation.

List the following steps to preparing a presentation in the order of what you believe is most difficult (1) to what is a piece of cake (8).

EXERCISE 7-10
Assessing Yourself

_____ Deciding on the type of speech

_____ Researching the material for the speech

_____ Choosing the main points of the speech and putting them in a sequence

_____ Writing engaging and memorable content for the speech

_____ Finding and using visual aids

_____ Wrapping up the speech

_____ Speaking in front of people

_____ Making eye contact with the audience

_____ Fielding questions after the speech

For the most difficult step, don't stop by merely identifying it. You *must* give yourself a solution to make that step easier for you. Make sure it is a solution that is actually "doable" for you.

> *Anything you have to acquire a taste for was not meant to be eaten.*
> —Eddie Murphy

WRITTEN COMMUNICATION

You're probably wondering why that statement is here. Well, if you think about it, whether or not you agree with Mr. Murphy's philosophy of food, those are words for any writer to live by. In other words, *the reader shouldn't have to do hard labor to understand you.*

If you remember that simple fact any time you have to write something in any form, you will be appreciated for many reasons—among them being considerate of others' time and energy. Good writing is a necessary skill throughout life, as it is yet another facet of how you present yourself to the world. In fact, in almost any career, some people in your life will know you *only* through your writing!

When you sit down to write, always know two things: the *purpose* and the *audience*. Sounds a lot like what you should first do when preparing a speech or presentation! It also follows that most written communications contain an introduction, body, and conclusion, just like your speech. See how communication principles are universal? Do Exercise 7-11 to assess your skills.

EXERCISE 7-11 Assess Yourself

Check each sentence that applies to you.

_____ I am confident in my ability to complete writing assignments.

_____ I write some type of outline, even an informal one, before I begin a writing assignment.

_____ I am aware of my strengths in writing.

_____ I am aware of the areas where I need to improve my writing.

_____ I am aware of the expectations and conventions about using secondary sources.

_____ I cite my sources when I write research papers, even when the material is in my own words.

_____ I ask friends or family members to give me feedback on my writing.

_____ I am willing to approach a faculty member with questions about writing assignments.

_____ I am comfortable writing under time constraints.

_____ I organize my time so I am not rushed to complete a writing assignment at the last minute.

Eight or more checked answers indicate that you're pretty confident and quite likely prepared for writing assignments. Six or seven checked answers indicate that you would benefit from some of the ideas in this chapter. If you have five or fewer checked answers, pay close attention to the advice that follows.

FIGURE 7-4
Section of a memo.

Template

TO: [the main addressee, or if two or more are equally important as addressees, list them here separated by commas]
FR: [you]
SUBJECT OR RE: [should be a brief statement of memo's subject, like a heading]
DATE: [current date]

CC: [anyone who should receive the memo "FYI"]

Example

TO: Members of the Business Society
FROM: Maria Sanchez, Chairperson
SUBJECT: Organizational Meeting
DATE: March 10, 2008

CC: Faculty Advisors

Memos

A memo is an excellent way to get across a brief idea, an "FYI" (for your information), or a request for information to one or more people. In printed (hard copy) form, it should always begin as shown in Figure 7-4.

The text should be brief and to the point with no excess baggage! Pretend you have to pay by the word for the memo as you would if you took out a newspaper advertisement. Lists are okay if they are not wordy. Remember that a memo's information should be easy to grasp at first reading. Also, don't overlook the importance of a succinct subject line (RE) or (SUBJ). Recipients should know at a glance exactly what your memo is about *before* they read it.

Before you distribute your hard copy memo, you must sign it. Some people like to sign at the bottom of the memo, directly below the body. Others simply put their initials next to their name at the top (next to FROM).

E-Mail Memos.

In e-mail form, the heading of your memo is more or less handled by your e-mail program, but you should still remember the hierarchy of addressees. The person to whom your memo is directed goes in the "To" section, and if it is directed to more than one person equally, put them all in there. Do not put just the first addressee in your alphabetical address book in the

"To" section and the rest in the "cc" section if the e-mail is equally important to all. Save the "cc" section only for those who are receiving your e-mail "FYI."

Once again, pay attention to the value of your subject line. The subject line is perhaps even *more* important in an e-mail because many people organize their e-mails or search for previous e-mails by subject line. If you are forwarding an e-mail to a third party, be *absolutely sure* you are not forwarding any personal, confidential, or proprietary information from the original sender to that third party. The consequences can range from lost friendships to lost business. Some people hit "reply to all" carelessly rather than selecting only the people they want to see the pertinent information in the content of the new message.

Because e-mails start in a window separate from the various headings, it is always appropriate and polite to open the content with a greeting, even in an e-mail that is just a memo or even a note to a friend. Start the message with a brief but appropriate greeting: "Hi folks" for holiday pictures to scattered family, and "Good morning, club members" if you're sending out a calendar of events, for example. Even just a "Hi Cathy" (providing, of course, that the person's name is Cathy) is a good way to start. (Speaking of Cathy, is it "Kathy"? Always be certain of spelling!)

Professional e-mails should always include contact information in the signature under your name. Most e-mail programs have the ability to format several different signatures for different situations; for the more formal ones, repeat your e-mail address below the other contact information as a courtesy.

WRITING THAT BIG PAPER

Writing, for class or for work, is challenging for many reasons. Perhaps the main difficulty is the need to do several things at once. Writing a paper, in a sense, is similar to driving an automobile. When you drive, you can't perform each function of driving in isolation. You simultaneously have to steer, brake (or accelerate), check for oncoming traffic and traffic behind you, and attend to traffic signs and signals.

Writing is similar. While you need to attend to higher-order concerns such as paper organization and development of ideas, you also need to consider sentence-level issues like punctuation, grammar, syntax (sentence structure), and semantics (word choice). You need to perform satisfactorily in all of these areas to earn a good grade. It's no wonder many students find writing to be stressful. However, following our advice in the following areas will help put your mind at ease.

Prewriting

Remember there are three main parts to any written paper: the **introduction, body,** and **conclusion** (sound familiar?). The introduction catches the reader's attention and states the purpose or topic of the paper. It is followed by the body of the paper, which presents the supporting facts. Finally, the end of the paper contains a summary and conclusion about your chosen topic. Given this simple overview, let's get a little more specific.

Point of View: Usually referred to as the *thesis statement,* a sentence in your introduction lets the reader know your point of view on a topic and how you'll organize the body of the paper. For example, if we were to write an essay on the challenges of essay exams, we might have a thesis statement like the following:

Taking an essay exam is very similar to taking the exam for obtaining a driver's license.

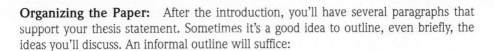

Organizing the Paper: After the introduction, you'll have several paragraphs that support your thesis statement. Sometimes it's a good idea to outline, even briefly, the ideas you'll discuss. An informal outline will suffice:

- Introduction and working thesis statement
- The writer, like the driver of a car, has to demonstrate many skills simultaneously
- Like taking a driving test, a student writing an essay exam has to demonstrate her skills in an artificial situation, not the ideal environment
- Both situations involve working under time constraints and under the eye of a critical examiner
- In both testing situations, students can improve their odds of performing well with practice
- Conclusion

Drafting the Paper

Many students have a hard time writing a particular section of the paper. For some, it's the introduction. For others, it's the conclusion. Some students struggle with titles. In the computer age, the good news is you do not have to start from the beginning. Feel free to start in the middle. If you were writing the essay comparing writing and driving, you could begin by developing the last body paragraph about the benefits of practice.

Peer and Faculty Review

Ask another student or trusted friend to read your draft and to give you feedback and suggestions. The more feedback you receive, the better, as long as your reader is honest with you. Some peers may hesitate to criticize your work. One strategy might be to share with the reader what you perceive to be the strengths and weaknesses of your writing. You might also share examples of feedback you've received from instructors, so the peer reviewer will know what kinds of suggestions to make.

Whenever possible, ask questions of your instructor. Some instructors respond best when students ask specific questions about an assignment rather than just handing over a draft and asking if it's OK. Prepare for a meeting with your instructor by asking specific questions about the assignment.

Revision

Revise several times before submitting a paper. With each revision, seek feedback from faculty and/or peers. If your school has a writing center or tutorial center, take advantage of that service to have a trained professional consult with you on your writing assignments.

Be careful of relying too heavily on spell checking in your word processor. You may have typed "form" instead of "from," and your spell checker will view it as correct. Always print out a hard copy because sometimes it is easier to see your mistakes on paper versus the computer screen.

Time Management and Writing

Many of your writing assignments will take time to do, so it's important to revisit the time management principles from Chapter 3. One of the key principles in time management is good strategic planning: Create a timeline for completing all the parts of writing a paper. Practice this technique in Exercise 7-12.

EXERCISE 7-12
Planning Your Time
for a Research Paper

Situation: If your instructor gives you an assignment three weeks in advance, you have 21 days (counting weekends) to work on it. Figure out what you would need to do each week by completing the chart provided.

Week 1	Amount of Time	Week 2	Amount of Time	Week 3	Amount of Time
Select a topic	~ 1 hour				
Develop a working thesis	~ 1 hour				

Compare your answers with a peer. Do you now feel you might have underestimated the length of time it would take to complete each step? Did you leave enough time for prewriting and drafting? Did you leave enough time for revising and editing?

Let's take a more complicated example and say that you have to write a 10- to 12-page research paper on a topic in your field. The steps involved would include the following:

- Select a topic (unless your topic has been predetermined)
- Decide the point of view you will present on that topic
- Research and gather information
- Retrieve print resources from the library
- Read your sources and decide which ones are most appropriate

- Develop a working outline
- Write a rough draft
- Get feedback from peers and others
- Revise the final paper

Plagiarism is falsely using someone else's work as your own. Every effort should be made to give credit where credit is due. Please complete Exercise 7-13 to learn more about plagiarism.

Place a check mark by each action that constitutes plagiarism.

_____ Submitting someone else's paper as your own.

_____ Purchasing a paper and submitting it as your own.

_____ Purchasing a paper on the Internet and borrowing some of the ideas for your own paper.

_____ Submitting the same paper for two or more courses.

_____ Using sources without providing endnotes, footnotes, or parenthetical citations.

_____ Using a direct quote without citation.

_____ Using your own words to explain another person's ideas, without citing the information.

_____ Using a direct quote and changing only one or two words, without citing the source.

Answers: All of the above constitute plagiarism.

EXERCISE 7-13
Plagiarism Quiz

Many of your assignments will require the use of *secondary sources* (such as journal articles, books, and online resources) to support your point of view. Different academic disciplines require different citation and footnoting models. Most humanities disciplines, including English composition, use MLA (Modern Language Association) style, whereas psychologists, educators, and social scientists often use APA (American Psychological Association) style. Historians rely on Chicago style (*Chicago Manual of Style*), and chemists use the citation conventions of the American Chemical Society. Here, we simply focus on the common elements of research writing across disciplines.

In-Text Citation

It is important to cite any material that isn't your own. If you use direct quotations, use quotation marks (or block indent if the quote is longer than four lines or so) and cite your source. In other words, tell the reader where you got the information. Depending on the format you use, you can use footnotes (numbered citations at the bottom of the page), endnotes (numbered citations placed at the end of the paper, before the reference page), or parenthetical citations (citing the source in parentheses at the end of the quotation or paraphrased passage).

Reference Pages

Depending on the style, your reference page may be called Works Cited, References, or Bibliography. Regardless of the title, this is a list of all the references you cited in your paper. APA-style references are listed at the end of a paper, textbook chapter, or textbook.

COMMUNICATING A PROFESSIONAL IMAGE

We end this chapter with a very important but often overlooked communication concept. No matter what your chosen program of study, you need to communicate a positive professional image if you want both to land and keep that great job. A positive professional image keeps you noticed and helps you to move onward and upward in your chosen career. To communicate a professional image, it is important to show that you have these attributes:

- Strong technical expertise and a willingness to share it (in other words, you "know your stuff" and keep up with the latest and greatest)
- Good human relations skills and constant striving to improve these skills (you get along well with others)
- Pride in your job performance and your organization
- The ability to tolerate the dull and boring aspects of your job (we all have them) without whining
- The capacity to work unsupervised in meeting commitments
- The confidence in putting forth new ideas
- The insight to give credit to all who help you
- A positive attitude toward change as an opportunity and *not* as a threat
- Common sense and common courtesy in your dealings with others
- The desire to get involved and make yourself useful to the organization

If this is the attitude you project, you will be a success in any chosen career!

HEALTHY DECISION MAKING

Maria does well on her written exams and papers. She is very personable in small groups and is well liked by the rest of the class. However, she is quite anxious about getting in front of a group to give a speech. The class she is taking requires her to do a presentation and counts for 20% of the course grade. Her presentation is due in one month, and she is getting very anxious. If you were Maria's friend, how would you try to help her?

_____

_____

_____

_____

_____

Now that you have read this chapter and performed the assessments and exercises, go to your CD for this chapter to reinforce these concepts. The CD presents you with a fun and interactive journey back through forms of communication and styles, along with additional assessments to help track your progress.

References

Denney, N. H. (2002). On leading with charisma. In *Let Your Leadership Speak: How to Lead and Be Heard* (pp. 15–26). Paxton, MA: The Future Is Yours to Create!

Hecht, M. L., DeVito, J. A., & Guerrero, L. K. (1999). Perspectives on nonverbal communication: codes, functions, and contexts. In *The Nonverbal Communication Reader: Classic and Contemporary Readings* (2nd ed., pp. 3–18). Prospect Heights, IL: Waveland Press.

Group Interaction and Team Building

Working Together Works

OBJECTIVES

What you will discover by the end of this chapter:

- Understanding the difference between a group and a team
- Understanding team-building concepts and purpose
- Appreciating diversity
- Enhancing group creativity through brainstorming
- Assessing team effectiveness and improving team performance

Coming together is a beginning.
Keeping together is progress.
Working together is success.

Henry Ford

At work and at play, we see countless examples of individuals interacting in groups large and small. This process, commonly referred to as *teamwork,* is very natural. So many examples come to mind: our favorite sports team, our favorite television show with its actors, local volunteer firefighters, our families, our coworkers, and fellow students working together on a school project. Think about your own activities and actions and how each of us participates in groups or teams. The familiar acronym **T**ogether **E**veryone

Achieves **M**ore reinforces the importance of participating on a team: We benefit from teamwork in many ways. This chapter reveals the value of teamwork on many levels:

- Sense of belonging
- Sense of responsibility
- Sense of accomplishment
- Sense of unity
- Sense of support
- Sense of motivation
- Sense of satisfaction
- Sense of pride (individual/team)

Teamwork is truly a *sensory* experience, and we hope this chapter will be eye-opening.

As Monty Python would say, "And now for something completely different!" In the preceding chapters, we discussed many individual attributes of success, including stress management, time management, and study skills. To understand group dynamics and team concepts, we need to experience as well as read about these ideas. Therefore, your learning experience in this chapter will come from your group and team interactions.

What is the difference between a group versus a team? We want *you* to come up with that answer as we work together. Our hopes are that your initial groups will develop into effective and energetic teams.

WHAT IS THE DIFFERENCE BETWEEN GROUPS AND TEAMS?

We join groups for different reasons. In Exercise 8-1, we look more closely at why we participate. Discovering the reason might help us understand the difference better.

Remember a time (maybe recently) when you agreed to join a group. The group may be a social organization, a school club, several students working on a class project, a committee, or friends who meet to play a sport at lunchtime. Here is a short list of possible reasons you decided to join. Assign a number value to each reason to rank its importance.

EXERCISE 8-1
Self-Assessment on
Why We Join Groups

5 = Absolutely most important

4 = Very important

3 = Average importance

2 = Seemed like a good idea at the time

1 = Sorry I got involved

_____1. Looking for people who share my interests and goals.

_____2. Feeling counted on by others.

_____3. Sharing the "thrill of victory" or "agony of defeat" with others who tried their hardest, gave their best, and pulled together.

_____4. Looking for people to encourage me and help me so I feel good about myself.

_____5. Knowing that the work/activity goes easier and has a better chance of success with a group than with my work alone.

_____6. Doing my best and being recognized as a member and contributor.

_____7. Sharing the feeling that "we did more than we thought we could."

_____8. Feeling inspired, energized, and powerful when working with others toward a goal.

Evaluate Your Choices

_____1. Add your scores for statements 1 and 4. This total suggests your motivation lies in a sense of *belonging and support*. Security in social relationships and interaction is important to you.

_____2. Add your scores for statements 2 and 8. This total suggests your motivation lies in a sense of *responsibility and motivation*. The need to serve and help others motivates you more than going it alone.

_____3. Add your scores for statements 5 and 6. This total suggests your motivation lies in a sense of *accomplishment and satisfaction*. Understanding that more can be accomplished by a group than by an individual is important to you.

_____4. Add your scores for statements 3 and 7. This total suggests your motivation lies in a sense of *pride and unity*. Esteem and cohesiveness (we-*ness* versus me-*ness*) matter to you.

Further Questions for Discussion

1. In which area did you have the highest score? _____

   In which area did you have the lowest score? _____

2. What is one more reason in addition to the ones mentioned for joining a group?

   _____

FIGURE 8-1

Teams build on each other's strengths and support each other's weaknesses.

With a better understanding of why we join groups, let's touch on your own knowledge and experience before we explore the difference between groups and teams. A Chinese philosopher, Confucius, had a great approach to learning:

> I read and I forget.
> I see and I remember.
> I do and I understand.

First, we have *read* a bit about groups. Second, we can *see* the pictures of teams in action (see Figure 8-1). Finally, we now *do* a series of hands-on exercises to experience the differences. Please complete Exercises 8-2A–C *on your own.*

List examples of groups that you see everyday. These can include at home, school, or in your community.

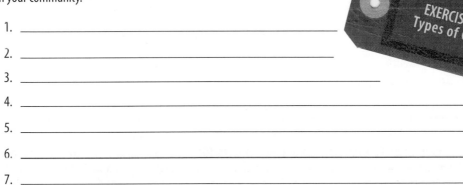

EXERCISE 8-2A
Types of Groups

1. _____

2. _____

3. _____

4. _____

5. _____

6. _____

7. _____

List groups in which you are a member.

1. _____
2. _____
3. _____
4. _____
5. _____

Describe your most memorable group experience.

_____
_____
_____
_____
_____
_____

The words *group* and *team* are often thought of as nouns, but for our purposes we must make them verbs. *Grouping* and *teaming* are processes in action. Remember, "I do and I understand." Next do Exercise 8-3.

Team up with a partner and compare your lists from Exercise 8-2A–C.

Together, build a list of the top-10 benefits of groups based on your lists and discussion from Exercise 8-2A–C.

1. _____   6. _____
2. _____   7. _____
3. _____   8. _____
4. _____   9. _____
5. _____   10. _____

Got your Top-10 List? Excellent! Thanks for your group effort. Now, in the words of America's favorite chef from New Orleans, Emeril Lagasse, "Let's kick it up a notch!" in Exercise 8-4.

Now let's work in larger teams. Group together two or three of the pairs of students from Exercise 8-3. This new expanded team should arrange desks or chairs for easier interaction and communication.

EXERCISE 8-4
Building Teams
from Groups

Situation: Your newly formed team is charged with developing ideas to market your school to attract qualified applicants.

Instructions

1. Introduce yourselves to each other and decide on a team name. Inform your instructor of your name.

2. All members must work together with each team member contributing ideas.

3. Assign someone from the team to record the ideas.

4. After the allotted time, select someone to present your ideas to the class.

After each presentation, answer the following questions about your own group's efforts:

What did each member contribute to the team?

_____

Did team members interrupt at any point?

_____

Did each person feel free to voice an opinion?

_____

Was there disagreement at any point? How was it handled?

_____

Where did the group most readily reach a consensus?

_____

Identify verbal behaviors that helped the group to progress.

_____

Identify nonverbal behaviors that helped the group to progress.

_____

Did suggestions from different members stimulate new ideas?_____

Did a leader emerge in the process?_____

What benefits occurred by working together on the project?

_____

_____

What, if anything, could your team do differently?

_____

_____

Did your class as a whole generate ideas that could help your school?

_____

_____

> *"When a team outgrows individual performance and learns team confidence, excellence becomes a reality."*
> —Joe Paterno, head coach of Penn State

Coach Paterno's statement seems to suggest that a team is something more than a group of individuals interacting. Did you think you were in a *group* or a *team* during the previous exercise? Let's improve our understanding by considering the definitions of groups and teams.

What Defines a Team?

Look at your earlier description of a memorable group experience (Exercise 8-2C). If the experience was a positive one, you probably enjoyed a sense of **camaraderie,** a spirit of cohesiveness and the inspiring enthusiasm, devotion, and strong regard for the honor of the group that is felt within a team. Team members can't explain the feeling, but they definitely know when they experience it.

A **group** is simply two or more people who interact with each other to complete certain tasks, achieve certain goals, or fulfill certain needs.

A t**eam** is a group whose members interact (work or play) with a focused intensity to complete a shared, mutually supported, specific, overriding goal. The key word in this definition is *intensity,* which is the primary difference between groups and teams. To demonstrate this difference, let's compare a team to a magnifying glass on a sunny day. If you look at Figure 8-2, the rays of sunshine represent the individual members. The specific goal is to start a fire to survive in the wilderness. Without the concentrated and intense focus of the magnifying glass, the goal of starting the fire would never be accomplished because the rays of the sun (team members) do not, at least individually, have enough intensity to accomplish this goal. A group is simply a collection of members who interact without that described point of focus or intensity. Figure 8-2 illustrates the point that every team is a group, but not every group is a team—but a group can develop into a team.

Different Types of Teams

Go back and look at the list of groups (Exercise 8-1A) you created. You probably see a variety of types. Now, can you differentiate which were *teams* and which were *groups?* Let's look at some of the different types of teams in more detail.

Two primary types of teams have to do with how the team was originally formed or started. **Formal teams** are set up by someone of authority who selects and assigns the members to work on a specific task. **Informal teams** occur when the members get together on their own because they share a common interest. Again, keep in mind the intensity level is what differentiates a team from a group.

Most other team types focus on the team's activity or purpose.

Work teams usually form around a specific process or function.

Examples:

1. **Advice teams** seek and provide information or research material, such as political advisers polling issues for popular opinion among voters.
2. **Project teams** produce, build, or create a new service or product, such as design teams who create new cars.
3. **Action teams** perform a specific operation or process for an organization, such as the organ transplant team within a hospital.
4. **Production teams** perform specific operations for producing a finished product, such as the shift crew at a fast-food restaurant.
5. **Maintenance teams** perform repair or preventative measures on equipment, such as the pit crew at a NASCAR race.
6. **Sports teams** are formed by members participating in their chosen sport, such as softball, football, soccer, bowling, or volleyball. A friendly pickup game would be a group, but a team has a schedule, a roster, and a competitive intensity to perform at their collective best.
7. Top **management teams** are executives who manage a company, such as a CEO and all his or her direct reports.
8. **Virtual teams** are individuals who meet and work together by Internet or media communication methods rather than face to face.
9. **Study teams** are collections of students who meet to encourage and support each other and complete assignments and projects.

> *"A group becomes a team when each member is sure enough of himself and his contribution to praise the skills of the others."*
>
> —Norman Shidle

FIGURE 8-2

The focus and intensity of the group members toward a goal determine if it is a team.

Rays of Sunlight
are
MEMBERS

Magnifying Glass
Is what intensifies and makes the
TEAM

Fire
Is the
ACHIEVED GOAL

REAL-LIFE APPLICATION
What Is Synergy?

An effective team creates synergy. Remember our definition from Chapter 3: "Synergy is the sum of the individual parts creating a greater whole." Let's look to nature for an example of synergy that is often used in team-building seminars. Please see Figure 8-3, a flock of geese flying in V formation.

What we learn from the team of geese is that overall performance and productivity increase significantly when a team works together to generate synergy. When you see geese flying in a V formation, you might be interested in knowing what scientists have discovered about why they fly that way. As each bird flaps its wings, the wind currents it creates produce an uplift for the bird immediately following.

These beautiful birds illustrate *teamwork* at its best:

FACT 1:   As each goose flaps its wings, it creates an uplift for the birds that follow. By flying in a V formation, the whole flock adds 71% greater flying range than if each bird flew alone.

Lesson: *People who share a common direction and sense of community can get where they are going more quickly and easily because they are traveling with the support of one another.*

FACT 2:   When a goose falls out of formation, it suddenly feels the drag and resistance of flying alone. It quickly moves back into formation to take advantage of the lifting power of the bird immediately in front of it.

Lesson: *If we have as much sense as a goose, we will stay in formation with those headed where we want to go. We are willing to accept their help and give our help to others.*

FACT 3:   When the lead goose tires, it rotates back into the formation and another goose flies to the point position.

Lesson: *It pays to take turns doing the hard tasks and sharing leadership. Like geese, people are interdependent on each other's skills, capabilities, and unique arrangements of gifts, talents, or resources.*

FIGURE 8-3

Geese in V formation personify a cooperative team.

FACT 4: The geese flying in formation honk to encourage those up front to keep up their speed.

Lesson: *When team members encourage each other, production is enhanced.*

FACT 5: When a goose gets sick, wounded, or shot down, two geese drop out of formation and follow it down to help and protect it. They stay with it until it dies or is able to fly again. Then, they launch out with another formation or catch up with the flock.

Lesson: *If we have as much sense as geese, we will stand by each other in difficult times as well as when we are strong.*

INNER WORKINGS OF A TEAM

The image of a well-oiled machine is commonly used to refer to a successful team. A well-oiled machine indicates smooth running, meshing of parts, minimal friction, little squealing or squeaking, low maintenance, and high productivity. Let's examine the inner workings, or the vital oils, of a team, which consist of rules, roles, and goals.

Team rules are the guidelines and instructions that all members agree to at the beginning of the team formation. The purpose of the rules is to specify what actions and corresponding behaviors the team members will use in achieving mutually determined goals.

Example: If you are on a sports team, you must learn and follow the rules of the game or your team will get repeated penalties and most likely lose the game.

Refer back to the marketing team from Exercise 8-1. Did your team establish any rules? What were they?

Team roles are those behaviors and tasks that a team member is expected to perform for the overall progress of the team. Have you ever been on a team and really didn't know what your job was? The term for that situation is **role ambiguity,** which can greatly decrease your team's effectiveness.

Example: The role of a point guard on a basketball team is to bring the ball up court and run the offense. The expected tasks and behavior include low or no turnovers, good passing, good shooting, and team spirit.

Refer back to the marketing team from Exercise 8-4. Which role did each person fill?

Team goals are specific and measurable results for a team to accomplish. Goals are whatever outcomes the team wants to achieve.

Example: A sports team goal is to win the championship.

In Exercise 8-4, what goal did your team want to achieve?

This trio of inner workings (rules, roles, and goals) must be determined by a team working together and making team decisions. Let's now look at the team decision-making process.

TEAM DECISION MAKING

Team interaction involves individuals making collective decisions. This ability to make a decision moves the team forward toward their goal(s). The measure of success for a team is directly related to the team's ability to reach its goal(s). Let's look at some different decision-making models.

The Three C's of Team Decision Making

1. **Command decisions** happen when a team member (self-appointed or team-appointed leader) dictates a decision. The member is very authoritative and exerts pressure on the other members to comply. An appropriate command type decision occurs on those infrequent occasions of crisis that demand immediate action (e.g., fire, accident, equipment breakdown, or illness, among others). The time to decide and implement is very short and, often, the team complies without a sense of buy-in or ownership.

2. **Consultative decisions** happen when a discussion takes place mainly among the team members who know about the issues at hand. Usually the individual who has the most expertise in the subject leads the consulting discussion, and others may be left out. The results lead to a decision based on a partial team contribution. Some team members may disagree with the final decision. Because resources and information often need to be collected from outside the team, the time to make and implement the decision is longer.

3. **Consensus decisions** happen when the entire team participates and every member expresses a view toward the ultimate decision. The discussion is spirited and energized, and all believe that the results of the decision are shared and equally owned. This type of decision takes the most time to complete; however, because the entire team participates, individuals become more committed to the decision, and the degree of ownership and buy-in is at the highest level. In addition, implementation is faster and more effective (Miller, 1984).

Each of the three C's can be used in different scenarios. No one decision-making type is correct in every circumstance. The two greatest factors that impact these three types of decision making are time and ownership:

Time: How much time is available to reach a decision? Is there a deadline? Balancing time and teamwork can be challenging.

Ownership: Does each team member feel a sense of commitment to the project and to other team members? Without that sense of ownership, your team is just a group.

Look at Figure 8-4 and then complete the exercise.

One other potential outcome is a team's inability to make a decision. Team members do not want to speak up, and progress stalls while everyone waits for someone else to take action and make a suggestion. Reluctance by team members to participate in the decision-making process inhibits the performance of a team. In some situations insufficient information or lack of resources justifies a nondecision. *It is a wise team that knows when to do nothing.* However, the amount of time involved in making a decision to do nothing varies. That nondecision can be reached quickly or can be a long drawn-out process of going round and round before the team decides to drop the discussion, take no action, and move forward. In Exercise 8-5, you'll think about types of team decisions.

FIGURE 8-4

Command decisions take the least amount of time, but buy-in may be small because only one person is involved. The decisions the team makes through consensus take the longest to reach, but everyone has taken ownership and the time for implementation is reduced. Cooperation and collaboration are increased, and the results are likely to be more positive.

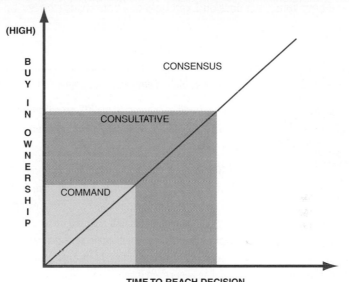

List some examples of the different types of team decision making that you have encountered in your own team experiences.

Command example:_____

_____

How did you feel about this decision?_____

_____

Consultative example:_____

_____

How did you feel about this decision?_____

_____

Consensus example:_____

_____

How did you feel about this decision?_____

_____

EXERCISE 8-5
Types of Team Decisions

If you ever encountered a situation where a team could not make a decision, describe it and explain the reasons behind the situation.

_____

_____

Let's see how your team does on Exercise 8-6, a consensus exercise on survival.

**EXERCISE 8-6
Consensus Exercise:
Wilderness and
Survival Exercise**

Join in teams of six to eight members. Now picture the following:

An old fashioned walk in the woods: no GPS, no cell phone, no pagers, no life lines—just your plain life experiences and common sense. Now let's add just a few challenges.

Here are 10 questions concerning survival in the wilderness. Your first task is *individually* to select the best of the three alternatives under each item. Try to imagine yourself in the situation depicted. Assume that you are alone and have minimal equipment, except where specified. The season is fall. The days are warm and dry, but the nights are cold.

After you have completed this task individually, you will again consider each question as a member of your small group. Your group will have the task of deciding, by consensus, the best alternative for each question. Do not change your individual answers even if you change your mind in the group discussion. Both individual and group solutions will later be compared with the "correct" answers provided by a group of naturalists who conduct classes in woodland survival and contributed to the *Worst-Case Scenario* book (Piven & Borgenicht, 1999). These answers can be found in the appendix after you complete the exercise.

You have 10 minutes to answer the questions individually and 25 minutes as a team. Appoint a team member to watch the time for your team.

Questions	Your Answer	Group Answer
1. You have strayed from your party in trackless timber. You have no special signaling equipment. The best way to attempt to contact your friends is to:	_____	_____
a) call "help" loudly, but in a low register.		
b) yell or scream as loud as you can.		
c) whistle loudly and shrilly.		
2. You are in "snake country." Your best action to avoid snakes is to:	_____	_____
a) make a lot of noise with your feet.		
b) walk softly and quietly.		
c) travel at night.		

3. The day becomes dry and hot. You have a full canteen of water (about 1 liter) with you. You should: _____   _____

    a) ration it—about a cupful a day.
    b) not drink until you stop for the night, then drink what you need.
    c) drink as much as you think you need when you need it.

4. You decide to walk out of the wild country by following a series of ravines where a water supply is available. Night is coming on. The best place to make camp is: _____   _____

    a) next to the water supply in the ravine.
    b) high on a ridge.
    c) midway up the slope.

5. An early snow confines you to your small tent. You doze with your small stove going. There is danger if the flame is: _____   _____

    a) yellow.
    b) blue.
    c) red.

6. Unarmed and unsuspecting, you surprise a large bear prowling around your campsite. As the bear rears up about 10 meters from you, you should: _____   _____

    a) run.
    b) climb the nearest tree.
    c) freeze, but be ready to back away slowly.

7. There are killer bees flying and swarming around you. Yes, they are stinging you. Ouch!   _____   _____

    a) Freeze and start to swat at them. Kill or be killed.
    b) Jump into the nearest swimming pool, river, lake, or body of water.
    c) Run away into the nearest bushes or high weeds.

8. You have just come around the bend in a trail and there is a ferocious mountain lion.   _____   _____

    a) Crouch down as much as you can.
    b) Run away like there is no tomorrow.
    c) Try to increase your size. Open up and spread wide your jacket or shirt.

9. You just crossed through a swamp and, sure enough, you just received a bite by an alligator. _____ _____

   a) Go completely limp and play dead.
   b) Make a loud screeching noise to shock the gator into opening its jaws.
   c) Use any weapon you can find and go for the eyes and/or tap the snout.

10. Finally, you are on your way out of the wilderness to safety. A thunder and lightning storm breaks out. Lightening strikes very near you. _____ _____

    a) If in an open area, drop and lie flat on the ground.
    b) Find a high place, open field, or ridge above timberline.
    c) If in an open area, lean on your knees and hands to minimize contact with the ground.

Question	Your Individual Answer	Mark Which Ones You Answered Correctly From the Appendix		Team Answer	Mark Which Ones Your Team Answered Correctly
1					
2					
3					
4					
5					
6					
7					
8					
9					
10					
Total		( )			( )

Now that you and your team have completed the Wilderness and Survival Exercise, answer the following questions:

Which score was higher, the team's score or yours?_____

Consensus decisions should be the best ones. None of us are as smart as *all* of us.

_____

How did your team do? Did one individual score higher than the collective team? Why?

_____

Did your team members listen to each other's suggestions and comments?

_____

Did your team members adopt different roles? Ex. leader–time keeper–recorder–encourager

_____

What have you learned about interactions between people attempting to solve a task? Did you reach consensus? If so, how long did it take?

_____

_____

What could you do differently to have a more effective outcome?

_____

_____

UNDERSTANDING TEAM DYNAMICS

Team dynamics refers to the basic nature of the team and how different personalities combine to create an evolving team personality. Just as every individual has a unique personality, each team forms a collective personality all its own. The growth of a team follows five steps, which are nicely demonstrated by the Tuckman Model of Group Development (Tuckman & Jensen, 1977). (See Figure 8-5.)

Diversity

Let's look at a story about teamwork and diversity, authored by Dr. Seuss. An excerpt from *Sneetches and Other Stories* (Geisel, 1961) describes a fictional community of strange-looking, long-beaked, spiky-haired, ruffled necked, tall bright yellow critters who live on a beach. A significant difference exists within this group of critters. Some have green stars on their stomachs and some do not. Surprisingly, the "star-bellied" Sneetches believe they are much better than the Sneetches with "plain bellies." This simple and clever children's story demonstrates a divided community with prejudice between the two groups of critters. The Stars are aloof and arrogant toward the meek and humble No Stars. Neither group socializes or interacts with the other.

The characters in this story certainly didn't experience teamwork. When one group or individual believes they have an edge and bring more to the team than anyone else, this

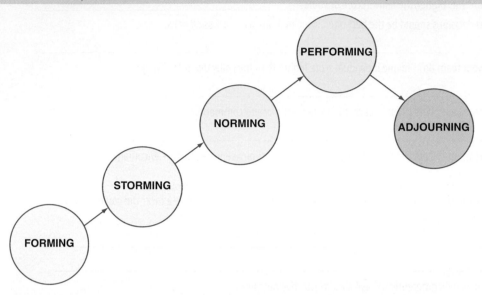

FIGURE 8-5

A representation of the Tuckman Model of Team Growth and Development.

STAGES	FORMING	STORMING	NORMING	PERFORMING	ADJOURNING
Individual Member Thoughts	Am I welcome? Can I trust these folks? Do they care about me? How do I fit in?	What is my role? Who leads? Why is that person in charge? Not ready to volunteer! Find someone to align with	What do you want me to do? Hey, these folks are OK! What's our goal and purpose? I can do that!	Enthusiasm Excitement Self-worth Belonging to part of something special Rely on teammates	Look at what we did! Next? Sorry it's over! Going to miss my teammates. What a great memorable experience!
Group Thoughts	Why are we here? Who are these people? Better not be any more work!	Disagreement over who leads! We won't get anything done this way (politics) Who does what?	Respect for one person to lead develops A spirit of teamwork begins to emerge	All tasks will be assigned and completed. Synergy is felt. Teaming is fun! Wow, look at us!	We were part of this! Hope next group works this well Need to find another project
Outcomes	Introductions Meet and greet Form opinions from first impressions Forming team identity	Testing of members and roles Leader emerges Awkwardness leaves Cliques form	Group trust builds cohesiveness Me-ness goes to We-ness Roles solidified	Open communication Conflicts resolved Cooperation Collaboration Goal/purpose met	Example of the power of teamwork Potential new team leaders trained

perception weakens and inhibits people from working together. And when team members allow another or others to gain a sense of superiority over them, energy, cooperation, productivity, creativity, and teamwork also suffer. A "me-ness" hinders the "we-ness."

This Dr. Seuss fable becomes interesting when a stranger, Sylvester McMonkey McBean, comes to town and offers to solve the inferiority complex for the Plain Belly Sneetches. McBean's revolutionary high-tech machine places Stars on Bellies for a small fee. Naturally, all the No-Star Sneetches embrace this quick fix. Now everyone on the beaches is starred the same. All this sameness was too much for the originally Starred Bellied Sneetches, so a town hall meeting is arranged to rectify this annoying sameness. Guess who arrives to save the day? Why, of course, Sylvester McMonkey McBean, with another high-tech machine that eradicates stars. Once again, the change involves a small fee. The frantic circus begins with everyone running to and fro, attempting to modify themselves differently from the other Sneetches. Into one machine and out the other machine, the Sneetches scurry all day long. After the vicious cycle begins, the results become rather confusing: No one knows who is who. But, with all their money spent, they collectively watch Sylvester McMonkey McBean drive off into the sunset with a grin of satisfaction, proclaiming, "They never will learn. No. You can't teach a Sneetch!"

Sylvester McMonkey McBean actually served as a catalyst between the different Sneetches. When all the money was spent and McBean got up and left, the Sneetches discovered a simple truth: We are all equal, and no one should determine our self-worth. The me-ness became we-ness that day on the beach, and diversity was well within everyone's reach!

This children's story teaches us a lot about teamwork and diversity. Sameness is not needed for equality. We should celebrate our differences. Often our team members look, think, act, and communicate differently. An effective team embraces these differences. Reflect on celebrating diversity in Exercise 8-7.

Answer the following questions, and then share your results with your team.

What are you most proud of concerning your heritage?_____

Describe a favorite food that reflects your heritage._____

What is your favorite family tradition?_____

Explain what diversity means to you._____

EXERCISE 8-7
Celebrating
Diversity

Share your answers with others on your team. Discuss these differences, and focus on the positives that grow from this diverse collection of team members. Remember: A team is a collection of people who have numerous differences, but the key is that they share a common goal. Let the richness of difference bring intensity to the solutions and ideas to meet the team's goal.

TEAM BRAINSTORMING

Now let's look at a strategy for generating breakthrough ideas and solutions. Of course we know that for a team to achieve its goals, ideas and solutions are an important step to success. **Brainstorming** is an all-inclusive method for complete team member involvement in generating ideas.

Team Creativity and Innovation: Brainstorming

A brainstorming session is an energetic, enthusiastic means to collect ideas and potential solutions for achieving a goal. Remember, the quantity of ideas is important, so building on the ideas of others and encouraging offbeat ideas are helpful. After studying the following list, do Exercise 8-8.

How to Conduct a Team Brainstorm

1. Define your goal, opportunity for change, or problem to be solved so all team members understand the objective of the session. (Remember MAPS in goal setting. If your goal is not measurable, attainable, personally chosen, and specific, the session focus will be too broad.)

    a. Good example: How can we increase the number of applicants to our school?

    b. Too broad: How can we improve our school?

2. Establish a time limit for the session. Depending on the subject, 20 to 30 minutes should be sufficient.

3. Choose a person to record comments. Note: Responses should be limited to five to ten words to expedite the process and maintain flow and energy.

4. The facilitator signals the start of the process, usually sits with the rest of the team at a table, and rotates around the group in one direction to seek input.

5. Teams participating in an active brainstorm session are similar to bags of microwave oven popcorn "popping out ideas." Once the popping begins to slow—the ideas stop flowing—the process is complete. Also, if the predetermined amount of time expires, call the session finished.

6. The facilitator coaches the team participants in categorizing the collected ideas.

7. The facilitator leads the team on a consensus prioritization of the top-five ideas.

8. The team focuses on finding a workable solution incorporating the potential idea(s) from the top-five priority list.

9. An action plan (including person, responsibilities, and completion times) is formulated to implement the idea or ideas. The team's problem-solving mission has begun.

Within your classroom, multiple teams should be completing their Festival Planning Tables. An interesting class discussion would include listing the best of the best ideas from the entire collection of ideas for all the teams. Your entire class can then be considered a team.

This process of small teams evolving into one large team is often used within an organization to gather ideas and maximize the participation of a greater number of people. Use Exercise 8-9 to assess team performance.

Have your team brainstorm the following:

Your school would like to have an ethnic festival to celebrate diversity and involve the local community. They have asked your class to help them brainstorm ideas concerning this event. They have given you a list of areas to consider:

1. Location

2. Theme

3. Music/food and Refreshments/activities

4. Marketing ideas

5. How the students can contribute

6. How the school can contribute

Conduct a brainstorming session for each of the elements of the festival. In brainstorming, no idea is too unrealistic or far-fetched. Don't judge one another's ideas—just throw them out there. Go for it!

Complete the Festival Planning Table with your team's final answers.

Topic Areas	Top Ideas
1. Location	
2. Theme	
3. Music/food and Refreshments/activities	
4. Marketing ideas	
5. How the students can contribute	
6. How the school can contribute	

How did your team do? Rate the following questions:

3 = fantastic   2 = good   1 = poor   0 = nonexistent

The goal or purpose was clear _____

Team energy and enthusiasm _____

Number and types of ideas _____

Level of participation _____

Support and encouragement _____

Open and effective communication _____

Team spirit and pride _____

Comfort level _____

Mutual respect _____

Ability to resolve conflict _____

EXERCISE 8-8
Brainstorming in Action

EXERCISE 8-9
Assessing Team
Effectiveness and
Performance

Scoring

25–30:	You were on a very synergistic and effective team.
20–24:	You were on a good team that, with work, can become a great team.
19–15:	Your team is OK but needs some work in the low-rated areas.
10–14:	Your team needs a lot of work to improve.
Below 10:	Hope you used this as a learning experience!

APPLICATION OF TEAMWORK TO SCHOOL, WORK, AND COMMUNITY

A parable about masons (bricklayers) best summarizes Chapter 8:

One day while out for a carefree walk, I came across three bricklayers working on the same project.

I asked the first bricklayer what he was doing.

"Laying bricks," he told me.

I asked the second what he was doing.

"Making a brick wall," he told me.

I asked the third.

"Building a cathedral," he explained. (St. Benedict, approximately A.D., 530 quoted in Chittester, 1999)

Everyone approaches work, tasks, and assignments from a different perspective. The question for a group of people who have transformed into a team is, "What are you going to do with the new skills that you have acquired? Lay bricks or build cathedrals?" An effective team looks for and embraces the next new challenge. Please consider using your new knowledge of teaming in every facet of your daily activities. Working together works—in school, work, and in your community.

Please complete Exercise 8-10 to assess teams in your school and community.

SUMMATION EXERCISE 8-10

Describe a team within your school._____

_____

What is its purpose? _____

What are its strengths?_____

How can it be improved?_____

Describe a team within your community._____

_____

What is its purpose? _____

What are its strengths?_____

How can it be improved? _____

HEALTHY DECISION MAKING

Dave and Selma joined a study group for a particularly difficult class. Their time is very limited because they both work outside of school. However, when this particular study group meets, other team members spend a lot of time complaining about the class and gossiping about other classmates. Dave and Selma feel the group should be more of a study team and have an intensity about their goal of doing well in this course. What are some of Dave and Selma's options?

_____

_____

_____

_____

 Now that you have actively participated in team-building activities, go to your CD and discover ways to reinforce the concepts in Working Together Works! The CD will further explore team building and the interaction and relationships of team members. *"All of us can do more than one of us."*

References

Chittester, J. (1999). *Wisdom from living the daily rule of St. Benedict.* San Francisco: Harper.

Geisel, T. S. (1961). *Sneetches and other stories.* New York: Random House.

Miller, L. M. (1984). *American spirit: Visions of a new corporate culture.* New York: Warner. pp. 40–43.

Piven, J., & Borgenicht, D. (1999). *The worst-case scenario survival handbook.* San Francisco: Chronicle Books. pp. 60–63, 54–56, 57–59, 155–158.

Tuckman, B. W., & Jensen, M. A. C. (1977). Stages of small-group development revisited. *Group & Organization Studies,* 419–427.

Job Seeking and Leadership Development

Your Future Begins Now

OBJECTIVES

In this chapter, you will learn strategies to enhance your career opportunities in four specific areas:

- Academic preparation: You will begin to find the right career and major.
- Out-of-class experience: You will learn how to increase your marketability with involvement in community, clubs, and organizations that will, in turn, develop your leadership and organizational skills.
- The job search: You will learn how to secure that great job by writing effective résumés and cover letters and performing well during your interview.
- Leadership: You will explore some ideas about leadership and how to develop the leader within *you*!

Preparing for your career is not something you do right before you graduate. Rather, preparation for your career begins early while you are still in school. The first step is to select your career and/or major, and, for most students, this is not a onetime process. The overwhelming majority of students change their minds at least once, even if they feel certain about their initial decision.

The reality is that most people change not just jobs but also career tracks several times in their lives. Today's economy isn't your grandparents' economy when employees often worked for the same organization from the start of their working career until retirement. Workers need to be able to adapt to changes in the workplace. One way to prepare for working in the 21st century is to explore and develop a wide range of knowledge, skills, and abilities.

Even if you have chosen your career and feel that the material in this section might not pertain to you, it is still very important. This information might confirm your choice, which is a great motivator to move on. However, some might find that they weren't as committed to their choices, and this exploration will help them with their decision-making process. Of course, for those of you who haven't got a clue as to what you want to do, this is a great place to start. Let's begin with Exercise 9-1.

Mark each statement with a "T" for true or "F" for false:

EXERCISE 9-1
What Do You Know?

1. Good grades are the only factor behind getting a good job after graduation. _____

2. Students who enter school with a chosen major or career have an advantage over those who do not. _____

3. For most professions, there is only one major that can prepare a student for an entry-level job. _____

4. Liberal arts majors such as English, psychology, and philosophy do not prepare students for professional careers. _____

5. Changing career plans require a change in major. _____

6. Most technology employers are not interested in skills like speaking and writing when they make hiring decisions. _____

7. Newspaper advertisements are the primary source for finding jobs. _____

8. If you interview well, you do not have to be as concerned with the appearance and format of your résumé. _____

9. You should join as many clubs and organizations as you can, even if you do not attend any meetings or plan to be actively involved. _____

10. Volunteer experience and service are never as valuable as a paid job in terms of your professional and career development. _____

The answer to all of the above is … false! Each of these statements addresses the many myths behind preparing for the world after school.

THE ACADEMIC CURRICULUM AND YOUR CAREER SEARCH

Career Fact
The average student changes his or her career choice or major at least once.

Selecting a Program That Fits You

You may already have chosen a program of study. However, circumstances may change, or you may change your mind. You need to consider the following issues in selecting or changing your program

- Why did you select your current program?
- Who, if anyone, influenced your choice?
- What do you know about the program and the opportunities in it?

No matter what your program, you may need to take courses in a number of areas. Requirements typically involve developing and demonstrating skills in writing and mathematics as well as knowledge in humanities, social sciences, and natural sciences.

Many students choose programs without knowing much about them. This chapter will give you the tools you need to make informed decisions about your academic and career options, starting with Exercise 9-2.

EXERCISE 9-2
If I Had a Million Dollars . . .

If you were independently wealthy and could study anything, what would it be? For this activity, do not be concerned about constraints such as what programs your institution offers, what others think, and the needs of other people such as parents, spouse, and children. This exercise is purely hypothetical, so be as imaginative and impractical as you would like to be.

Now that you've answered the question, do some homework. Go to the U.S. Bureau of Labor Statistics (2006) Occupational Outlook Handbook at www.bls.gov. There is a search box on every page. Search for your dream career. (Please note that you might have to change the wording slightly. If you type English literature, you will not find any results. You will, however, find several results for English and for literature.)

Let's use art history as an example. If you search art history, you will find links on the following:

1. Archivists, curators, and museum technicians

2. Graphic designers

3. Advertising, marketing, promotions, public relations, and sales managers

4. Artists and related workers

If you chose health careers, you will be amazed at the numbers of professions in addition to nurses and doctors. There are more than 80 allied health professions alone. Some of the results of your search might not interest you, but others likely will. Write the search items that are either interesting or pleasantly surprising to you:

_____

_____

_____

_____

Let's go back to our art history example and look at the third item on advertising, public relations, and related careers. You will see links to the following:

Nature of the Work

Working Conditions

Training, Other Qualifications, and Advancement

Fmployment

Job Outlook

Earnings

Related Occupations

Sources of Additional Information

Now it's your turn to explore. Go to the Occupational Outlook Handbook at www.bls.gov. Complete this exercise by researching a career path that looks interesting to you. Summarize the key points under each heading:

Nature of the Work: _____

_____

_____

Working Conditions: _____

_____

_____

Training, Other Qualifications, and Advancement: _____

_____

_____

Employment: _____

_____

_____

Job Outlook: _____

_____

_____

Earnings: _____

_____

Related Occupations: _____

_____

Sources of Additional Information: _____

_____

_____

Matching Your Skills

Achieving career success requires you to demonstrate certain skills. These skills can come from courses within your program of study, but oftentimes outside courses (and soon, we will find, experiences) will greatly enhance your marketability. For example, students interested in business careers will do what seems to be obvious and take business accounting and marketing classes. However, many of these students would benefit from liberal arts courses that might teach them a second language, help them to write and communicate more effectively, or give them an international view of the world.

To illustrate the importance of assessing and developing skills for the workplace, the U.S. Department of Labor (1991) identified the skills needed for career success in the *Secretary's Commission on Achieving Necessary Skills*, or SCANS report.

This government document can be distilled to the workplace competencies and foundation skills that *any* worker needs to be successful in the rapidly evolving workplace. Many of these skill areas are covered in this book and CD.

SCANS Workplace Competencies

According to the SCANS report, effective workers can productively use:

Resources: They know how to allocate time, money, materials, space, and staff.

Interpersonal skills: They can work on teams, teach others, serve customers, lead, negotiate, and work well with people from culturally diverse backgrounds.

Information: They can acquire and evaluate data, organize and maintain files, interpret and communicate, and use computers to process information.

Systems: They understand social, organizational, and technological systems; they can monitor and correct performance; they also can design or improve systems.

Technology: They can select equipment and tools, apply technology to specific tasks, and maintain and troubleshoot equipment.

SCANS Foundation Skills

Competent workers in the high-performance workplace need:

Basic skills: Reading, writing, mathematics, speaking, and listening.

Thinking skills: The ability to learn, to reason, to think creatively, to make decisions, and to solve problems.

Personal qualities: Individual responsibility, self-esteem and self-management, sociability, and integrity.

These are the skills that many employers want to see, and many programs can help you to develop these skills. This is one reason, among many, for general education courses in addition to technical and professional training. Experience in a breadth of areas contributes to being a well-rounded and educated person, but it can also make you more employable. Do Exercise 9-3 now.

For each of the SCANS areas listed, fill out the table as instructed.

**EXERCISE 9-3
How Can You and Your Program Develop Your Skills?**

Academic: What curricular opportunities (i.e., classes) does your institution provide to help in the development of each skill? Which classes are you taking or do you plan to take (as electives or requirements) that will address this area?

Cocurricular: What involvements does your campus offer that will help you to develop this skill?

Extracurricular: What activities outside of the campus afford opportunities to develop each skill?

The first row is filled out as an example, although you can feel free to add your own ideas. Complete the rest of the chart on page 182 on your own or with a classmate.

SCANS Skills	Academic	Cocurricular	Extracurricular
Using resources	*Courses that involve research, such as writing and library science.*	*Holding an office in a club or organization.*	*A part-time job. A volunteer project in the community.*
Interpersonal skills			
Information			
Systems			
Technology			
Basic Skills: Reading			
Basic Skills: Writing			
Basic Skills: Mathematics and quantitative reasoning			
Basic Skills: Speaking and listening			
Thinking Skills: Learning and reasoning			
Thinking Skills: Creativity			
Thinking Skills: Decision making and problem solving			
Personal Qualities: Responsibility			
Personal Qualities: Self-esteem and self-management			

Personal Qualities: Sociability			
Personal Qualities: Integrity			

You now have an idea of how your skill sets will develop as you continue your education. Did you have any areas that were difficult to fill in? These might require additional attention.

What Experiences Can Help My Career?

Although grades are certainly important, they are just one ingredient in the mix. Things you do while in school (cocurricular activities) will tell a potential employer a great deal about who you are and what you can do. These experiences will also show the employer how well you work with others, a major consideration in hiring.

Consider these two students, who are about to begin a job search upon graduation. Both are seeking entry-level jobs in business management.

Jane is a psychology major with a 2.8 grade point average. She struggled during her first year, but her grades have averaged B or B+ during the last three years of college. Because she has to pay for part of her education with a part-time job, she maintains a work study job in the campus library. In addition to her job, she has also gotten involved in some campus organizations, particularly SIFE (Students Involved in Free Enterprise) but also her residence hall governing council and Circle K, a community service organization. She became president of Circle K during her junior year, and in each organization she has attended personal and professional development programs as well as participated in community service projects. Given the demands of coursework and keeping a job, Jane has to limit her cocurricular involvements somewhat, but she makes the most of the organizations in which she is a member.

Bill is a business administration major and a successful one at that. With the exception of one semester, he has earned dean's list honors each term by achieving a minimum grade point average of 3.3. He always maintains a part-time job, usually working in food service or retail. He has declined invitations to join organizations such as the math club, Habitat for Humanity, and student government, citing his need to study and to maintain his strong grades. His efforts have paid off with his grades, which include A+ in marketing research, human resource management, and business information systems.

Answer the following questions:

1. Which student has the stronger academic record?
2. Which student is more marketable in terms of employment?
3. Each student has identifiable strengths. What are they?
4. Each student has identifiable weaknesses. What are they?

Both students will enter the job market with strengths and with liabilities, just like anyone searching for a job. Good arguments could be made for either student having an advantage in the job market, but the edge ultimately goes to Jane. Her grades are not

Fact

Students who work on campus rather than off campus report greater satisfaction with their school experience.

quite as good as Bill's, it's true. However, she has done something Bill has not: She has learned from every facet of the college experience, in and out of the classroom. Refer back to the SCANS list. Jane has more relevant experiences in each of these areas than Bill.

Soon you will see sample résumés for Jane and Bill. Both can structure their résumés and cover letters to highlight their strengths, which is what you will need to do. Exercises 9-4 and 9-5 will help you get started.

**EXERCISE 9-4
Develop a Plan**

Juanita is about to begin an 18-month program to become a respiratory thera-pist. She has one child and wants to secure employment at a local hospital upon graduation so her parents can continue to help her raise her child. However, the local hospital typically only has one or two openings per year, and the class size averages 15 to 20, with many wanting to remain in the area. What can Juanita do, beyond getting good grades, to maximize her chances of being chosen for the position? List one specific cocurricular and one specific extracurricular activity that will help her.

Cocurricular activity _____

_____

_____

Extracurricular activity _____

_____

_____

_____

**EXERCISE 9-5
Opportunities on
Your Campus**

For information on your curriculum, you can refer to your student catalog, which lists course descriptions, academic policies, and academic program requirements. For cocurricular options, you should have access to similar documents, including a student handbook.

Get a copy of your student handbook (or find it on your school's website, if a hard copy is not available).

Identify the names of clubs and organizations that are relevant to your major or career interests:

_____

_____

_____

Identify the names of clubs and organizations that are relevant to your personal interests:

_____

_____

_____

Follow-up: Contact an officer or faculty adviser of one organization. Most clubs and organizations meet regularly, so schedule a time to attend the next meeting. Find out the following: Who are the student officers? Who is the faculty or staff adviser? What are some upcoming projects the group has for the year? Does the organization do any service projects? If so, where? How can you get involved in this organization? This involvement will give you something substantial to add to your experience and will help you to network in an area related to your future career.

Internships or Service Learning Experiences

Mark Twain once said, "People who grab a cat by the tail know 45% more about cats than people who do not." You learn from your experiences, both good and bad. One of the best experiences can be in the form of internships, service learning, or clinical experience. In these situations, you learn by actually doing and getting a taste of the working world while still in school. The benefits to these kinds of experiences include:

- Applying classroom learning
- Experiencing challenging assignments and duties
- Getting an edge in the job market
- Improving communication skills
- Establishing a work routine
- Enhancing critical and creative thinking
- Improving teamwork and time management skills
- Clarifying your career direction

Internships and service provide a chance to learn from your experiences before you enter the work world. You

Job Search Fact

Newspaper advertisements are one way to learn about job vacancies, but most job searchers find employment through networking and word of mouth. Begin developing your network by meeting people through campus involvements and service in addition to part-time work.

will sharpen your skills and ensure that when you officially begin your career, your first impression will be a positive and lasting one.

BEGINNING THE JOB SEARCH: YOUR RÉSUMÉ

It should be clear by now that your résumé is a work in progress, and it should continue to evolve as you do. It is best to have a résumé written when you begin your program and to update it as you progress through your program.

Your first point of contact for obtaining a job is to present your qualifications in writing. Interviewing is very important, but you will not get to an interview if your written presentation isn't appealing to a potential employer.

A résumé details the qualifications you can offer a potential employer. Because it is often the first screening tool for potential applicants, your résumé should be complete, neat, and error free. This shows you have taken pride in preparing the résumé and, therefore, are likely to take pride in your future work.

You can use a number of formats, but the most commonly used are chronological and functional résumés. **Chronological résumés,** the most frequently used, provide a listing of your experiences in order, with the most recent listed first. **Functional résumés** focus on skill sets and qualifications more than actual work experience, which can be beneficial for job applicants with limited experience.

Before deciding on a format, complete the following information, which you will use to write your résumé.

Education Level

Start with the most recent, and list your degree, field, and graduation date along with the institution you attended. Here's an example:

> *Bachelor of Science in Nursing, Superior University*
>
> *Anticipated Graduation Date: May 2008*
>
> *Associate Degree in Forensic Sciences, Superior Community College May 2002*

Write your own here: _____

Work Experience

List your jobs in chronological order, the most recent first. Include your job title, the organization that employed you, start and end dates, and responsibilities. Here's an example:

> *Cashier, JC Penney, 2004–present. Greeted customers. Balanced cash register. Assisted with annual inventory.*

Note: Use action verbs to begin each description of your responsibilities. Examples include "facilitate," "manage," "assist," "help," and "coordinate."

List your work experiences here, using action verbs to describe responsibilities:

_____

_____

_____

_____

Skills

List any knowledge, skills, and abilities you have that would be useful to an employer. Many students include their knowledge of computer software programs. Here's an example:

> *Proficient with MS Office; Knowledge of basic Web design.*

List your own here :_____

References

Most résumés end with the reference section. It is perfectly appropriate to write "available upon request," as you will see on the examples. Before your job search, though, be sure to ask current and past employers for permission to use their names as references, and make sure you have accurate contact information for each. It is good form to let them know in advance about jobs you are applying for so they can anticipate being called.

Take a look at the chronological résumés of our two students in the beginning of this chapter. See Figure 9-1 for the chronological résumé of Jane Smith.

Because Jane's cocurricular experiences are more extensive than her work experience, she highlights those involvements in a separate section.

Now, let's take a look at Bill Jones's chronological résumé in Figure 9-2.

Even though Bill has more work experience than Jane, his résumé is less detailed because Jane has so much more leadership experience to highlight. Bill might benefit from writing a functional rather than chronological résumé, which would highlight his knowledge and downplay his lack of experience. See Figure 9-3 for an example of Bill's functional résumé:

Note that although both students were creative in their organization, they do not exaggerate accomplishments. Their résumés share the following:

- Both are professionally written.
- Both highlight accomplishments and downplay deficits.
- Both use action verbs to describe accomplishments.
- Both are free of errors in grammar and punctuation.

In Exercise 9-6, it's your turn.

FIGURE 9-1

Chronological résumé of Jane Smith.

Jane E. Smith

Grove University
Campus Box #0001
Pittsburgh, PA 16901

Phone: (412)555-1111
Cell: (412) 555-0000
E-mail: jsmith@yahoo.com

Education

Grove University
Bachelor of Arts in Psychology
Anticipated Graduation Date: May 2007

Work Experience

Grove University Library
Circulation Assistant (2002–present)
Responsibilities: Assisted students, faculty, and staff with library requests. Maintained records for interlibrary loan requests. Mailed correspondence regarding overdue materials. Organized and shelved returned materials.

Jo's Diner
Table Server (2001–2002)
Responsibilities: Served customers during dinner. Helped greeters during peak hours.

Leadership Experience

President, Circle K (2005–present)
Achievements: Inaugurated annual fundraising drive for Juvenile Diabetes Association. Increased membership by 20 percent. Increased programming budget. Participated in monthly service projects, including delivering gifts to the local senior center and raising funds for charity clothing drive.

Member, Students Involved for Free Enterprise (2004–present)
Achievements: Developed marketing plan for locally owned drugstore. Presented plan at the annual SIFE conference.

Representative, Grove University Residence Hall Council (2003)
Responsibilities: Attended monthly hall council meetings. Reported on building programs and events. Discussed maintenance and facility issues. Met weekly with residence hall director to discuss resident complaints and suggestions.

Skills

Fluent in Spanish
Computer skills: MS Office, Web Design

References

Available upon request

FIGURE 9-2

Bill Jones's chronological résumé.

Bill A. Jones

Grove University
Campus Box 9999
Pittsburgh, PA 41290

Phone: (412) 555-1234
Cell: (412) 555-8989
E-mail: bjones@yahoo.com

Education

Grove University
Bachelor of Science in Business Administration
Anticipated Graduation Date: May 2008

Work Experience

Ward Clothing and Retail
Sales Clerk (2005–present)
Responsibilities: Waited on customers in men's-wear department. Balanced cash register at the end of each shift. Assisted with annual inventory.

Pizza Place
Waiter (2004–2005)
Responsibilities: Waited on customers during evening shift. Assisted with cleaning tables and closing restaurant. Responsible for night deposits for evening earnings.

Burger Palace
Customer Service (2002–2004)
Responsibilities: Waited on customers at fast-food restaurant. Supervised drive-through station. Coordinated staff schedule on weekends.

Skills

Computer: MS Office, Visual Basic, Web Design

References

Available upon request

FIGURE 9-3

Bill Jones's functional résumé.

Bill A. Jones

Grove University
Campus Box 9999
Pittsburgh, PA 41290

Phone: (412) 555-1234
Cell: (412)555-8989
E-mail: bjones@yahoo.com

Objective: To obtain an entry-level position in business management

Education

Grove University
Bachelor of Science in Business Administration
Anticipated Graduation Date: May 2008
Dean's List honors, 2006–2008

Course Work Highlights

Microcomputer Applications
Marketing Research
Human Resource Management
Current Issues in Management
Business Law

Skills and Abilities

Presentation and Communication Skills

- Participated in group presentations on diverse issues, including diversity in the workplace, technology education.
- Led presentation on marketing plan for a local company as part of marketing research methods course.
- Interviewed applicants for positions at local restaurant.
- Addressed customer complaints professionally and punctually.

Technology

- Proficient in MS Office, including PowerPoint.
- Experience in developing and maintaining Excel and Access databases.

Research

- Assisted management professor in gathering articles for research.
- Conducted focus groups for faculty member's research project, "Millennials' Perceptions of the Management Landscape."

Work History

Ward Clothing and Retail
Sales Clerk (2005–present)

Pizza Place
Waiter (2004–2005)

Burger Palace
Customer Service (2002–2004)

References

Available upon request

Using the information in this section, construct your own résumé. Give it to two trusted people to read and evaluate. Then revise your finished copy and update it as you go through your program.

EXERCISE 9-6
Writing Your Résumé

WRITING COVER LETTERS

Your résumé is a critical document in your job search. To get an employer to read your résumé, though, you must also write a good cover letter. One of the secrets to a good cover letter is to focus less on why *you* want the job and focus on explaining why the *company* should want you *in* the job. To that end, avoid statements like the following:

> *I would really like to work for your organization because I think it would be a great move for my career.*

Even the most caring employer will be more interested in knowing what you can provide the company as opposed to what the company can do for your advancement. Instead, try a statement like this:

> *My education and experience provide the qualifications your company needs in its next accounts manager.*

> ### Helpful Hint
>
> A number of websites provide templates for entry-level résumés. You can use one of those templates to design your résumé, which may save you time with formatting and organizing. If you use MS Office, see www.office.microsoft.com for examples, including both chronological and functional formats.

Tips for Writing a Cover Letter

Professionalism: Create letterhead to make the letter attractive and professional looking.

Organization: Remember what we discussed in Chapter 7 ("Communication in Action") about thesis statements and topic sentences. Your introduction should explain why you are writing and should include a thesis. Your thesis: Explain why you are qualified for this position.

> *I am writing in regard to the second-grade teacher vacancy in the Cornfield school district (as advertised in the New York Times on 7 September 2007). My work experience and educational background have given me the skills needed for this position.*

Topic sentences: Each paragraph should provide a different reason to persuade your reader to give you an interview. For example, introduce yourself in the first paragraph. In the second paragraph, explain how your work experience provides you with qualifications. If your work experience is limited, focus on cocurricular achievements. In the third paragraph, perhaps you can highlight your educational achievements and how some of the course work you have taken applies to the position.

> *I earned my undergraduate degree and teaching certificate at Grove University, where I majored in secondary education/English with additional certification in elementary literacy and reading. In my course work, I learned the history and most recent theory about whole-language and phonetics approaches, using my knowledge to develop my own philosophy of language arts education.*
>
> *My experience in the classroom was very much influenced by my work and volunteer experience in the local school system. I applied my learning to practical situations as a classroom assistant at Grove City Elementary School before beginning my practicum and student teaching assignments at the same school. Although most of my classroom experience was with third-grade students, I have been working since then as an after-school tutor for students in all grades. This breadth of experience has prepared me to work with students at a number of grade levels.*

Note that each paragraph focuses on a different facet of the student's qualifications: first, her academic background, and second, her experience.

Your closing paragraph is very important. Here, you want to thank the reader for considering your application, express your availability for an interview, and remind the reader how to contact you.

> *My academic transcript and résumé (both enclosed for your review) attest to my qualifications for the second-grade teacher vacancy in your school district. I would be happy to discuss my qualifications in person at any time. If you would like additional information about my application, feel free to contact me at (555) 555-1111. Thank you for considering my application.*

Conciseness: When applying for an entry-level position, your cover letter should be no more than one page long. Cut to the chase!

Focus on the reader: It's not all about you. Focus on the employer's needs rather than your own, using the pronoun "you" over "I" whenever possible. For example, "If you would like additional information . . ." "Thank you for considering my application . . ." "You will find my credentials to be worthy of review."

Of course, the cover letter should be neat, error free, positive, and professional looking. The cover letter and your résumé will get you to the next step: the interview. You may also be asked to fill out an application at your interview, so it is a good idea to bring a copy of your résumé to help you provide accurate and complete information. In addition, this level of preparation will show how organized and responsible you are.

THE INTERVIEW

Your written materials (cover letter and résumé) are designed to get you an interview. Now you will be evaluated face to face on your interpersonal skills and professionalism. The following qualities are critical.

The Three P's: Punctuality, Professionalism, and Preparation

You've heard the saying, "You never get a second chance to make a great first impression." If you are late for your interview, the interviewer will notice. Anticipate any obstacles, such as traffic or child-care arrangements, and make sure you have a contingency plan.

Your personal appearance is important in making that first impression. Make sure you are dressed in appropriate business attire. Avoid colognes and perfumes in case someone on the search committee has allergies. If you carry a cell phone, make sure it is off during your interview.

Research the company and organization. At minimum, be familiar with their Web page. If the company has a mission statement, be prepared to discuss how you fit in with their philosophy. Make sure you are aware of the organizational structure and how you might fit into it.

Interview Questions

The following are typical interview questions you should be prepared to answer:

- Tell us about yourself.
- What assets would you bring to this position if we were to hire you?
- What are your strengths?
- What are your weaknesses?
- Where do you see yourself five years from now? Ten years from now?
- What types of work situations do you enjoy?
- What types of work situations do you find frustrating? How do you handle them?

This list is not all inclusive. Remember, most schools have a Career Services office with staff who can help you prepare by doing mock interviews.

Your Own Interview Questions for the Interviewer:

- What opportunities does your organization provide for professional development?
- What qualities are you looking for in the next (name of position)?
- What is the best thing about working for this organization?
- Does your organization provide any type of tuition assistance for further education?
- How do you measure and reward high-quality and excellent performance?
- Would it be possible to talk with some of your employees currently working in this or a similar position?

Other Interview Tips:

- Treat everyone with respect and courtesy during the interview process. Others, such as the receptionist in the waiting area, may be asked their opinion.
- Be friendly and open. Greet everyone you meet with good eye contact, firm handshake, and positive facial expressions.

> *"Interview fact from a contributing author: Be yourself, be confident, and remember you are the competition."*
> —Doug Reed

- Don't criticize past employers.
- Follow up after the interview with a brief thank you letter for their time and consideration.
- Go on many interviews to get practice. Try Exercise 9-7, a mock interview.

EXERCISE 9-7
Mock Interview

Position Announcement

The information desk at the campus center has a vacancy for a student worker. The position requires a working knowledge of campus office functions and locations, the ability to multitask, and strong customer service skills. Résumés and cover letters can be submitted to the Student Life Office, and interviews will be scheduled within the next two weeks.

With another student, conduct a mock interview with each of you taking turns as the interviewer and the applicant. Prepare a list of questions or use the ones listed earlier. Evaluate each other on the following:

Quality of answers: _____

_____

Quality of appearance: _____

_____

Communication skills: _____

_____

Job knowledge: _____

_____

Suggestion for improvement: _____

_____

Web Resources That Can Help Career Exploration and Assessment

Strong Interest Inventory: Self-assessment available at the publisher's website, www.cpp-db.com/products/strong. You can also see if your career services office or personal counseling center offers this inventory, which asks questions about course work preferences, work preferences, and personality traits to determine possible career paths to research.

Keirsey Temperament Sorter: This assessment can be taken at www.keirsey.com. It measures personality traits, which can be helpful before beginning a job search. Click on the link to Keirsey Temperament Sorter II, register, and take the assessment.

The Occupational Outlook Handbook: Published annually by the U.S. Department of Labor, this resource provides an overview of many occupations, including majors and educational preparation for those occupations. In addition, the handbook projects the job outlook for different fields. The handbook can be accessed online at www.bls.gov/oco. Many libraries carry hard copies as well.

CHANGING COURSE (NOT REALLY): DEVELOPING YOUR LEADERSHIP POTENTIAL

As you near the end of your journey through this text and CD, you have the skills not only to succeed in your chosen profession but to emerge as a leader. More and more, employers are looking for leadership potential in the people they hire. This project has already helped you with the first steps in leadership development by helping you learn more about yourself. Let's begin with Exercise 9-8, a simple Internet exercise.

Choose your favorite search engine, such as Google (www.google.com), and enter the word "Leadership."

How many results did you receive?

_____

The author got 877 million sites —wow!

Now search for "Leadership Development + Books."
How many results did you get?

_____

Identifying Leaders and Their Characteristics

Interestingly, just about everyone has written something about the subject of leadership, as evidenced by Exercise 9-8. Here, though, we ask you to reflect on your thoughts and experiences to formulate your own understanding of leadership. Then we consider a basic definition or description and ask the one fundamental question: Do *you have* what it takes to be a leader?

One of the best methods to learn about any subject is to study examples. Leaders serve as excellent role models, or examples, for us to investigate questions such as Who are effective leaders? What characteristics or traits do they possess that make them successful? Let's see what you think by completing Exercise 9-9.

EXERCISE 9-9
What Makes a
Leader?

Complete the chart by:

1. Listing people you believe are outstanding leaders in their respective fields. You may select two or three from each area.

2. Listing specific characteristics they possess that make them successful.

Name	Field or Profession	Characteristics		
	Sports			
1.		1.	2.	3.
2.		1.	2.	3.
3.		1.	2.	3.
	Business			
1.		1.	2.	3.
2.		1.	2.	3.
3.		1.	2.	3.
	Government			
1.		1.	2.	3.
2.		1.	2.	3.
3.		1.	2.	3.
	Historical Figure			
1.		1.	2.	3.
2.		1.	2.	3.
3.		1.	2.	3.
	Entertainment			
1.		1.	2.	3.
2.		1.	2.	3.
3.		1.	2.	3.

	Religion			
1.		1.	2.	3.
2.		1.	2.	3.
3.		1.	2.	3.
	Family			
1.		1.	2.	3.
2.		1.	2.	3.
3.		1.	2.	3.
	Educator			
1.		1.	2.	3.
2.		1.	2.	3.
3.		1.	2.	3.
	You Pick a Field			
1.		1.	2.	3.
2.		1.	2.	3.
3.		1.	2.	3.

With a group of friends or as an entire class, prepare a list of the most frequently selected leaders. Generate a chart of the top choices. Discuss among your team or class what makes these leaders special. Make a list of the common characteristics shared by your top choices. Perhaps a top-10 list would be appropriate. Now in Exercise 9-10, create your own list.

From the collective list of leaders and their characteristics, create your own list of the most important characteristics of a leader.

1. _____

2. _____

3. _____

4. _____

5. _____

EXERCISE 9-10
Self-Discovery: Your Characteristics of a Leader

Now you have each built your own definition of a leader.

Key Ingredients of Effective Leaders

Look at the key ingredients of effective leadership and develop a guide to personal and professional success. Remember our metaphor of teamwork where the magnifying glass with pinpoint focus could bring on the fire? A leader is that individual who can unite and ignite us.

Some people see leaders as superheroes: Most valuable player/person, Academy Award winner, Gold Medal winner, Congressional Medal of Honor recipient, and so on. But think about the fact that each of us leads our own personal growth and professional careers by our daily actions, goals we strive to achieve, the teams we join, and the sum total of our choices and decisions.

In effect, we are all potential leaders. We must embrace those characteristics we identified in Exercise 9-10 as our own. Let's look to those leaders we respect as our guides, role models, and coaches for the rich valuable examples they are. The modeling of our own behavior to match those characteristics of our leader's list is a great place to start our own leadership development.

What Do Leaders *HAVE* That Make Them Leaders?

Often people say leaders are born that way. "Who, me?" "No! I just don't *have* what it takes to be a leader." The authors feel you *all* have what it takes; you just need to rise to your full potential.

Let's look at four primary ingredients to developing our individual leadership potential. We know that leaders *have* something different and special.

HAVE Leadership?   *H*eart   *A*ttitude   *V*ision   *E*nergy

Heart

One thing that we all share is the desire to be recognized and appreciated when we do something well. This sense of accomplishment, followed with recognition, is a key to our motivation. As leaders, we need to build relationships and demonstrate that we care and want others to succeed. Sincerity and recognition of work done well provides encouraging heartfelt feedback.

All leaders must earn the respect and trust of the people they choose to lead. We know when someone is leading from the heart. These leaders are the ones who bring hope and possibility.

How can you be a caring leader to others if you struggle with your own self-esteem? Leadership is largely about self-development. Let's do a brief self-esteem exercise, Exercise 9-11, to prepare us to become the leaders we can be.

EXERCISE 9-11
Analyzing Yourself

To answer the following questions, identify the last time you were part of a team at home, work, or school: _____

1. Were you fully involved and energized in your activities with others?

2. Did you frequently review your own actions and work? Did you develop a plan on how to improve?

3. Did you accept responsibility for your actions and choices?

4. Did you speak up for yourself and your beliefs?

5. Did you set goals and monitor your progress?

6. Did you do what you said you were going to do?

If you said "no" to any of these questions, then you have identified some areas for improvement. Effective leaders always strive for improvement. Perhaps a brief positive statement about those *no* areas can be written to capture your feelings about what and how to improve. Perhaps a frank discussion with someone you respect and admire can bring some suggestions to strengthen those identified areas. Solid self-esteem is a critical element of effective leaders.

Attitude

Ever hear the expression, "Oh, she or he has an attitude!" What attitude do you project? Simply put, attitudes really come in two types: positive and negative. We pretty much pick an attitude and run with it each day. (An interesting question: Because each of us has two choices, why would anyone want to pick the negative one?)

One characteristic of attitudes, both positive and negative, is their contagious nature. A negative attitude can tear down a team, and a positive attitude can lift up a team. A leader must embrace a positive attitude, providing hope and promise to his or her followers. We all know individuals who exude a positive attitude and possess a bright outlook on life. They are much more fun to be around, in both work and play, and help contribute to a more productive work environment.

Leaders must set the tone for the task at hand. Embracing a "Can-Do Attitude" gives the team hope and the sense of reaching its potential. Leaders must light the way with a positive attitude. Explore the power of attitude in Exercise 9-12.

Write down an experience in which keeping a positive attitude produced a positive outcome:

EXERCISE 9-12
Power of a Positive Attitude

_____

_____

_____

_____

_____

_____

Vision

When we think of vision, we think literally of our ability to see an object. But when leaders have vision, we are in a totally different mindset. Vision could be defined as a combination or a collection of goals that create a greater, more complex result. More simply stated, *Leaders are individuals who have a vision and energize themselves and others to make that vision become a reality.*

One description of a leader is the person you could follow to a place you wouldn't go by yourself. To reinforce this description, let's look at Martin Luther King, Jr.'s famous 1963 speech, which painted a vision of a dream that led to a destination.

I say to you today, my friends, that in spite of the difficulties and frustrations of the moment I still have a dream. It is a dream deeply rooted in the American dream. . . .Free at last!

Martin Luther King's speech that afternoon painted a vivid image, or vision, of a destination that inspired others to want to arrive at that destination. Write about your personal vision in Exercise 9-13.

**EXERCISE 9-13
Visioning Exercise**

What is your personal vision for your life during the next five years? You can include any categories, including family, career, education, spiritual, financial, personal, anything and everything you can think of:

_____

_____

_____

_____

_____

MAP out a plan: What actions must you take between now and then to accomplish your vision?

1. _____

2. _____

3. _____

Remember: Vision with action can change the world ... and your future as well.

Energy

A leader needs to motivate self and others to fulfill objectives, reach goals, achieve purposes and, ultimately, realize a vision. Motivation is all about creating desired movement and overcoming inertia. The engine that drives this movement requires fuel to produce energy. The fuel is energy, or enthusiasm. Ralph Waldo Emerson's statement, "Nothing great was ever accomplished without enthusiasm," holds true today.

A leader must be energized and be able to energize others, which provides the fuel necessary to fill up the tank. (The greatest advantage of this energy is that there are no rising costs and no immediate shortages!). In Exercise 9-14, describe where you get *your* energy.

**EXERCISE 9-14
Where Do You Reach
for the Energy
Necessary?**

Think of a time when you had to complete a major project (at school, home, or work), and you needed a significant amount of energy to bring the project to completion. Describe how you got your energy.

_____

_____

_____

SUMMATION EXERCISE 9-15: BASICS OF LEADERSHIP

A fitting last exercise gets right to the heart of leadership and even life. Explain in your own terms what the following quote means to you: "The best way to lead is by example."

_____

_____

_____

_____

Remember, when you secure that great job, your work has just begun. It is important to make positive and lasting impressions by demonstrating that you have commitment to your work. In addition, you need to show dependability, interpersonal skills, leadership, and team skills—along with a desire for continuous improvement.

HEALTHY DECISION MAKING

Robert's résumé and cover letter have secured him an interview with a company he knows little about but has heard is a great place to work. The position seems like it is a perfect fit. He knows the competition is tough but feels if he presents himself well at his interview, he has a good chance of getting the job. What steps can Robert take to ensure he performs at his best during the interview process?

_____

_____

_____

_____

Now that you have read this chapter and performed the assessments and exercises, please go to your CD to reinforce these concepts. The CD will present you with more information concerning job-seeking skills.

References

U.S. Bureau of Labor Statistics. (2006). *Occupational outlook handbook, 2006-07 edition.* Retrieved April 23, 2007, from www.bls.gov/oco/

U.S. Department of Labor. (1991). The secretary's commission on achieving necessary skills. Retrieved from http://wdr.doleta.gov/SCANS/

Enhancing Your Personal Health

Take Care of Yourself Along the Journey

OBJECTIVES

What you will discover by the end of this chapter:

- How to develop a personal fitness plan for your body, mind, and spirit
- Healthy eating and sleeping habits
- Disease prevention or how not to be sick for that big test
- Understanding depression
- Understanding and preventing addiction

WHY LEARN THIS SKILL?

The journey through this textbook began with a focus on you and then discussed your interactions with others. We conclude this journey by bringing the focus again back to you. The three elements you will carry throughout your journey in life, no matter where you go, are your body, mind, and spirit. This chapter discusses these areas.

We've all been inundated with messages about health and wellness. In terms of physical health alone, the contradictory messages are overwhelming: Eat carbohydrates and avoid fats! No, wait—do the opposite! Strength training versus aerobic exercise: Which is more important? One consistent message in recent years is the need to avoid substance abuse, but for those with addictions to illegal drugs (heroin, cocaine, marijuana) and legal drugs (nicotine and caffeine), it's "easier said than done."

One of the most important personal choices you will ever make will be the decision about what kind of lifestyle you want to live. Choices you make now will have a *profound* effect on your future health and quality of life. Will you eat properly and exercise? Will you get enough sleep to recharge your body? Will you avoid doing illegal drugs, smoking, and drinking alcohol in excess? Will you avoid risky behaviors that can have serious consequences? These are *your* choices; what you choose will greatly impact your health, wealth, and success in life.

Let's begin with the effects of peer pressure. We often talk about peer pressure as a negative influence, but what about peers and role models who promote good, healthy lifestyles? Think about it. Do you know people or have friends who make healthy decisions? It is a conscious choice to surround yourself with the type of people who model positive choices.

Individual accountability and *informed choices* are two key concepts in deciding your lifestyle. To make good choices you need to be adequately informed. This chapter provides a foundation of information concerning your overall health. Over your lifetime, you will be bombarded with health information from many sources. Just look at the number of "miracle diets" and "miracle pills" on TV and the Internet. Read—and analyze what you read. Utilize multiple *reliable* sources. Even though the Internet is a wonderful source of information, it includes a lot of junk science that contains more opinion than fact. Also, be very careful and skeptical of those jazzy TV commercials with fine print you can never read.

(Please note: None of the information in this chapter is meant to substitute for medical advice. Consult with your physician or health care provider about any changes.)

If you have ever been seriously ill, you know that without your health, nothing seems to matter except getting better. When you hear the word *health*, you may connect it merely to avoiding illness. However, there is so much more to it. The term *wellness* is more encompassing. To achieve overall wellness, we come back to common themes found in this textbook. The first theme is the powerful connection between the mind and body; physical and mental wellness must be addressed together. Second is maintaining balance and moderation in life. Ben Franklin, an accomplished statesman, scientist, writer, and philosopher, believed that the key to a happy, successful life is balance and moderation.

Although there are many conflicting beliefs about wellness, we have chosen the commonly held beliefs that have stood the test of time: the "back to basics" approach that always seems to work. In this chapter, you will read some background information for each topic, which is followed by key points to take home for the future. With each topic, we ask you to commit to *one* change that will help you to create a healthier life, no matter where you stand right now. Let's get started with the basic health issues, so you can make the best choices.

PHYSICAL AND MENTAL WELLNESS

Several lifestyle factors affect our physical and mental wellness. These include how we nourish and exercise our bodies, our quality of sleep, steps we take to prevent disease, and behaviors we choose. We explore each of these areas separately, but they are all connected.

Nutrition

First assess your nutritional habits in Exercise 10-1.

**EXERCISE 10-1
Evaluate Your
Current Nutritional
Practices**

Answer the questions using the following point scale:

3 points = daily

2 points = 3 — 5 days per week

1 point = 1 — 2 days a week

0 points = less than 1 — 2 days a week

_____I eat several servings of fresh fruits and vegetables.

_____I drink 6 to 8 glasses of water every day.

_____I eat a variety of foods.

_____I eat sweets and high-cholesterol foods sparingly.

_____I make sure my diet includes essential vitamins and minerals.

_____I eat a diet low in saturated fats and cholesterol.

_____I only eat when I'm hungry not when I feel the emotional need to eat.

_____I eat to maintain a healthy weight.

_____Point total

Where did you score?

24 points:	You have excellent nutritional habits.
20–23 points:	You have good habits but could improve.
16–19 points:	You are doing okay but could improve.
Below 15 points:	You have poor nutritional habits that are greatly affecting your health.

Basic Nutritional Concepts

You would not want to put bad gas, with dirt and other contaminants, in your car. Your car would run poorly or break down. The same can be said for our bodies. Food provides the nutrients, or fuel, our bodies need for energy and growth.

The three basic types of food are proteins, carbohydrates, and fats. *Protein*, found in meat, fish, eggs, some nuts, and dairy products, is needed for growth and repair of our bodies.

Carbohydrates, found in grain products, fruits, and vegetables, provide our primary sources of energy. Some carbohydrates contain fiber, which helps digestion. *Fats,* found in meat, nuts, oils, and dairy products, are needed for energy storage, insulation, some vitamin absorption, and proper immune system function. Fats are either saturated (solid at room temperature such as butter) or unsaturated (liquid at room temperature such as corn and vegetable oil).

The foods we eat have traditionally been broken down into the five food groups shown in Table 10-1.

> ## Erroneous Fact
>
> It is a common misconception that fat is bad for you. This is not true. Our bodies need all three food types: carbohydrates, proteins, *and* fats. Again, the key is maintaining the proper balance and eating the right types of food.

At some time in our lives, we have seen a version of the traditional food pyramid, which told us what portion of our diet should be dairy, what portion of our diet should be vegetables, and so forth. One problem with this pyramid was that it was designed to fit *everyone*. However,

TABLE 10-1
The Five Basic Food Groups

Food Group	Example of Foods	Nutritional Note
Grains	Whole-grain bread, cereals, rice, pasta	Be careful of sweetened cereals and doughnuts, which contain grains but also high levels of sugar (which should be eaten sparingly in your diet).
Vegetables	Broccoli, carrots, corn, peas, spinach, lettuce	Fresh vegetables are better and are all very good for you. Canned vegetables lose most of their nutritional value and often have sugar, salt, or other additives. It is a good idea to wash all vegetables and fruits to remove any potentially harmful residue.
Fruits	Apples, peaches, pears, oranges	Fresh fruit is again best because many canned fruits contain added sugar and much lower nutrient values.
Dairy	Milk, ice cream, cheese, yogurt	Skim and 1% milk and nonfat yogurt have the least fat. Whole milk, ice cream, and cheese have a higher fat content.
Meat, poultry, fish, eggs, beans, and nuts	Turkey, beef, tuna, salmon, peanuts, walnuts	This group is high in protein and fat. However, fat can be trimmed on meat or reduced—for example, in canned tuna packed in water versus oil. (Also, watch for peanut allergies.)

not everyone is the same sex, height, shape, age, and level of activity. Go to the Internet and enter MyPyramid.gov. This site will show you the USDA's (U.S. Department of Agriculture 2005b) newest spin on the food pyramid, which now takes into account your age, sex, and activity level when determining the best diet for *you*. There is still some controversy surrounding the pyramid. Most research, however, still holds true to the following key concepts:

- Eat a balanced diet with a variety of foods.
- Eat several servings of fruits and vegetables (especially raw) per day.
- Eat fats in moderation *only*. Although you need fats, high levels of saturated fats can lead to higher levels of bad cholesterol, a fatty acid found in animal products that can contribute to obesity and heart disease. Cut down on fat (especially saturated) and cholesterol in your diet.
- Limit sweets in your diet. Sweets (sugar, jellies, candy, soft drinks) contain sugar that has a lot of empty calories and can lead to diabetes.
- Avoid or limit alcohol.
- Drink 6 to 8 glasses of water. Water is present in most foods and liquids. It is present in all our cells and needed to transport waste and nutrients, in addition to performing the countless chemical reactions going on in our bodies.

Vitamins and Minerals

Vitamins and minerals are trace (found in small amounts) nutrients, each of which has a specific job (USDA, 2005a "Inside the Pyramid"). Vitamins help perform specific functions in the body (see Table 10-2). Minerals like calcium are needed for strong bones and teeth. Calcium supplements may prevent osteoporosis, a disease that causes bones to become brittle. However, be careful and informed about supplements. Excessive dosages or megadoses of fat-soluble vitamins (A, D, E, and K) can actually harm the body because they can build up to toxic levels and harm the liver and kidneys.

So what are the key points about vitamins and minerals?

- Although you can take vitamin and mineral supplements, most studies still suggest it is best to get vitamins from natural sources—in other words, from eating a healthy, well-balanced diet.
- Most experts agree that natural food sources provide the best source of vitamins and minerals, but in some situations responsible use of supplemental vitamins and minerals can play an important role in your health. Stay informed, and consult your physician concerning nutritional supplements.

Healthy Skin Facts

Proper diet and hydration (fluid in your body) is important for healthy skin. This is another reason why it is important to drink *at least* 6 to 8 glasses of water a day. Other fluids, such as alcohol and caffeine, are actually diuretics and can cause a net water loss. Smoking also affects your skin by causing premature aging. Sun exposure is important for the production of vitamin D in your body, but limiting the amount of sun exposure to prevent skin cancer is equally important. Some forms of skin cancer are treatable; others can be lethal. The effect of the sun is cumulative, and severe sunburns as a child can have severe consequences in adulthood.

There are several ways to prevent excessive sun exposure. First, minimize your time in the sun between 10 A.M. and 4 P.M. because this is when the sun's rays are most intense. Wear long-sleeved shirts when possible, brimmed hats, sunglasses (preferably wraparounds), and, of course, use sunscreen properly. See Figure 10-1.

TABLE 10-2

Vitamins: Functions and Sources

Vitamin	Needed for	Examples of Food Containing This Vitamin
Vitamin A	Vision, development of bones and teeth, infection resistance, healthy skin	Meat, eggs, dairy, dark green and yellow vegetables, carrots and fruits (tomatoes)
Vitamin B (several types)	Healthy nervous system, energy, normal digestion	Whole-grain products, meats, poultry, vegetables
Vitamin C	Infection resistance, development of teeth and bone, wound healing	Citrus fruits, many raw fruits and vegetables
Vitamin D	Development of strong bones and teeth	Dairy products (also produced in skin on exposure to sunlight)
Vitamin E	Muscle growth, wound healing (may help fertility and prevent certain cancers)	Wheat germ, vegetables
Vitamin K	Needed for proper blood clotting	Green leafy vegetables

FIGURE 10-1

Skin cancer.

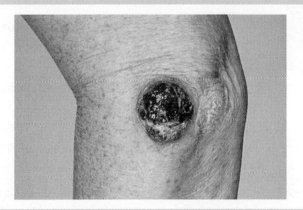

To view a video on skin cancer, please go to your CD for this chapter.

Now that you are informed, what changes would you make? Set a goal in Exercise 10-2.

**EXERCISE 10-2
MAP Out a Plan**

Changing your diet is difficult because much of it has become habit. From what you have read so far, pick *one* strategy to improve your diet, and write a specific goal. Remember to include a target date for successful attainment of your goal. Many behavioral psychologists feel you need to practice the new habit for at least 30 days for it to become a permanent change. When this *one* positive diet change becomes a way of life, pick another.

Positive Diet Change Goal:_____

_____

_____

_____

Exercise and Wellness

First, assess your status in Exercises 10-3.

**EXERCISE 10-3
What Is Your Current
Level of Physical
Activity?**

Place a check mark beside any description that fits your life:

_____ I exercise at least 3 days a week so my heart gets pumping and I sweat.

_____ I walk and take stairs whenever I can.

_____ I do strength training exercises at least two times per week (weight lifting, push-ups, etc.

_____ I stretch my muscles at least two times per week.

_____ I'm involved in a sport or recreational activity (such as hiking or bicycling) that requires physical activity.

Ideally all of these items should all be checked unless you have a medical reason to limit any of these activities. For any items you did not check, make it your goal to have one of them checked next month. Remember to work on just one at a time.

Although a proper diet is important, it is just one factor in your overall wellness. Diet and exercise go hand in hand. Benefits of exercise and a healthy diet include:

- **Growth and protection of your bones:** A diet rich in calcium and vitamins helps maintain good bone growth and development. In addition to diet, weight-bearing exercise is also beneficial in maintaining healthy bones over a lifetime.
- **Percentage of muscle versus fat:** A higher percentage of muscle makes you stronger, more energetic, and releases endorphins ("feel-good" peptides).
- **Aging:** Some studies show that exercise increases the number of brain cells, prevents Alzheimer's disease, and slows the aging process. (See, exercise can help your grades!)

Of course, always check with your physician before beginning any exercise program.

There are two basic types of exercise: *aerobic* (also known as cardiopulmonary) and *nonaerobic* (also known as strength and flexibility). You should do a form of each. Aerobic exercise gets your pulse pumping and sweat pouring. Examples include running and basketball. Aerobic exercise is best for cardiopulmonary (heart and lung) health and in turning body fat to muscle. Nonaerobic exercise involves exercise to improve muscle strength, endurance, and flexibility, such as weight lifting, yoga, and stretching. (See Table 10-3.)

Now, take a minute to view the Activity Pyramid shown in Figure 10-2. Assess your level of activity in Exercise 10-4.

Heart-Healthy Facts

A heart-healthy diet low in saturated fats (remember, we all need some fat for proper function), high in fiber, and rich in fruit and vegetables will help maintain an optimal cardiovascular system. However, diet alone is not sufficient for a healthy heart. Regular exercise, even something as simple as brisk walking for 30 minutes a day, three to four times a week, also helps condition the heart. Of course, the level of your exercise program depends on many individualized factors.

TABLE 10-3		
Types of Exercise		
Exercise Type*	**Benefits**	**Examples**
Aerobic or cardiopulmonary	Strengthens your heart and lungs	Aerobic dance, running, swimming, and active sports such as basketball
Strength (nonaerobic)	Strengthens and develops different muscle groups	Weight training, push-ups, and sit-ups
Flexibility (nonaerobic)	Helps prevent injuries	Stretching and yoga

*Note: Some of these types can be combined. For example, using light weights with many repetitions can help you include aerobic exercise in your weight training.

Exercise is a key ingredient to health.

EXERCISE 10-4
How Active Are You?

Circle the number that best describes you.

The type of exercise I do causes

1. No change in pulse (watching TV)

2. Little change (slow walking)

3. Small increase in pulse (moderate-pace walking, golf)

4. Some heavy breathing, sweating, and large increase in pulse (tennis)

5. Sustained high heart and respiratory rate with sweating (jogging, basketball)

FIGURE 10-2

The activity pyramid.

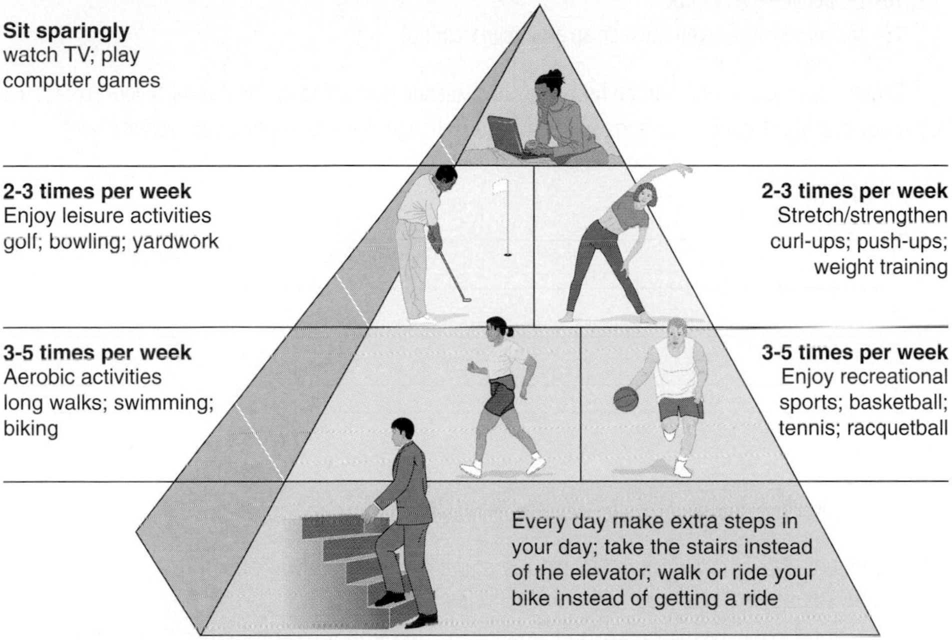

Sit sparingly
watch TV; play
computer games

2-3 times per week
Enjoy leisure activities
golf; bowling; yardwork

2-3 times per week
Stretch/strengthen
curl-ups; push-ups;
weight training

3-5 times per week
Aerobic activities
long walks; swimming;
biking

3-5 times per week
Enjoy recreational
sports; basketball;
tennis; racquetball

Every day make extra steps in
your day; take the stairs instead
of the elevator; walk or ride your
bike instead of getting a ride

Source: Colbert, Bruce J.; Ankney, Jeff; and Lee, Karen. *Anatomy and Physiology for Health Professionals: An Interactive Journey,* First Edition. Copyright © 2007. Electronically reproduced by permission of Pearson Education, Inc., Upper Saddle River, New Jersey.

I exercise for _____ minutes per session.

1. 0–5 minutes

2. 5–15 minutes

3. 16–30 minutes

4. 31–45 minutes

5. More than 45 minutes

I exercise _____ times a week.

1. 0–1

2. 2

3. 3

4. 4

5. 5 or more

Total score _____

3: inactive—couch potato

4–6: mildly active

7–9: moderately active—satisfactory but could improve

10–12: active—very good

13–15: very active—you must be an athlete in training!

Regardless of your score, you can find a way to challenge yourself to the next level. If your score is 9 or below, however, we strongly encourage you to make *one* change that will improve your activity level.

MAP out a plan:

_____

_____

_____

_____

Here are some main points to keep in mind concerning exercise:

- Avoid being a couch potato or, in this computer generation, "a mouse potato." Make proper exercise a vital part of your daily life.
- Walk as much as possible, even in small increments. For example, don't spend time and gas looking for that one parking place that is just a little closer to the store. Walk and enjoy the scenery. Take stairs whenever you can.
- Enjoy physical activity, such as shoveling snow or mowing the grass.
- Find a recreational sport or activity (skiing, hiking) that requires exercise, and make it fun. Variety will help you to stay with an exercise program, so mix it up.
- Try to socialize while exercising. Choose a partner who will help you stick with a program. Sign a contract so you both stick with it. Use goal-setting principles, such as writing down specific goals and rewarding yourself when you reach them.
- Be careful of muscle enhancement drugs. Many are dangerous and have serious side effects. Again, careful critical investigation is the best rule to follow.
- Always consult your physician about an appropriate and safe exercise program.

> *"Eat to live, and do not live to eat."*
> —Ben Franklin, statesman, scientist, and writer

Maintaining a Healthy Weight

Many charts will tell you your ideal body weight given your age, height, weight, sex, and body frame (see Figure 10-3). You should have an idea of your ideal weight and be within a few pounds of it. Being too overweight increases your risks of high blood pressure, heart disease, stroke, and diabetes. Being too far underweight increases your chance of osteoporosis (weak brittle bones) and, on average, decreases longevity, in comparison with healthy-weight people.

FIGURE 10-3

Chart to find your ideal body weight.

Ideal Body Weight for Women

Height Feet Inches	Small Frame	Medium Frame	Large Frame
4' 10"	102–111	109–121	118–131
4' 11"	103–113	111–123	120–134
5' 0"	104–115	113–126	122–137
5' 1"	106–118	115–129	125–140
5' 2"	108–121	118–132	128–143
5' 3"	111–124	121–135	131–147
5' 4"	114–127	124–138	134–151
5' 5"	117–130	127–141	137–155
5' 6"	120–133	130–144	140–159
5' 7"	123–136	133–147	143–163
5' 8"	126–139	136–150	146–167
5' 9"	129–142	139–153	149–170
5' 10"	132–145	142–156	152–173
5' 11"	135–148	145–159	155–176
6' 0"	138–151	148–162	158–179

Ideal Body Weight for Men

Height Feet Inches	Small Frame	Medium Frame	Large Frame
5' 2"	128–134	131–141	138–150
5' 3"	130–136	133–143	140–153
5' 4"	132–138	135–145	142–156
5' 5"	134–140	137–148	144–160
5' 6"	136–142	139–151	146–164
5' 7"	138–145	142–154	149–168
5' 8"	140–148	145–157	152–172
5' 9"	142–151	148–160	155–176
5' 10"	144–154	151–163	158–180
5' 11"	146–157	154–166	161–184
6' 0"	149–160	157–170	164–188
6' 1"	152–164	160–174	168–192
6' 2"	155–168	164–178	172–197
6' 3"	158–172	167–182	176–202
6' 4"	162–176	171–187	181–207

If you are overweight, you need to lose pounds by burning more calories than you consume. This can be accomplished through eating less and exercising more. If you need to gain weight, you need to increase your eating (calories) and still exercise. Let's explore these two situations in more depth, beginning with being overweight.

Have you heard the not-too-flattering term "Freshman 15"? This term means that some students can expect to gain 15 pounds during their first year of school, mainly due to stress eating and consuming fast foods. It doesn't happen to everyone, but even a 5-pound gain sets the pace for a lifelong problem. Here are some basic but effective ways to avoid the Freshman 15:

- Use the concepts on nutrition and diet in this chapter as a lifelong choice.
- Be careful of fad diets. These diets can be dangerous because many don't supply the necessary nutrients and vitamins, stress your kidneys, and can cause heart disease. Always consult your physician before beginning a diet.
- Drink more water. It is healthy and will take away some of your hunger.
- Eat more slowly. The brain takes 10 to 20 minutes to register you are full. Give it time, so you don't overeat. Your digestive system will also be less stressed if you eat slowly.
- Eat at regular times, and don't skip breakfast. Eating breakfast is a good idea, especially if you eat foods such as fruit, whole-grain cereal or bread, low-fat or skim milk, and an occasional egg.
- Avoid emotional eating.
- Keep away from vending machines.
- Avoid eating late at night, especially right before bed when your body will not have the opportunity to burn the calories.
- As we've already said, maintain a diet that is low in fat and cholesterol, contains plenty of fresh fruits and vegetables, and uses sweets and salt sparingly.
- If you drink alcohol, do so in moderation.

There is also the other extreme of being too far underweight. This will cause the body to be malnourished and starving for nutrients vital for growth, repair, and proper function. People who are excessively underweight often have contributing psychological issues, which may include eating disorders. Eating disorders result from out-of-control eating habits.

Anorexia nervosa, an eating disorder that usually affects females, occurs when individuals starve themselves because they fear looking fat. Even someone with a skeletal frame still sees a fat person in the mirror and continues to search for the impossible "ideal body." Bulimia, often called the binge-and-purge disease, is a condition in which an individual

To view videos on eating disorders such as anorexia nervosa and bulimia, please go to your CD for this chapter.

consumes a large amount of food and then deliberately vomits. This disorder can cause serious digestive system problems. People with bulimia are usually aware that what they are doing is abnormal, whereas many with anorexia nervosa are not. Both conditions require psychological and medical help.

> *"To sleep, per chance to dream."*
> —Shakespeare

Quality Sleep

Sleep is needed for the body to repair and recharge. Poor sleep leads to less energy, lack of focus, illness, irritability, forgetfulness, and a decreased reaction time. It also means you are most likely wasting precious study time, not reading effectively, and making more mistakes. Naturally, your academic and personal life will suffer.

In ancient times, sleep was based on the natural cycle of light and darkness. The invention of light bulbs, TVs, and computers has changed this cycle. Most studies

> ### Safety Fact
>
> Sleep deprivation accounts for thousands of auto accidents each year.
>
> If you have any of the following symptoms while driving—excessive yawning, head nodding, inability to remember the last few miles, or drifting between lanes—you need to pull over immediately and get some rest. It is always best to have a driving partner.

still show we need between 7 and 8 hours of quality sleep each night (Shuman, 2005). Quality sleep means that we spend most of our time in the deeper stage of sleep, non-rapid eye movement (NREM) sleep, and a smaller portion in the lighter stage, or rapid eye movement (REM) sleep. NREM is the longer period of sleep, during which brain and body activity really slows down to regenerate. REM, which occurs when we dream, normally occurs in brief spurts.

Healthy sleep includes both stages of sleep, but usually 80 minutes of NREM is followed by 10 minutes of REM cycled throughout the night. If this cycle is interrupted, your sleep quality is affected. In other words, if you spend more time in the lighter stage of sleep (REM), your body doesn't recharge even if you get 10 hours of sleep. Quantity (7 to 8 hours) and quality (most time spent in deeper sleep stage) are required for healthy sleep.

Here are some tips to help ensure a healthy sleep:

- You can test yourself if you are not getting quality sleep. If you nod off or yawn excessively during class, you are sleep deprived.
- Keeping a steady schedule can classically condition your body to connect sleep to a certain time. Get 7 to 8 hours of sleep, and follow a regular schedule even on weekends.
- Reduce noise or, if necessary, reduce distracting noise by substituting with soothing noise.
- Avoid naps because they may disrupt your normal sleep cycle.
- Lights out: Even when you get to sleep, light can keep you in the lighter stages of sleep.
- Avoid all-night study sessions.
- Wind down, not up, before bedtime. If you need to wind down, listen to soothing music, meditate, or take a hot bath. Reduce alcohol and caffeine (coffee, tea, chocolate, and cola) because they will cause you to sleep lightly and not get into deeper restorative sleep stages. To help sleep, exercise regularly (but not within 3 hours of sleep).

- Make sure your sleeping area is comfortable.
- Don't lie in bed and worry about not sleeping. Get up and do something boring until you get tired.

Do Exercise 10-5, and improve the quality of your sleep by making one positive change. Happy dreams!

EXERCISE 10-5
Improving the Quality of Your Sleep

MAP out a plan: From what you have learned about getting quality sleep, choose *one* positive change you will make to improve your sleeping habits. Be specific and write a specific goal and place it by your bed. Once you are successful in making this positive change, work on a new goal.

_____

_____

_____

_____

Preventing Illness

Proper diet, exercise, and quality sleep are all needed for the immune system, which is responsible for preventing disease. Other factors can assist your immune system:

- One of the simplest and most effective ways to prevent the spread of disease is proper hand washing.
- Current immunizations are important so the immune system can resist certain pathogens. For recommended immunization schedules, refer to the Centers for Disease Control and Prevention (CDC 2007a). Many schools recommend meningitis vaccines because outbreaks are related to living in close quarters, such as schools. Some individuals mistakenly believe immunizations are only needed in childhood. Flu vaccines are just one example of an immunization that is particularly important for the adult and geriatric population.

- While taking an antibiotic, make sure you consume the full dose. Don't stop after you feel better. If you stop short of the full dose, surviving bacteria may present a stronger, resistant strain. They are now free to reproduce even stronger drug-resistant offspring. This situation has led to small epidemics of drug-resistant infections.

- Prevent the spread of sexually transmitted diseases (STDs). STDs can have serious effects on the reproductive system—and lethal

Sobering Sexual Fact

As Ross Geller found out in an episode of *Friends* , condoms aren't 100% safe in preventing pregnancies. Sex with condoms isn't totally safe, just less risky. You can still get a STD, although the risk is greatly reduced, and condoms are 94% effective in preventing pregnancy.

TABLE 10-4

Sexually Transmitted Diseases

Disease	Organism	Symptoms
Herpes	Herpes simplex virus -2 Virus that can't be cured and flares up; some drugs can reduce the reoccurrence	Male: fluid filled vesicles on penis Female: blisters in and around vagina
Gonorrhea	Bacterial; cured with antibiotics	Discharge of pus, painful and frequent urination, can lead to sterility
Chlamydia	Bacterial; cured with antibiotics	Discharge, burning, and itching in genital area; can lead to sterility
Syphilis	Bacterial; cured with antibiotics	Chancre sores, systemic infection can lead to serious damage.
Genital warts	Human papilloma virus (HPV)	Cauliflower like growths on penis and vagina
AIDS (acquired immune deficiency syndrome)	HIV virus that cripples immune system; no cure, but drugs can slow the disease	Several symptoms related to weakened immune system

effects on the body. Many diseases and organisms can be transmitted through unprotected sex (including oral sex). Please see Table 10-4 for a listing of STDs (Centers for Disease Control and Prevention, 2007b). The spread of STDs can be reduced or stopped by using safe sex practices, such as the use of condoms or practicing abstinence.

 To view a videos on AIDS and STDs, go to your CD for this chapter.

Even with the best precautions, you can get sick. See a physician when you have an illness. Sometimes it is difficult to know when to go. When in doubt, you should always go because it is "better to be safe than sorry." Exercise 10-6 will help you begin a personal record of your health.

**EXERCISE 10-6
Keeping Your
Health Records**

Complete the following questions and activities to construct a personal health profile. File the information in a convenient, accessible location so you can access it when necessary.

Health insurance policy numbers and phone numbers

_____

Physician address, phone number, and fax number

_____

Immunizations record: (If you have a written record from your physician, just include it in your file.)

_____

_____

_____

Your personal medical history:

Surgeries (include dates) _____

Hospital stays (dates and reason) _____

Allergies _____

Diseases_____

Prescribed drugs and dosages _____

Any adverse drug reactions _____

Family medical history (diseases your parents, grandparents, or brothers and sisters have)

_____

_____

You have a right to copy any of your medical records, blood work, eyeglass prescriptions, and so on. Keep these copies in your file. In addition, keep photocopies of your insurance cards in case you lose them or your wallet or purse is stolen. In fact, it is a good idea to photocopy the front and back of all your credit cards, insurance cards, and licenses so you know what you have to replace and have easy access to phone numbers to cancel cards and order replacements.

Avoiding Harmful Substances

Drugs can play a role in maintaining health and wellness, particularly when prescribed to treat illness. Drug abuse is the nonmedicinal use of drugs, which alters physical, emotional, and mental characteristics and behaviors. Basically, drug abuse harms the mind, body, and spirit.

People abuse drugs for many reasons: pleasure, peer pressure, or escapism. Continued use, usually by people with low-self esteem and self confidence, leads to addiction. You can become

physically dependent (your body needs it to function) or **psychologically dependent** (you believe you need it to function) on drugs. Drug abuse causes harm to the user and family, friends, coworkers, and employers.

Remember, drug abuse not only causes devastating personal health issues but also wreaks havoc in the lives of those close to the abuser. Let's start with tobacco use.

Tobacco.

Tobacco contains the addictive stimulant nicotine, which leads to physical and psychological addiction. Smoking is the number-one preventable cause of respiratory diseases. It can lead to damage of lung tissue and chronic diseases such as bronchitis, emphysema, and asthma.

> ## Sad Fact
>
> Approximately 400,000 people die in this country annually due to smoking-related diseases (Cable News Network, 2005).

In addition, smoking increases the occurrence of lung infections and colds as well as sinus infections. Approximately 80% of all lung cancers can be traced to smoking. Smoking also affects the heart by reducing the availability of oxygen to the heart muscle. Smoking, along with alcohol consumption, leads to an increase in stomach and mouth cancers.

Smoking hurts not only smokers but those around them. Secondhand, or passive, smoking occurs when a nonsmoker is near someone smoking and therefore inhales that person's smoke. (At least the smoker has a filter!) Secondhand smoking causes 3,000 deaths per year and is especially dangerous to children.

Mothers who smoke while pregnant tend to have babies of lower birth weights, a tendency toward premature births, and experience higher rates of SIDS (sudden infant death syndrome). And while we're talking about babies and children, don't forget about the hazards of secondhand smoke in the home. In homes that have at least one smoking parent, children have slower than normal lung development and also have increased incidences of bronchitis, asthma, and ear infections.

Smokeless tobacco, or chewing tobacco, is also very dangerous. Chewing can lead to increased risks of oral cancers and a host of digestive disorders. (Besides it is a pretty disgusting habit!)

If you smoke, quit! You must be motivated and truly want to stop causing harm to yourself and those around you. There is plenty of help available. Your physician can order nicotine patches and gum that will reduce the cravings. When you chew the gum, you still get nicotine but not the other 3,000 dangerous chemicals contained in the smoke. Here are some other hints for quitting smoking:

- Seek out support groups and friends who have quit (or want to)
- Avoid situations that make you want to smoke

> ## Successful Smoking Story
>
> When the author was in college, a good friend of his smoked two packs of cigarettes a day. Every day for one year, the author put back the money his friend spent on cigarettes and at the end of the year bought a large TV. At that time, cigarettes were 50 cents a pack. This shocked the author's friend so much that he stopped smoking. With today's prices, consider someone who is spending $6 a day on cigarettes. That is $6 × 365 days, about $2,200 a year. This is enough to buy a *great* TV, not to mention the benefits of being healthier.

Some Sobering Facts on Alcohol

- Nearly 600,000 students are injured because of alcohol consumption.
- Approximately 25% of students report poor academic performance due to alcohol-related issues.
- Over 2 million students drive under the influence each year.
- 400,000 students had unprotected sex while under the influence of alcohol.

Source: "College Drinking: Changing the Culture," 2005.

- Use healthy substitutes such as exercise or walking
- Some people get used to having cigarettes in their hands, so substituting carrots or celery is a healthy alternative
- Set goals and make contracts with trusted friends

Alcohol.

Although drinking at legal age and not driving is socially acceptable, alcohol is actually the most abused drug in the United States. It is a depressant that, when abused, can cause a host of physical and mental problems. Alcohol affects all body systems, with the liver getting the brunt of the assault. Alcohol also disrupts the quality of your sleep, inhibits the ability to absorb nutrients, slows your reflexes, and causes you to make poor or harmful decisions. For example, students' use of alcohol has been associated with missing class, having unprotected sex, and causing accidents. Take the quiz in Exercise 10-7 to assess your drinking.

EXERCISE 10-7
Do You Have a Problem with Alcohol?

Answer yes or no to the following questions:

_____Do you drink when you feel depressed?

_____Must you drink at certain times? (before bed or after meals)

_____Have you tried to stop drinking but found you couldn't?

_____Do other people tell you they are concerned about your drinking?

_____Do you try to hide your drinking?

_____Do you need larger and larger amounts to get the desired effect?

_____Do you continue to drink even if it is having an impact on your health?

_____Do you drink and drive?

_____Do you drink to escape or become someone else?

_____Do you drink every day?

_____ Do you drink alone?

_____ Do you feel "shaky" and need a drink to stop?

The scoring is pretty simple. You have a problem if you answered yes to any of the questions, and you need to seek professional counseling. In addition, support groups such as Alcoholic Anonymous (AA) can help you with your problem.

Illegal Drugs.

Some people misuse common drugs that you can buy at the store, also known as over-the-counter (OTC) drugs. For example, overuse of antihistamines found in cold medicine can cause sleepiness and accidents. Some people choose to use illegal street drugs to get a desired feeling or to escape their problems. However, the desired feeling doesn't last long, and they need more and more of the drug, which leads to addiction. In addition, their problems get worse rather than better after they come down from their high. Often, they behave irresponsibly while high, which creates even more problems in their lives and those around them.

Table 10-5 lists some common abused drugs and some of their major adverse effects.

Most drug abuse occurs due to feelings of helplessness, low self-esteem, and the need to escape. Treatment in the form of counseling and support groups can change the underlying attitudes. Addictions can be treated with medical care in addition to counseling to help lessen the physical effects. Detoxification centers provide a controlled environment to help get past the withdrawal period. Of course, the *best* treatment is never to start.

TABLE 10-5

Abused Drugs and Their Adverse Effects

Drug*	Adverse Effects
Heroin	Overdose is deadly; many inject this drug and thus AIDS and hepatitis can be spread through infected needle use.
Cocaine (including crack)	Highly addictive stimulant that can cause a deadly overdose and heart damage.
Marijuana	Hallucinogen that alters the mind and causes lack of concentration, coordination, and slows reflexes. Can lead to car and other accidents because people think they can function.
Ecstasy	Combination stimulant and hallucinogenic drug that can cause nausea, vision problems, hallucinations, and depression. Long-term use causes permanent brain damage, depression, and memory loss.
Amphetamines	Stimulant that can lead to unhealthy weight loss, malnourishment, and pain. Prolonged use can cause violence and aggressive behavior.
Sedatives	Slows or stops breathing.
Inhalants (huffing glue and aerosols)	Damages brain, liver, and kidneys.
Anabolic steroids (muscle enhancers)	Many side effects; women become more masculine in appearance (shrinking of breasts, growth of body hair, baldness, and deepened voice). Men get high blood pressure, lowered sperm count, acne, heart problems, and sexual dysfunction; causes liver and kidney damage in both sexes.

*Note: All illegal drug use violates the law and can lead to a prison sentence.

If you are using a recreational drug and want to take an assessment and see if you have a drug problem, go back to Exercise 10-7. Take the same assessment but substitute your drug's name for alcohol.

HEALTHY LIFESTYLE CHOICES

So far, you have been introduced to a good bit of knowledge that can help you make informed decisions about proper eating, exercise, sleep, and avoiding harmful drugs. Some other lifestyle choices can help you achieve a longer, healthier, and happier life. Here are some basic choices, with examples:

Choose to Keep Safe:

- Statistics prove that one thing you can do to increase your life expectancy is wear your seat belt.
- Don't drink and drive.
- Don't walk alone at night, and keep your car and home locked and secure.

Choose Preventative Health:

- Prevent illnesses by maintaining a good diet and exercise program, along with healthy life choices.
- Make regular visits to your doctor, dentist, and eye-care specialist.
- Consult a specialist right away for new conditions, such as hearing loss.
- Cavities and poor oral hygiene can lead to diabetes and heart attacks. In fact, the simple act of flossing will enhance your health and prevent heart disease (Demmer & Desvarieux, 2006). That's because bacteria that grows in the mouth of an individual with poor oral hygiene can escape into the bloodstream and cause problems throughout the body.
- Know the possible causes and warning signs of cancer. Any number of triggers can make a cell cancerous, including genes, radiation, sunlight exposure, smoking, poor diet, viruses, and chemical exposure. Some of these triggers, like genes or some viruses, are difficult to avoid. However, many types of cancer can be prevented or managed with a healthy diet and exercise.

See Figure 10-4 for the possible causes and warning signs of cancer.

Choose a Safe Home and Work Environment:

- To avoid hearing loss, wear ear protection to safeguard against loud noise. Damage to the ear is cumulative, so there is no better time to start than right now.
- Protective eyewear should be worn to safeguard against eye injury at work and/or during recreational activities.
- Wear protective clothing and masks if you are going to come in contact with dangerous substances or fumes or if you work in dusty areas.
- One condition related to repetitive motion such as typing on a keyboard, playing a piano, or hammering is known as carpal tunnel syndrome. This causes nerve damage and can lead to numbness in the fingers.

FIGURE 10-4

Causes and signs of cancer.

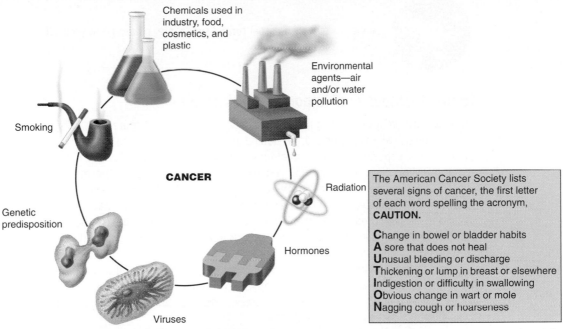

Chemicals used in industry, food, cosmetics, and plastic

Environmental agents—air and/or water pollution

Smoking

CANCER

Radiation

Genetic predisposition

Hormones

Viruses

The American Cancer Society lists several signs of cancer, the first letter of each word spelling the acronym, **CAUTION.**

Change in bowel or bladder habits
A sore that does not heal
Unusual bleeding or discharge
Thickening or lump in breast or elsewhere
Indigestion or difficulty in swallowing
Obvious change in wart or mole
Nagging cough or hoarseness

Source: Colbert, Bruce J.; Ankney, Jeff; and Lee, Karen. *Anatomy and Physiology for Health Professionals: An Interactive Journey,* First Edition. Copyright © 2007. Electronically reproduced by permission of Pearson Education, Inc., Upper Saddle River, New Jersey.

Noise protection will save hearing loss in later years.

To view a video on carpal tunnel syndrome, please go to your CD.

Choose to Understand Important Health Issues

An important wellness issue is mental health. One study shows more than 30% of first-year students often feel overwhelmed. We talked about stress and how to manage it, but what if these feelings continue to be overwhelming? Everyone has ups and downs in life, but depression is a feeling that no matter what you do, things will go wrong and never work out.

Depression affects about 20 million people in the United States each year (National Institute of Mental Health, 2002). This makes it a widespread illness that is often misunderstood and undiagnosed. Some people wrongly view depression as a personal weakness best handled by "being strong," but the fact is that there is often a biological and genetic component behind depression.

Being sad following a tragedy or loss of loved one is natural, but if that sadness continues for a very long time and affects daily living activities and work, it is most likely depression. Sometimes individuals are in a state of depression so long, they fail to recognize many symptoms. Here are some common symptoms:

- Loss of interest in life
- Frequent crying
- Sleep changes (either increased or decreased)
- Decreased energy and sex drive
- Appetite changes (either increased or decreased)
- Feeling of worthlessness, helplessness, and "gloom and doom"

TEST YOURSELF
Depression

State whether the following is true or false:

_____ "Real" depression is not suffered by teenagers.

_____ Depressed individuals are just weak.

_____ Talking about depression makes it worse.

_____ People who talk about suicide never commit it.

These statements are all false. There are many misconceptions about depression—and mental illness, for that matter. Too often, mental health issues have been stigmatized, causing sufferers to hide their conditions. We don't hide the fact that we have the flu or a broken arm. Why should we hide the fact that we may be sad for long periods of time (depression) and need help to resolve that condition?

- Increased irritability
- Problem with concentration and memory
- Suicidal thoughts
- Decreased academic/work performance
- Isolation from friends and family

Depression is treatable. Symptoms are relieved with medication, psychological therapy, or a combination of both. If you see these signs in a friend, do all you can to get the friend to seek professional help. If you see it in yourself, reach out to a trusted friend and seek professional help.

SPIRITUAL WELLNESS

Just what is spiritual wellness? The human spirit is that undefinable thing that makes us question who we are, why we exist, and what our purpose is. Although many debate religion and the existence of the soul, no one argues that human beings have the capacity to question things beyond their day-to-day existence. It is this questioning nature or spirit that we are discussing, nothing more and nothing less. The mere fact of this questioning spirit often drives us to better ourselves, our communities, and indeed the world in which we live. In Exercises 10-8, you'll have an opportunity to explore your essence.

EXERCISE 10-8
Exploring Who You Are

Part of this exploration in life is trying to find out who we are. During the Middle Ages, most people could not read, and symbols and pictures were used for communication. Knights had a coat of arms painted on their shields to identify just who they were.

Reflect and answer the following questions, and then draw a coat of arms that symbolically represents you. Have fun, and be creative!

Who are the special people in my life?

_____

What is my ethnic background and heritage?

_____

What are some traditions and customs that are important to me and my family?

_____

What do I do best?

_____

What kind of books, movies, and music do I like?

_____

What are my dreams for my future?

_____

What activities do I like?

_____

Coat of arms.

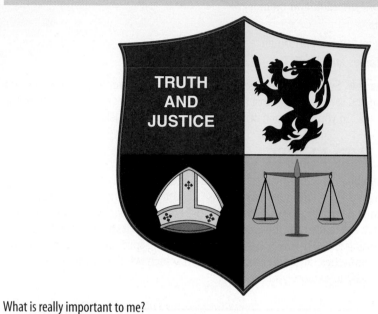

What is really important to me?

_____

If I had a motto, what would it be?

_____

What do I do that improves my family, friends, and/or community?

_____

Draw your "coat of arms."

_____

Some suggestions to develop your spiritual wellness:

- Always search for a higher meaning to your life.
- Commit to making your community a better place. You can volunteer for organizations such as the American Cancer Society, American Heart Association, Easter Seals Foundation, or local help centers.
- You can give back by reading books at a children's hospital or donating blood.
- Work with Habitat for Humanity, an organization that builds houses for the poor.
- Volunteer for Special Olympics, where you can make a big difference by simply cheering and hugging someone.

Now that we have come to the end of the text, we wish you a happy, safe, and successful journey through life. We hope this text and interactive CD serve as helpful travel guides.

HEALTHY DECISION MAKING

Jules's father died of lung cancer and smoked two packs of cigarettes a day. Jules misses his father, especially because he has become a father himself and has a 2-year-old daughter. Jules has returned to school to better his life, but the added stress he feels has caused him to begin his smoking habit again. In addition, he has stopped exercising and notices a drop in energy. He's concerned about doing well in school and also feels the fear is driving him to smoke more. What are some suggestions you can give Jules to help him (and his family)?

_____

_____

_____

KNOW YOUR SCHOOL

Your school has support services to help enhance and maintain your overall wellness. Identify school resources that can help you. Examples would include any personal counseling services, school health center, and any wellness centers or gyms. List the information here, and for quick reference place the information in a prominent place such as your refrigerator.

Resource Name _____

Office Location _____

Phone Number _____

E-mail Address _____

Now that you have read this chapter and performed the assessments and exercises, please go to your CD to reinforce these concepts. The CD will present you with an interactive journey back through wellness.

References

Cable News Network. (2005). Smoking causes 400,000 premature deaths per year, study finds. Retrieved April 23, 2007, from www.cnn.com

Centers for Disease Control and Prevention. (2007a). 2007 childhood & adolescent immunization schedules. Retrieved April 23, 2007, from www.cdc.gov

Centers for Disease Control and Prevention. (2007b). Sexually transmitted diseases. Retrieved April 23, 2007, from www.cdc.gov

College drinking: Changing the culture. (2005). A snapshot of annual high-risk college drinking consequences. Retrieved April 23, 2007, from www.collegedrinkingprevention.gov

Demmer, R. T., & Desvarieux, M. (2006). Periodontal infections and cardiovascular disease: The heart of the matter. *Journal of the American Dental Association, 137,* 7–8.

National Institute of Mental Health. (2002). Depression. Retrieved April 23, 2007, from www.nimh.nih.gov

Shuman, T. S. (Ed.). Sleep 101. WebMD. Retrieved April 23, 2007, from www.webmd.com/ sleep-disorders

U.S. Department of Agriculture. (2005a). Inside the pyramid. Retrieved April 23, 2007, from http://mypyramid.gov

U.S. Department of Agriculture. (2005b). Steps to a healthier you. Retrieved April 23, 2007, from http://mypyramid.gov

Wilderness Survival Answer and Rationale Sheet

Here are the recommended courses of action for each of the situations on the Wilderness Survival Worksheet. These answers come from the comprehensive course on woodland survival taught by the Interpretive Service, Monroe County (New York) Parks Department. These responses are considered to be the best rules of thumb for most situations; however, some might require other courses of action.

1 (a) **Call "help" loudly but in a low register.** Low tones carry farther, especially in dense woodland. There is a much better chance of being heard if you call loudly but in a low key. "Help" is a good word to use, because it alerts your companions to your plight. Yelling or screaming would not only be less effective, but it might be passed off as a bird call by your friends far away.

2 (a) **Make a lot of noise with your feet.** Snakes do not like people and will usually do everything they can to get out of your way. Unless you surprise or corner a snake, there is a good chance that you will not even see one, let alone come into contact with it. Some snakes do feed at night and walking softly may bring you right on top of a snake.

3 (c) **Drink as much as you think you need when you need it.** The danger here is dehydration, and once the process starts, your liter of water will not do much to reverse it. Saving or rationing will not help, especially if you are lying unconscious somewhere from sunstroke or dehydration. So use the water as you need it, and be aware of your need to find a water source as soon as possible.

4 (c) **Midway up the slope.** A sudden rain storm might turn the ravine into a raging torrent. This has happened to many campers and hikers before they had a chance to escape. The ridge line, on the other hand, increases your exposure to rain, wind, and lightning, should a storm break. The best location is on the slope.

5 (a) **Yellow.** A yellow flame indicates incomplete combustion and a strong possibility of carbon monoxide build-up. Each year many campers are killed by carbon monoxide poisoning as they sleep or doze in their tents, cabins, or other enclosed spaces.

6 (c) **Freeze, but be ready to back away slowly.** Sudden movement will probably startle the bear a lot more than your presence. If the bear is seeking some of your food, do not argue with him and let him forage and be on his way. Otherwise, back very slowly toward some refuge (trees, rock outcrop, etc.).

7 (c) **Run away into the nearest bushes or high weeds.** If bees are flying around or stinging you, do not freeze. Run away; swatting at them only makes them more angry. If no shelter is available, run through bushes or high weeds. This will help give you cover. Do not jump into a swimming pool or other body of water—the bees are likely to be waiting for you when you surface.

8 (c) **Try to increase your size. Open up and spread wide your jacket or shirt.** Upon sighting a mountain lion, do not run. Do not crouch down. Try to make yourself appear larger by opening wide your coat. The mountain lion is less likely to attack a larger animal. Hold your ground, wave your hands, and shout. Show it that you are not defenseless.

9 (c) **If attacked, go for the eyes and snout.** Use any weapon available, even your fist. If its jaws are closed on something you want to remove (like an arm, hand, or leg), tap or punch it on the snout. Alligators open their mouths when tapped lightly. They may drop whatever it is they have taken hold of and back off.

10 (c) **If in an open area, squat down; to minimize contact with the ground, do not kneel on hands or knees.** Avoid high places, open fields, and ridges about the timberline. If in an open area, do not lie flat or kneel with your hands on the ground. Squat to minimize contact with the ground and keep your head low. Avoid isolated tress, unprotected picnic or rain shelters, and shallow depressions in the ground. Current traveling through the ground may use you to bridge the hollow area in the earth. Avoid baseball dugouts, communication towers, flagpoles, and metal or wooden fences/ bleachers. Avoid bodies of water.

GLOSSARY

Acronym   A type of mnemonic device that is similar to acrostics. Acronyms are words formed from the first letters of the terms you need to memorize.

Acrostic   A learning aid in which you take the first letter of every item to be memorized and form a sentence that will help you to remember vocabulary, terms, or concepts.

Action teams   Teams that perform a specific operation or process for an organization, such as the organ transplant team within a hospital.

Active listening   The process of paying close attention to what the speaker is saying and feeling. Key points to active listening include facing the individual who is speaking, maintaining good eye contact, and genuinely focusing on what they are saying.

Advice teams   Teams that seek and provide information or research material, such as political advisers polling issues for popular opinion among voters.

Analytical thinking   Thinking process that aids decision making.

Auditory learner   Learners who understand material best by listening are termed *auditory learners.* They tend to prefer lecture classes.

Bad stress   Negative stress that detracts from your performance and impacts your health.

Bloom's taxonomy   A framework of classifying different types and levels of examination questions developed by psychologist Benjamin Bloom.

Body of speech or paper   The portion of a speech or paper that immediately follows the introduction. The body usually represents about 75% of your speech or presentation and should cover the main points with supporting facts.

Budgeting   Planning and controlling the use of your money.

Camaraderie   A spirit of cohesiveness and inspiring enthusiasm, devotion, and strong regard for the honor of the group that is felt within a team.

Chronic stress   Harmful stress that remains over a prolonged period of time and can cause poor performance, poor decisions, and poor health.

Chronological résumés   A job-seeking document that provides a listing of your experiences in order, with the most recent listed first.

Classical conditioning   The repeated process of using an established relationship between a stimulus and a response to cause the learning of the same response to a different stimulus. Also called Pavlovian conditioning.

Command decisions   Dictated decisions reached from a self-appointed or team appointed leader. The leader is very authoritative and exerts pressure on the other members to comply. An appropriate command type decision occurs on those infrequent occasions of crisis that demand immediate action (e.g., fire, accident, equipment breakdown, or illness, among others).

Conclusion of speech or paper   The last portion of a speech or paper that provides closure with a brief summary and strong final statement that should leave a lasting impression.

Conscious mind   Being aware and having perception. The portion of the mind that deals with day-to-day thoughts about what to wear, how to pay the bills, and what the future holds.

Consensus decisions   Decision-making process in which the entire team participates and every member expresses a view toward the ultimate decision. This type of decision takes the most time to complete; however, because the entire team participates, individuals become more committed to the decision, and the degree of ownership and buy-in is at the highest level.

Consultative decisions   Decisions reached when a discussion takes place mainly among the team members who know about the issues at hand. Usually the individual who has the most expertise in the subject leads the consulting discussion.

Cornell method   A method to organize study material and check for learning retention developed by Walter Pauk of Cornell University.

Creative thinking   Thinking process that generates new ideas or new ways to look at a situation.

Deductive reasoning   Form of logical thinking in which you reach a conclusion based on true facts called premises.

Evocative speech   Speech meant to bring forth, or create, certain feelings. Evocative speeches can entertain, inspire, or commemorate a person or event. Examples can include a sermon or a testimonial dinner.

Expenses   What you spend your money on. Expenses can be broken down into fixed and variable expenses.

External stress   The stress that results from events outside of yourself and includes the physical environment, social interactions, and major life events.

Fixed expenses   Expenses that are the same during a given time period, usually each month. Examples include your rent or mortgage (home) payment, utility bills (phone, TV, Internet service), and loan payments.

Formal teams   Teams that are set up by someone of authority who selects and assigns the members to work on a specific task.

Functional résumés   Résumés that focus on skill sets and qualifications more than actual work experience, which can be beneficial for job applicants with limited experience.

Goals   Desired outcomes or what we aim for and want to achieve in our lives.

Good stress   Positive stress that enhances your performance.

Grant   Form of monetary aid that does not need to be repaid.

Gross income   The total amount of income before any tax deductions or withholdings.

Group   Two or more people who interact with each other to complete certain tasks, achieve certain goals, or fulfill certain needs.

Impromptu speech   Off-the-cuff or unrehearsed presentations.

Income   Money you receive that can come from a variety of sources such as your salary, allowance, child support, social security, tax refunds, gifts, interest, money made on investments, and so on.

Inductive reasoning   Form of logical thinking in which you make your *best guess* based on the premises or facts. Your conclusion has a high probability of being true but is not guaranteed to be true.

Informal teams   Teams that develop when the members get together on their own because they share a common interest.

Informative speech   Speech in which you explain something to a person or group of people. Examples include teaching a class, giving a workshop, or demonstrating a technique such as CPR.

Interest   The extra charge for borrowing money usually determined by the annual percentage rate (APR).

Internal stress   The stress resulting from personal characteristics such as lifestyle choices, personality traits, and negative thinking styles such as being pessimistic or too self-critical.

Introduction of speech or paper   The first portion of a speech or paper in which the main goal is to state your purpose and get the audience's attention. This sets the tone for everything that follows and should be short but powerful to be effective.

Kinesthetic learner   A learning style that responds best to hands-on education. This style tends to prefer classes with lab work, group activities, and fieldwork.

Lateral thinking   Thinking that creates new ideas by making connections with no set pathway. Lateral thinking generates the ideas that will later be evaluated by vertical or logical thinking modes. Some people consider this "sideways thinking," where you make cross connections with other thoughts in contrast with the vertical "step-by-step" thinking.

Maintenance teams   Teams that perform repair or preventative measures on equipment, such as the pit crew at a NASCAR race.

Management teams   Teams usually comprised of executives who manage a company, such as a CEO and all his or her direct reports.

Mnemonics   A learning aid in which words, rhymes, or formulas improve your memory.

Multiple intelligences   A theory developed by Howard Gardner that states we have different types of intelligences, and, within each person, some intelligences are better developed than others.

Net income   Your actual take-home pay after all deductions and withholdings.

Nonverbal communication   Communication without the use of sound. This can include a handshake, smile, wink, or people rolling their eyes in disgust.

Objectives   Specific actions you need to do to achieve your stated goal.

Persuasive speech   Speech that attempts to convince or influence an audience about your topic. Examples could be a political speech or sales pitch.

Physical dependence   Dependence on a drug or substance in which your body craves the substance to function.

Plateau period   A period of slowed progress toward your goal that often occurs after you first make rapid progress. This is the crucial stage where you should not give up!

Proactive thinking The process of focusing on problem solving or "thinking ahead" to avoid future problems.

Procrastination The inefficient habit of putting off doing something until the last possible minute or not doing it at all.

Production teams Teams that perform specific operations for producing a finished product, such as the shift crew at a fast-food restaurant.

Project teams Teams that produce, build, or create a new service or product, such as a design for a new car.

Psychological dependence Dependence on a drug or substance in which you believe you need it to function. Often leads to drug abuse that harms the user, family, friends, coworkers, and employers.

Reactive thinking The process of focusing on problem solving when a problem or crisis occurs.

Reframing Looking at situations, people, and things in a positive way.

Role ambiguity A team situation where the expected roles of each member are not well defined and can lead to confusion, poor communication, and team inefficiency.

Scholarship Free money that does not need to be paid back. Scholarship money can be based on your need or on your achievements, community service, or your ability to write an essay.

Self-fulfilling prophecy The theory that states if you believe something strongly enough and plant it firmly in your mind, it will eventually become reality.

Sports teams Teams formed by members participating in their chosen sport, such as softball, football, soccer, bowling, or volleyball.

Stress reaction The reaction of both the mind and body to an event, person, or situation. The reaction is largely influenced by the environment and the individual's perception.

Study teams Collections of students who meet to encourage and support each other and complete assignments and projects.

Subconscious mind The portion of the mind where mental processes takes place that you are not aware of.

Subsidized student loan Loans available to finance your education that have low interest rates because they are subsidized (assisted) by the federal government. Student loans are often not required to be paid back until after graduation.

Synergy The sum of the individual parts creates a greater whole.

Team Group whose members interact (work or play) with a focused intensity to complete a shared, mutually supported, specific, overriding goal.

Team goals Specific and measurable results for a team to accomplish.

Team roles Behaviors and tasks that a team member is expected to perform for the overall progress of the team.

Team rules The guidelines and instructions that all members agree to at the beginning of the team formation. The purpose of the rules is to specify what actions and corresponding behaviors the team members will use in achieving mutually determined goals.

Variable expenses Expenses that can change over time and can't be as easily predicted as fixed expenses. These can include your food, clothing, entertainment, gas, car repairs, and educational expenses.

Verbal communication Communication that includes all communication forms that produce sound. This can include conversations, lectures, songs, stories, animal sounds, grunts, and so on.

Vertical thinking Thinking that relies on logic in which each idea relates to the next. Vertical thinking allows one to make assumptions based on past experiences.

Virtual teams Teams in which individuals meet and work together by Internet or media communication methods rather than face to face.

Visual learner Learning style that responds to educational material best by seeing it. Visual learners tend to be organized readers and note takers, and they may like to highlight or write notes in different colors.

Work teams Teams usually formed around a specific process or function.

Written communication Communication in the visual realm; can be letters, memos, reports, e-mails, charts, and pictures, among many others.

SUBJECT INDEX

Hearing, 137–138
Highlighting, 80
Hobbies, 16
Humor therapy, 16–17, 33–35
  positive effects of, 33–34
  suggestions for, 34
Idea generation, 118
Ideal body weight, 212–215
Identity theft, 69
Illegal drugs, 220–221
Impromptu speeches, 140
In-text citation, 151
Income, 62–63
Incubation period, 122
Individual accountability, 203
Inductive reasoning, 125
Informal communication, 136–137
Informal teams, 160
Informative speech, 139
Informed choices, 203
Innovation, 172
Integrated thinking process, 111–114
  environmental assessment,
    112–113
Interest, 68
Internal biological clock, 58
Internal stressors, 7–8
Internships, 185
Interpersonal intelligence, 94, 96
Intrapersonal intelligence, 94–95
Intrapersonal skills, 133
Introduction of speech, 140–141
Introduction of written paper, 148
Intuition, 24
Job interview, 192–195
  preparation for, 193
  professionalism and, 193
  punctuality, 193
  questions and tips for, 193–194
Job search
  résumé for, 186–191
  writing cover letters, 191–192
Jokes, 141
Keirsey Temperament Sorter, 195
Kinesthetic learners, 91–93, 95
King, Martin Luther, Jr., 199–200
Knowledge questions, 106
Lack of organization, 47–49
Lateral thinking, 119
Lateral Thinking (De Bono), 119

Leadership potential, 195–201
  attitude, 199
  energy, 200–201
  identifying leaders/characteristics,
    195–197
  key ingredients for, 198
  self-assessment for, 198–199
  vision, 199–200
Learning styles, 89–91
  assessment of, 89–90
  auditory learners, 90, 92
  kinesthetic learners, 91–92
  visual learners, 90–92
  working with, 91–92
Leisure time, 16
Lifestyle, 203
Linguistic intelligence, 93–94
Listening, 84, 137–139
  active listening, 138–139
  hearing vs., 137–138
Logical thinking, 124–125
Logical/mathematical intelligence,
  93–94
Long-term goal, 37
Maintenance teams, 161
Management teams, 161
Manuscript speech, 143
MAPS (goals), 36
Marginal notes, 80
Matching exams, 103
Mathematical intelligence, 93–94
Meditation, 18, 32–33
Medium-range goal, 37
Memory aids, 36, 96–99
  grouping, 97
  mnemonics, 97–99
Memory skills, 89
Memos, 147
Mental health, 224–225
Mind-body connection
  classical conditioning, 75
  stress and, 6
Mind talk, 8, 23
Minerals, 206–207
MLA (Modern Language Association)
  style, 151
Mnemonics, 97–99
Money, 60–61
  basics of, 62–63
Multiple choice exams, 103

Multiple intelligences. *See* Gardner's
  multiple intelligences
Music, 16
Musical/rhythmic intelligence, 93, 95
Naturalistic intelligence, 94–95
Nebraska Book Company *Buyer's
  Guide*, 80
Negative attitudes, 25, 27, 29
Nervous habits, 15
Net income, 62
Networking, 185
Newspaper advertisements, 185
Nonaerobic exercise, 209
Nonverbal communication, 134–136
Norming stage, 170
Note-taking skills, 83–85
  Cornell method, 84–85
  listening, 84
  organization, 84–85
  revising lecture notes, 86
Notebooks and other materials, 74
Nutrition, 16, 204–208
  basic concepts of, 204–206
  five basic food groups, 205
  USDA's food pyramid, 206
  vitamins and minerals, 206–207
Objective exams, 103
Objectives, 39
Occupational Outlook Handbook,
  178–179, 195
Old sayings (adages), 27
Opportunity for positive change,
  115–117
Organization skills, 47–49, 73
  note-taking skills and, 84–85
Outlining, 100
Ownership, 164
Paterno, Joe, 160
Pauk, Walter, 84
Pavlov, Ivan, 75
Peak periods, 58
Peer and faculty review, 149
Peer pressure, 203
Perceptions, 6–7
Performing stage, 170
Personal brainstorming, 122
Personal creativity, 122
Personal goal, 40
Personal habits, 52–53
Personal stories, 141